P9-CFX-279

BALANCED SCORECARD STEP-BY-STEP FOR GOVERNMENT AND NONPROFIT AGENCIES

BALANCED SCORECARD STEP-BY-STEP FOR GOVERNMENT AND NONPROFIT AGENCIES

Paul R. Niven

John Wiley & Sons, Inc.

Library of Congress Cataloging-in-Publication Data:

Niven, Paul R.
  Balanced scorecard step-by-step for government and not-for-profit
agencies / by Paul R. Niven.
      p. cm.
  ISBN 0-471-42328-9 (CLOTH)
  1. Total quality management in government. 2. Administrative agencies–
Management–Evaluation. 3. Nonprofit organizations–Management–Evaluation.
4. Benchmarking (Management) 5. Performance standards. 6. Organizational
effectiveness–Measurement.
I. Title.
  JF1525.T67N58   2003
  352.3'57–dc21

                                                          2003003949

/5///

For my wife Lois, with much love and many thanks

Contents

Preface

While researching this book, I had the pleasure to speak with many people working in, and involved with, both the nonprofit and government fields. Intent on supplementing my own knowledge of these organizations, I subjected those charitable enough to share their time with me to dozens of questions on every conceivable topic of even remote relevance to the Balanced Scorecard. One person, however, turned the tables on me. Dennis Feit, of the Minnesota Department of Transportation, began our interview by putting forth these questions to me: "You're trying to change something with this book. What is it?"' And, second, "Why is that important?" In many respects this entire book represents my answer to his challenging and valuable questions. However, in this short space I will provide a condensed response, and in so doing introduce you to what lies ahead.

In the early 1990s, Robert Kaplan and David Norton sought to solve a measurement problem plaguing corporations around the globe. The dynamics of business were changing rapidly; globalization, customer knowledge, and the rise of intangible assets were all rapidly converging to forever change the way business was conducted. Strategy was considered a potent defense for succeeding in this changing landscape. However, the facts suggested that approximately 90 percent of organizations were unable to execute their strategies.

Kaplan and Norton made the startling discovery that performance measurement systems utilized by most firms were not capable of providing the information needed to compete in this new knowledge economy. Most were remarkably unchanged from those developed by the early industrial giants at the turn of the twentieth century. Characterized by an almost exclusive reliance on financial measures of performance, these systems were ill prepared for the challenges faced by modern organizations. Kaplan and Norton believed that organizations should attempt the introduction of balance to their measurement systems. Specifically, the historical accuracy and integrity of financial measures must be balanced with the drivers of future financial performance in an attempt to view a wider spectrum of performance and execute strategy. Their radical, yet profoundly simple approach was labeled the Balanced Scorecard, and featured measurement in four distinct, yet related areas: customer, internal processes, employee learning and growth, and financial.

Since its introduction in 1990, the Balanced Scorecard has been embraced by corporations around the world. Recent estimates suggest at least 50 percent of Fortune 1000 organizations use a Balanced Scorecard system. For-profit companies have used the system to generate improved financial results, align employees with strategy, base resource allocation decisions on company goals, and improve collaboration.

Public and nonprofit agencies have been slower to accept the Balanced Scorecard system of performance measurement. Many possible explanations exist, including the reluctance to experiment with tools conceived with a for-profit audience in mind, and the notion that measurement efforts may obscure the true mission orientation of the organization. These justifications, and others like them, are what I am attempting to change with this book. In my work as a Scorecard practitioner and consultant, I have seen this remarkably adaptable tool successfully applied in organizations large and small, public, private, and nonprofit alike. Now, why is this important?

Are nonprofit and government organizations so dissimilar to their private sector colleagues that a Balanced Scorecard approach to measurement is irrelevant? While you're considering your response, review this quote: *"The issues are many and complex, but taken together they might be characterized by two superordinate and related challenges—sustainability and the ability to adapt to a rapidly changing world. Organizations must cope with increased competition, more diversity among constituents, higher expectations from the public, increasing costs, declining support, rapidly changing technology, and substantially different ways of conducting business. Surviving in such an environment (sustainability) depends upon the ability to adapt."*[i] If you believed this was written in reference to modern corporations, you're wrong. This quote was specifically directed toward nonprofit organizations. Your challenges, as clearly articulated, are remarkably similar to those of private-sector firms. Modern corporations facing increased competition, increasing costs, and diverse constituents have embraced the Balanced Scorecard as a beacon to guide them through these dark woods of change all around us. There is no reason to believe nonprofits, facing virtually identical challenges, will not derive the same, if not greater, benefits.

The lines separating public and private organizations are equally blurry. In an era when investor demands of greater disclosure and increased governance are pounding boardrooms across the nation, public-sector agencies face equally vexing challenges. Demands of accountability and transparency in public-sector performance are ringing ever louder. A consistent information and reporting framework for performance is widely viewed as inhibiting their ability to draw the curtain on performance and results. Forward-thinking public-sectors agencies, representing all levels, are beginning to see the benefits offered by a Balanced Scorecard system in this arena. The City of Charlotte, North Carolina, profiled in Chapter Thirteen, has been using the system for several years and credits it with focusing employees on strategy and improving overall city results.

Making the transition to this new world of measurement is not without its share of potential pitfalls. This book has been written to help you navigate this sea of change and to capitalize on the many benefits of the Balanced Scorecard, while concurrently avoiding costly implementation errors. Here's a look at what you'll find in the chapters ahead.

HOW THE BOOK IS ORGANIZED

Our Balanced Scorecard journey together consists of 14 chapters separated into four distinct, yet related, parts. Part One serves as an introduction to the field of Performance Measurement and, more specifically, the Balanced Scorecard. Chapter One introduces the Scorecard tool, providing an historical perspective and discussing the many facets of this tool. Adapting the Balanced Scorecard to the public and nonprofit sectors is the subject of Chapter Two. You'll learn that with only minor "geographical" modifications, the Balanced Scorecard is well suited to meet your measurement challenges.

Upon embarking on a Balanced Scorecard implementation, you'll quickly discover it is more than a "measurement" initiative. In fact, the Scorecard will touch many disparate elements of your organization. Part Two of the book, "Pouring the Foundation for Balanced Scorecard Success," outlines the many and varied elements that must be in place to ensure your Scorecard outcomes are successful. Chapter Three, entitled "Before You Begin," discusses a number of items that you must consider prior to building a Scorecard, including: your rationale for developing a Scorecard, gaining executive sponsorship for the initiative, and building an effective team. Many organizations rush into the Scorecard building process without the aid of training on the subject. Poorly designed Scorecards, and little if no alignment throughout the organization, frequently result from this decision. Chapter Four provides a training curriculum for your Balanced Scorecard initiative and discusses the importance of communication planning. Chapter Five begins the transition to the core elements of the Balanced Scorecard, specifically addressing mission, values, and vision. The Scorecard will ultimately act as a translation of these critical enablers of organizational success. In this chapter we'll explore the nature of these critical enablers and I'll offer tools for developing or refining your current statements. Strategy is at the core of every Balanced Scorecard, and Chapter Six examines this widely discussed, but often poorly understood subject. A straightforward approach for developing strategy is offered. Part Two ends with an examination of the Balanced Scorecard's place within the larger context of your performance management framework. The Scorecard will not exist in a vacuum, so you must determine how it complements your current management framework.

In Part Three of the book, "Developing Your Balanced Scorecard," you'll take a guided tour through the development of a strategy map and Balanced Scorecard. Chapter Eight outlines the strategy map concept, that of graphically displaying the key objectives that serve as the translation of your strategy. The critical concept of cause and effect is also explored. Chapter Nine fills in the remaining pieces of your Scorecard, with measures, targets, and initiatives. You'll learn how to develop measures in each of the four perspectives, why targets are critical, and how initiatives can mean the difference between success and failure on performance.

The final part of the book, Part Four, "Maximizing the Effectiveness of the Balanced Scorecard," is dedicated to helping you get the most out of your Balanced Scorecard system. We begin in Chapter Ten, which probes the concept of cascading the Balanced Scorecard. This term refers to the process of generating goal alignment throughout the organization through the development of Balanced Scorecards at each and every level of the agency. In an era of shrinking budgets, we're constantly reminded of the importance of aligning spending with results. Chapter Eleven provides a method of linking the Balanced Scorecard to your budgeting process, and in so doing aligning spending with strategy. Chapter Twelve canvasses the many reporting options available to Scorecard-adopting organizations. Whether you choose to buy an automated software package or develop your own tool, in this chapter, you'll find the information you need to make an informed decision. In Chapter Thirteen we're treated to an insider's view of the highly successful Balanced Scorecard implementation at the City of Charlotte, North Carolina. These pioneers of public sector Scorecard use share the secrets of their success, along with the challenges they've faced. The book concludes in Chapter Fourteen with a glimpse into what is necessary to sustain your Scorecard success. We'll examine the dynamic nature of the Balanced Scorecard and consider key roles necessary to maintain your momentum. The book also includes a glossary of key Balanced Scorecard and Performance Management terms.

It's a pleasure to serve as your guide through the rewarding territory that is the Balanced Scorecard. My goal is to steer you through the terrain that follows by offering a text that is exhaustive in scope without being excessively complex or unduly simplistic. Let's get started!

Paul R. Niven
San Diego, California
January 2003

---

[i] Thomas Wolf, *Managing a Nonprofit Organization in the Twenty-First Century* (New York: Fireside, 1999), p. 314.

Acknowledgments

Isaac Newton once remarked, "If I have seen farther than others, it is because I was standing on the shoulders of giants." And so it is that I am able to deliver this book to you. The individuals mentioned below, and countless others, are largely responsible for giving me the opportunity to share the ideas in this book with you. In many ways, I am merely a vessel through which their ideas, inspiration, and wisdom passes from me to you, and hopefully from you to many others.

My deepest gratitude is extended to the many individuals kind enough to share their time and information with me. Special thanks to Bobbi Bilnoski at the Concitti Network, Colleen Tobin formerly of Women's World Finance, Rhonda Pherigo from the Center for Nonprofit Management, Bruce Harber of the Vancouver Coastal Health Authority, Dr. Howard Borgstrom from the Department of Energy, Nancy Foltz at the State of Michigan, Rick Pagsibigan from the Red Cross of Southeastern Pennsylvania, Abbi Stone and Katy Rees from the San Marcos campus of the California State University, consultant Donald Golob, author and consultant William P. Ryan, Jake Barkdoll and the Balanced Scorecard Interest Group, Betty Cabrera at the Dallas Family Access Network, Diane Williams of the Safer Foundation, Dennis Feit from the Minnesota Department of Transportation, Philippe Poinsot from the United Nations Development Programme, and Jeff Celentano from the City of North Bay, Ontario.

I've also benefited tremendously from knowledge gained during many consulting engagements focused on Balanced Scorecard development. The following individuals have been particularly influential in my thinking: From the County of San Diego, California, Nicole Alejandre, Jackie Baker Werth, Tom Phillip, Chris Heiserman, John Ramont, and Randall Krogman. Bob Whip of Horizon Fitness, Art Rothberg of Fusura, Jay Forbes, Allan MacDonald, and Dennis Barnhart at Aliant, Ed VanEenoo, Cheryl Fruchter, and Dave Rowlands at the City of Chula Vista, California, and Isaac Hashem from Southwest Properties.

An innumerable number of other individuals have an imprint on this book. Let me conclude by mentioning just a few: Lisa Schumacher, Tiffany Capers, and Matt Bronson from the City of Charlotte, North Carolina. My open and insightful interview with them was a highlight of this project. Joe and Catherine Stenzel have been wonderful friends and great supporters for many years, my thanks to both of you. Steve Mann provided invaluable assistance with early interviews and research on this book, despite recently retiring! Brett Knowles provided me with wise counsel and provided contacts who are featured in this book. Andra Gumbus of Sacred Heart University offered insight and assistance that is greatly appreciated. From the Balanced Scorecard Collaborative I would like to thank Bob Kaplan and Michael Contrada. Both have offered me guidance and encouragement as we attempt to advance the Scorecard field. Teemu Lehto at QPR Software has been a great business partner, and I thank him for his many valuable ideas. Jeannine Owens from PB Views has been a mentor, coach, and great source of inspiration. Finally, I would like to thank Teri Anderson. Teri gave me my start in the performance measurement field several years ago, and has been a supporter and great friend ever since.

PART ONE

Introduction to Performance Measurement and the Balanced Scorecard

CHAPTER 1

Introduction to the Balanced Scorecard

Roadmap for Chapter One Before you can begin developing a Balanced Scorecard for your organization you must have a solid foundation of Scorecard knowledge and understanding from which to build. This chapter will provide that base.

We'll begin by considering just why measurement is so important to the modern public and nonprofit organization. We'll then look at three factors that have led to the rising prominence of the Balanced Scorecard since its inception over a decade ago. You'll learn that accounting and business scandals in the for-profit world have led to a demand for greater accountability and disclosure from all organizations. Next we'll examine financial measurements and their significant limitations. The final factor escalating the growth of the Balanced Scorecard is the inability of most organizations to effectively execute their strategies, so we'll also review a number of barriers to strategy implementation.

The Balanced Scorecard has emerged as a proven tool in meeting the many challenges faced by the modern organization. The remainder of the chapter introduces you to this dynamic tool. Specifically, we'll examine the origins of the Scorecard, define it, look at the system from three different points of view, and consider just why the word "balance" is so important to the Balanced Scorecard.

WHY MEASUREMENT IS SO IMPORTANT

Recently I read about an historical incident that I'd like to share with you. In the dense fog of a dark night in October 1707, Great Britain lost nearly an entire fleet of ships. There was no pitched battle at sea; the admiral, Clowdisley Shovell, simply miscalculated his position in the Atlantic and his flagship smashed into the rocks of the Scilly Isles, a tail of islands off the southwest coast of England. The rest of the fleet, following blindly behind, went aground as well, piling onto the rocks, one after another. Four warships and 2,000 lives were lost.

For such a proud nation of seafarers, this tragic loss was distinctly embarrassing. But to be fair to the memory of Clowdisley Shovell, it was not altogether surprising. Though the concept of latitude and longitude had been around since the first century B.C., still in 1700 no one had devised an accurate way to measure longitude, meaning that nobody ever knew for sure how far east or west they had traveled. Professional seamen like Clowdisley Shovell had to estimate their progress either by guessing their average speed or by dropping a log over the side of the boat and timing how long it took to float from bow to stern. Forced to rely on such crude measurements, the admiral can be forgiven his massive misjudgment. *What caused the disaster was not the admiral's ignorance, but his inability to measure something that he already knew to be critically important—in this case longitude.*[1]

We've come a long way since Clowdisley Shovell patrolled the seas for his native Great Britain. If sailing is your passion, today's instrumentation ensures that any failure of navigation may be pinned squarely on your shoulders. But for those of you who spend your days leading public and nonprofit organizations, and not cruising the high seas, how far have you come in meeting the measurement challenge? Can you measure all those things you know to be critically important? Today's constituents and donors are better informed than at any time in history. That knowledge leads to a demand of accountability on your part to show results from the financial and human resources with which you've been entrusted. To do that you must demonstrate tangible results, and those results are best captured in performance measures.

Over 150 years ago the Irish mathematician and physicist Lord Kelvin reminded us: *"When you can measure what you are speaking about, and express it in numbers, you know something about it; but when you cannot measure it, when you cannot express it in numbers, your knowledge is of a meager and unsatisfactory kind...."* The goal of this book is to help you do just that: to measure all those things that you know to be important, those areas that truly define your success and allow you to clearly demonstrate the difference you're making in the lives of everyone you touch. Welcome to your Balanced Scorecard journey.

WHY THE BALANCED SCORECARD—AND WHY NOW?

Before we explore the Balanced Scorecard in detail, let's look at some of the factors that have given rise to this new framework for tracking organizational performance. Simply put, performance measurement and management have never been hotter. Three factors have fueled the need for improved performance reporting: the recent spate of corporate accounting scandals, a longstanding reliance on financial measures of performance as the one true way to gauge success, and the inability of many organizations to successfully execute their strategies. We'll look at each of these and discover how they've contributed to the need for a Balanced Scorecard system. We'll then return to an overview of the Balanced Scorecard and learn how this deceptively simple tool is revolutionizing the management of performance (see Exhibit 1.1).

Doing Business in the Post-Enron Era

As I write this in late 2002, it's difficult to pick up a newspaper, turn on a radio or television, or open up a news magazine without almost immediately hearing or seeing a reference to yet another corporate scandal. Everywhere you turn there is news that another organization has run afoul of the law in its almost maniacal pursuit of pleasing shareholders. Leading this infamous pack is of course Enron. Once the seventh largest company in the United States, Enron has become the butt of endless jokes; but more importantly, it's also become the defendant in countless lawsuits launched by those who have collectively lost billions since the company's demise. Of course Enron's $63.4 billion bankruptcy was later dwarfed by that of fellow-wrongdoer WorldCom. WorldCom sought Chapter 11 protection in a $107 billion disaster. The list goes on and on: Tyco, Xerox, Global Crossing, Adelphia, and dozens of others. Even those organizations once considered paragons of corporate virtue have been tainted by the sting of scandal. Johnson & Johnson, for example, an organization renowned for

Exhibit 1.1   The Balanced Scorecard Solves Business Issues

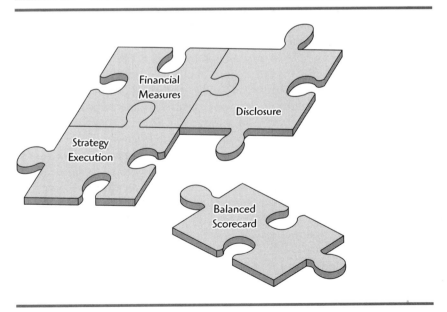

ethical business practices, was cited for irregularities at a manufacturing facility in Puerto Rico.[2] Not surprisingly, these activities have not gone unnoticed by you and me. Trust in organizations has never been lower. In one recent poll, 57 percent of respondents said they don't trust corporate executives to give them honest information.[3] Clearly, something has to change.

In response to the much-publicized shenanigans taking place in boardrooms around the country, the public is demanding greater disclosure of information. The rationale is that the more we know about a company's financial situation, the better equipped we are to discern the true state of its operations. On July 30, 2002, President George W. Bush took a great stride forward in this direction by signing into law the Sarbanes-Oxley Act. All companies required to file periodic reports with the Securities and Exchange Commissions (SEC) are affected by the Act. Proponents suggest it represents the most far-reaching U.S. legislation dealing with securities in many years.

While the act contains many provisions, two are particularly relevant to this chapter. First, Section 906, which is effective immediately, requires certification by the company's chief executive officer (CEO) and chief financial officer (CFO) that reports fully comply with the requirements of securities laws and that the information in the report fairly presents, in all material respects, the financial condition and results of operations of the company. Basically, company executives are making a pledge that what is in their financial reports is accurate and true. The act also requires plain English disclosure on a "rapid and current basis" of information regarding material changes in the financial condition or operations of a public company as the SEC determines is necessary or useful to investors and in the public interest.

Reforms such as the Sarbanes-Oxley Act represent tremendous advances in the pursuit of increased disclosure, but they miss a fundamental point: We need more than just financial information and disclosure to judge the health of an enterprise. To make an informed decision about any organization's true state of affairs, we require information that covers a broader perspective. This is the case whether we're talking about a Fortune 100 company, a local nonprofit health services organization, or state governments. We need to uncover the real value-creating and destroying mechanisms that are ultimately reflected in financial results. Even Wall Street is beginning to carry a torch for broader reporting. The accounting firm PricewaterhouseCoopers asked institutional investors and stock analysts what measures were most important to them. As you would expect, earnings and costs were consistently cited. But so too were nonfinancial indicators such as market share, new product development, and statements of strategic goals.[4] They could be on to something. Hewitt Associates found evidence that companies highly aligned with traditional metrics (financial) tend to be the worst performers in shareholder returns.[5]

All of the developments just described have prompted leaders and those who work in, and follow, organizations to further embrace concepts that place a premium on providing a balanced view of performance. Calls for use of the Balanced Scorecard are ringing out from observers around the globe. In

Canada, for example, the Society of Certified Management Accountants (CMA) has developed a new management accounting guideline entitled, "The Balanced Scorecard for a Board of Directors." The document serves to address corporate governance and management issues that have arisen in the wake of the Enron collapse.[6] France now mandates what it calls "sustainability reporting" for all publicly traded companies. The government has outlined indicators—in the areas of workplace, community, and environment—that companies must legally report on in annual reports.[7] Here in the United States, the American Institute of Certified Public Accountants (AICPA) has noted its support of the Balanced Scorecard in annual reporting to satisfy enhanced reporting requirements. Harvard University professor Jay W. Lorsch very nicely sums up the value of the Balanced Scorecard in this capacity: *"If directors were getting a Balanced Scorecard, they would be much more likely to be informed about their companies on an ongoing basis. The Scorecard's emphasis on strategy (linking it to all activities, day-to-day and long-term) could help directors stay focused."*[8]

Limitations of Financial Measurements

As the preceding discussion has clearly demonstrated, we require balanced performance information to fully assess an organization's success. Despite this realization, recent estimates suggest that 60 percent of metrics used for decision-making, resource allocation, and performance management are still financial in nature.[9] It seems that for all we've learned, we remain stuck in the quagmire of financial measurement. Perhaps tradition is serving as a guide unwilling to yield to the present realities. You see, traditionally, the measurement of all organizations has been financial. Bookkeeping records used to facilitate financial transactions can be traced back thousands of years. At the turn of the twentieth century, financial measurement innovations were critical to the success of the early industrial giants like General Motors. The financial measures created at that time were the perfect complement to the machinelike nature of the corporate entities and management philosophy of the day. Competition was ruled by scope and economies of scale, with financial measures providing the yardsticks of success.

Over the last hundred years, we've come a long way in how we measure financial success, and the work of financial professionals is to be commended. Innovations such as Activity-Based Costing (ABC) and Economic Value Added (EVA) have helped many organizations make more informed decisions. However, as we begin the twenty-first century, many are questioning our almost exclusive reliance on financial measures of performance. Here are some of the criticisms levied against the over-abundant use of financial measures:

- *Not consistent with today's business realities.* Tangible assets no longer serve as the primary driver of enterprise value. Today it's employee knowledge (the assets that ride up and down the elevators), customer relationships, and cultures of innovation and change that create the bulk of value provided by any organization. In other words, intangible assets. If you buy a share of Microsoft's stock, are you buying buildings and machines? No, you're buying a promise of value to be delivered by innovative people striving to continually discover new pathways of computing. Traditional financial measures were designed to compare previous periods based on internal standards of performance. These metrics are of little assistance in providing early indications of customer, quality, or employee problems or opportunities. For more on the rising prominence of human capital, see Exhibit 1.2.

- *Driving by rear view mirror.* This is perhaps the classic criticism of financial metrics. You may be highly efficient in your operations one month, quarter, or even year. But does that signal ongoing financial efficiency? As you know, anything can, and does, happen. Financial results on their own are not indicative of future performance.

- *Tendency to reinforce functional silos.* Working in mission-based organizations, you know the importance of collaboration in achieving your goals. Whether it's improving literacy, decreasing HIV rates, or increasing public safety, you depend on a number of teams working seamlessly together to accomplish your tasks. Financial statements don't capture this cross-functional dependency. Typically, financial reports are compiled by functional area. They are then "rolled-up" in ever-higher levels of detail and ultimately reflected in an organizational financial report. This does little to help you in meeting your noble causes.

- *Sacrifice of long-term thinking.* If you face a funding cut, what are the first things to go in your pursuit to right the ship? Many organizations reach for the easiest levers in times of crisis: employee training and development, or maybe even employees themselves! The short-term impact is positive, but what about the long-term? Ultimately, organizations that pursue this tactic may be sacrificing their most valuable sources of long-term advantage.

- *Financial measures are not relevant to many levels of the organization.* Financial reports by their very nature are abstractions. Abstraction in this context is defined as moving to another level and leaving certain characteristics out. When we roll up financial statements throughout the organization, that is exactly what we are doing: compiling information at a higher and higher level until it is almost unrecognizable and useless in the decision-making process of most managers and employees. Employees at all levels of the organization need performance data they can act on. This information must be imbued with relevance for their day-to-day activities.

Exhibit 1.2   Rising Prominence of Human Capital

Writing in the Economist, Peter Drucker noted, *"They (knowledge workers) now account for a full third of the American workforce, outnumbering factory workers two to one. In another twenty years or so, they are likely to make up close to two-fifths of the workforces of all rich countries."[i]* Our organizational world is clearly in a time of change as we make the transition from an economy based on physical assets to one almost fully dependent on intellectual assets.

While this switch is evident to anyone working in today's business world, it is also borne out by research findings of the Brookings Institute. Take a look at the chart to the right which illustrates the transition in value from tangible to intangible assets. Since this research was completed the pace of change has continued unabated. Speaking on National Public Radio's Morning Edition, Ms. Margaret Blair of the Brookings Institute suggests that tangible assets have continued to tumble in value: *"If you just look at the physical assets of the companies, the things that you can measure with ordinary accounting techniques. These things now account for less than one-fourth of the value of the corporate sector. Another way of putting this is that something like 75% of the sources of value inside corporations is not being measured or reported on their books."[ii]*

While Ms. Blair used the term "corporations" in the above quote, public and nonprofit organizations are certainly not immune to these changes. The challenges represented by this switch are well known in Washington. David M. Walker, Comptroller General of the United States said in a February, 2001 testimony to the U.S. senate that *"human capital management is a pervasive challenge in the federal government. At many agencies human capital shortfalls have contributed to serious problems and risks."[iii]*

This transition in value creation from physical to intangible assets has major implications for measurement systems. Financial measurements were perfectly appropriate for a world dominated by physical assets. However, the new economy with its premium on intangible assets demands more from our performance measurement systems. Today's system must have the capabilities to identify, describe, monitor, and provide feedback on the intangible elements driving organizational success. The Balanced Scorecard focuses on identifying and translating all of an organization's value-creating mechanisms, including intangibles, into objectives, measures, targets, and initiatives. As such, organizations are turning to the Scorecard in ever-increasing numbers as a powerful framework in both measuring and managing intangible assets.

[i] Peter F. Drucker, The New Society, *"The Economist,*" September 15, 2001.
[ii] Interview on National Public Radios Morning Edition October 27, 2000.
[iii] Testimony by David M. Walker, Comptroller General of the United States before the Subcommittee on Oversight of Government, Management, Restructuring, and the District of Columbia Committee on Governmental Affairs, U.S. Senate.

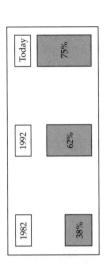

Thus far in the chapter, I've taken a hard line on financial measures of performance. We just reviewed their many limitations; and a little earlier I suggested that a single-minded focus on financial success might have been among the causes for the epidemic of scandals currently plaguing the corporate world. With all that in mind, the question is: Do financial metrics deserve a place on your Balanced Scorecard? Absolutely. Despite their many shortcomings, financial yardsticks are an entirely necessary evil. This is especially the case in the public and nonprofit sectors. In an era of limited, often decreasing, funding, you must consistently tread the delicate balance between effectiveness and efficiency. Results must be achieved, but in a fiscally responsible manner.

Your stakeholders will be looking to you to achieve your missions, thus nonfinancial measures of performance become critical in your efforts. However, pursuing your goals with no regard to the financial ramifications of your decisions will ultimately damage everyone: You'll be the victim of decreased funding as it becomes clear that you're unable to prudently manage your resources. Your funders will be discredited and, potentially, unwilling to support you in the future. But most important, your target audiences will not receive the services they need as a result of your inability to reach them in both an effective and efficient way.

Strategy: Execution Is Everything!

When I was conducting research for my book on private-sector Balanced Scorecard development (*Balanced Scorecard Step-by-Step: Maximizing Performance and Maintaining Results*, John Wiley & Sons, 2002), I knew I'd come across many references to strategy. After all, strategy is probably among the most discussed and debated topics we encounter in the world of organizations. But of course it's not just organizations that wrestle with strategy. The concept has entered the mainstream of our society. Professional sports teams all have a strategy to beat their opponents (and their owners have a strategy to separate us fans from our money!). I have a strategy for writing this book, and I'm sure you all employ strategies in achieving your daily tasks, both at home and at work. The interesting thing about strategy in the business sense of the word is that nobody seems to agree on what it is, specifically. There are as many definitions for the term as there are academics, writers, and consultants to muse on the topic. In fact there is even a book titled *Strategy Safari*.[10] I enjoy conjuring up that image of strategy—I picture myself cutting through the dense forest of research, attempting to find my quarry: the holy grail of strategy.

One point on which strategy gurus do seem to agree is this: The *execution* of a strategy is more important, and more valuable, than the *formulation* of a strategy. It's one thing to sit down and craft what is seemingly a winning strategy, but successfully implementing it is another thing entirely. For those who can execute, the rewards are significant. In the for-profit world, a 35 percent improvement in the quality of strategy implementation, for the average firm, is associated with a 30 percent improvement in shareholder value.[11] While shareholder value is not the end game of your organizations, you too will benefit greatly from an ability to carry out your strategies. Unfortunately, the vast majority of organizations fail miserably when attempting to execute their strategies. In fact, a 1999 *Fortune* magazine story suggested that 70 percent of CEO failures came not as a result of poor strategy, but of poor execution.[12] Why is strategy so difficult for even the best organizations to effectively implement? Research and experience in the area have suggested a number of barriers to strategy execution, and they are displayed in Exhibit 1.3. Let's take a look at these in turn.

The Vision Barrier

Employee empowerment, two-way communication, and information sharing—executives and managers alike frequently espouse the benefits of these concepts. Talk is cheap. The fact of the matter is that the vast majority of organizations have a long way to go when it comes to getting their most important messages—their vision and strategy—out to their most important constituents: their employees.

Exhibit 1.3   Barriers to Implementing Strategy

Adapted from material developed by Robert S. Kaplan and David P. Norton.

The previous section pointed out that many financial measures were developed at the turn of the twentieth century. Transport yourself back in time for a moment and put yourself inside one of those fortresses of industry, complete with towering walls and smokestacks billowing who-knows-what into the atmosphere. Chances are, as an employee there, you'd be told what to do, when to do it, where to do it, and how to do it. Would knowledge of the organization's vision and strategy have been the least bit relevant or helpful in your task? Probably not. But the world today is an entirely different place. Value is created largely from intangible assets like customer knowledge and information-rich networks. Today, to contribute in a meaningful way, you must know where the organization is headed and what the strategy is to get there. Only then can you combine your talents with others from across your agency to create value for your stakeholders and, ultimately, achieve your mission.

People Barrier

Debate has raged for decades as to whether incentive compensation plans really do lead to improved performance. We may never know the answer, but it is probably safe to suggest that an incentive of any kind tends to increase focus—at least temporarily. The danger with incentive plans is the possibility that managers will sacrifice long-term value-creating activities and initiatives in order to reach a short-term financial target and receive a monetary award. Strategy cannot be executed if the focus is continually on the short term. By its very nature, strategy demands a longer-range view of an organization's landscape. Financial incentives can distort or entirely block an organization's strategic view.

Resource Barrier

Sixty percent of organizations don't link budgets to strategy. If that's the case, then what are they linking their budgets to? For many organizations, it's as simple as looking at last year's budget and adding or subtracting a few percentage points as appropriate. This is a particularly damaging blow to the hopes of executing strategy. What is a budget if not a detailed examination of the priorities of the enterprise for the next fiscal year? If the budget is not linked to some form of strategic plan and goals, then what does that say about the organization's priorities? Does it even possess any, or is it simply spinning its wheels and wasting precious resources in the process? We'll return to the important topic of budgets in Chapter Eleven.

Management Barrier

Have you ever heard the phrase "management by walking around?" It suggests an approach of staying close to your employees by speaking to them frequently and informally, ensuring communication is two-way and beneficial to all. By contrast, I believe most of us live in the age of "management by firefighting!" We move from one crisis to the next, never taking the time to pause and reflect on our larger objectives, strategies, and mission. A client of mine uses the analogy of "working in the business"; that is, fighting fires, versus "working on the business," taking the necessary break to examine things from a wider perspective.

Many would argue there is literally no time to slow down, not even for a minute. Undoubtedly, we live in an era of fast-paced organizations, but virtually all of us attend regular management meetings. In order to have any chance of executing strategy, these meetings must be transformed. No longer should we sit around and examine the "defects" that result when actual results do not meet budget expectations. Instead, these meetings should be used to discuss, learn about, and debate our strategy.

THE BALANCED SCORECARD

Reading the preceding pages could make you feel as though your back is up against the wall when it comes to effectively measuring your performance. Review the considerable hurdles we've discussed: First, there are the many scandals erupting around us, forcing all organizations to provide ever-greater disclosure. Second, for the most part, we've been limited in our measuring options because of an almost exclusive reliance on financial measures that definitely don't tell the whole story. And, finally, as important as strategy is, a number of significant barriers make its execution truly elusive.

What is needed is a system that provides real insight into an organization's operations, balances the historical accuracy of financial numbers with the drivers of future performance, and assists us in implementing strategy. The Balanced Scorecard is the tool that answers all these challenges. In the remainder of the chapter we will begin our exploration of the Balanced Scorecard by discussing its origins, reviewing its conceptual model, and considering what separates it from other systems.

> Note
> The focus here is on the for-profit Balanced Scorecard model, since the tool was originally conceived with that audience in mind. Chapter Two will detail how the "geography" of the Balanced Scorecard has been successfully adapted to fit both the public and nonprofit sectors.

Origins of the Balanced Scorecard

The Balanced Scorecard was developed by Robert Kaplan, an accounting professor at Harvard University, and David Norton, a consultant from the Boston area. In 1990, Kaplan and Norton led a research study of a dozen companies with the purpose of exploring new methods of performance measurement. The impetus for the study was a growing belief that financial measures of performance were ineffective for the modern business enterprise. Representatives of the study companies, along with Kaplan and Norton, were convinced that a reliance on financial measures of performance was affecting their ability to create value. The group discussed a number of possible alternatives but settled on the idea of a scorecard, featuring performance measures capturing activities from throughout the organization—customer issues, internal business processes, employee activities, and of course shareholder concerns. Kaplan and Norton labeled the new tool the Balanced Scorecard and later summarized the concept in the first of three *Harvard Business Review* articles, "The Balanced Scorecard—Measures That Drive Performance."[13]

Over the next four years, a number of organizations adopted the Balanced Scorecard and achieved immediate results. Kaplan and Norton discovered these organizations were not only using the Scorecard to complement financial measures with the drivers of future performance, but they were also communicating their strategies through the measures they selected for their Balanced Scorecard. As the Scorecard gained prominence with organizations around the globe as a key tool in the implementation of strategy, Kaplan and Norton summarized the concept and the learning to that point in their 1996 book, *The Balanced Scorecard.*[14] Since that time, the Balanced Scorecard has been adopted by nearly half of the Fortune 1000 organizations, and the momentum continues unabated. So widely accepted and effective has the Scorecard become that the *Harvard Business Review* recently hailed it as one of the 75 most influential ideas of the twentieth century.

Once considered the exclusive domain of the for-profit world, the Balanced Scorecard has been translated and effectively implemented in both the nonprofit and public sectors. Success stories are beginning to accumulate and studies suggest the Balanced Scorecard is of great benefit to both these organization types. In one public sector study funded by the Sloan Foundation, 70 percent of respondents agreed that their governmental entity was better off since implementing performance measures.[15]

WHAT IS A BALANCED SCORECARD?

We can describe the Balanced Scorecard as a carefully selected set of quantifiable measures derived from an organization's strategy. The measures selected for the Scorecard represent a tool for leaders to use in communicating to employees and external stakeholders the outcomes and performance drivers by which the organization will achieve its mission and strategic objectives.

A simple definition, however, cannot tell us everything about the Balanced Scorecard. In my work with many organizations, and in conducting Scorecard best-practices research, I see this tool as three elements: measurement system, Strategic Management System, and communication tool (see Exhibit 1.4).

The Balanced Scorecard as a Measurement System

Earlier in the chapter I discussed the limiting features of financial performance measures. To review: They provide an excellent review of what has happened in the past, but they are inadequate in addressing the real value-creating mechanisms in today's organization—the intangible assets such as knowledge and networks of relationships. We might call financial measures *lag indicators*. They are outcomes of actions previously taken. The Balanced Scorecard complements these lag indicators with the drivers of future economic performance, or *lead indicators*. But from where are these performance measures (both lag and lead) derived? The answer is: your strategy. All the measures on the Balanced Scorecard serve as translations of the organization's strategy. Take a look at Exhibit 1.5. What strikes me when I look at this diagram is that vision and strategy are at the center of the Balanced Scorecard system, not financial controls as we see in many organizations.

Exhibit 1.4 What Is the Balanced Scorecard?

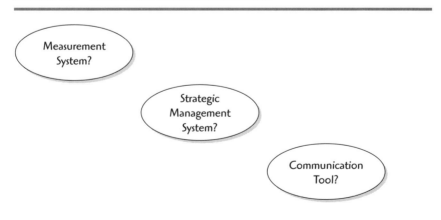

Exhibit 1.5 The Balanced Scorecard

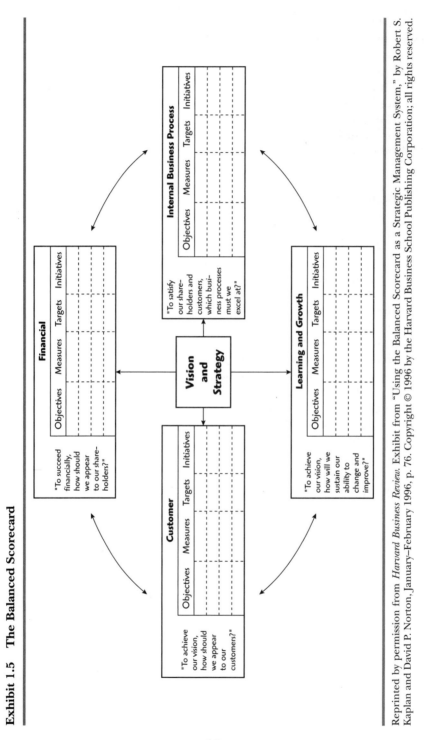

Many organizations script inspiring visions and compelling strategies, but then are often unable to use those beautifully crafted words to align employee actions with the firm's strategic direction. In his book, *The Fifth Discipline*, Peter Senge describes this dilemma when he notes, "*Many leaders have personal visions that never get translated into shared visions that galvanize an organization.*"[16] The Balanced Scorecard allows an organization to translate its vision and strategies by providing a new framework, one that tells the story of the organization's strategy through the objectives and measures chosen. Rather than focusing on financial control devices that provide little in the way of guidance for long-term employee decision-making, the Scorecard uses measurement as a new language to describe the key elements in the achievement of the strategy. The use of measurement is critical to the achievement of strategy. In his book *Making Strategy Work*, Timothy Galpin notes "measurable goals and objectives" as one of the key success factors of making strategy work.[17] While the Scorecard retains financial measures, it complements them with three other distinct perspectives: *Customer, Internal Processes,* and *Learning and Growth.*[18]

Customer Perspective

When choosing measures for the Customer perspective of the Scorecard organizations must answer two critical questions: Who are our target customers? and What is our value proposition in serving them? Sounds simple enough, but both questions present many challenges to organizations. Most organizations will state that they do in fact have a target customer audience, yet their actions reveal an "all things to all customers" strategy. Strategy guru Michael Porter suggests this lack of focus will prevent an organization from differentiating itself from competitors.[19] Choosing an appropriate value proposition poses no less of a challenge to most organizations. Many will choose one of three "disciplines" articulated by Michael Treacy and Fred Wiersema in *The Discipline of Market Leaders*.[20] They are:

- *Operational excellence.* Organizations pursuing an operational excellence discipline focus on low price, convenience, and, often, "no frills." Wal-Mart provides a great representation of an operationally excellent company.
- *Product leadership.* Product leaders push the envelope of their firm's products. Constantly innovating, they strive to offer simply the best product in the market. Nike is an example of a product leader in the field of athletic footwear.
- *Customer Intimacy.* Doing whatever it takes to provide solutions for unique customer's needs help define the customer intimate company. They don't look for one-time transactions, but instead focus on long-term relationship building through their deep knowledge of customer needs. In the retail industry Nordstrom epitomizes the customer-intimate organization.

As organizations have developed, and experimented with, value propositions, many have suggested it is difficult, if not impossible, to focus exclusively on just one. A more practical approach is to choose one discipline in
which the organization possesses particularly strong attributes and maintains
at least threshold standards of performance in the other disciplines.
McDonald's, for example, is a truly operationally excellent organization, but
that doesn't stop it from continually introducing new menu items. In
Chapters Eight and Nine, we will take a closer look at the Customer
perspective and identify the specific steps your organization should take to
develop customer measures. Included in the discussion will be ideas you can
use to apply the "value proposition" concept to your organization.

Internal Process Perspective

In the Internal Process perspective of the Scorecard, we identify the key
processes at which the organization must excel in order to continue adding
value for customers. Each of the customer disciplines outlined previously
will entail the efficient operation of specific internal processes in order to
serve your customers and fulfill your value proposition. Your task in this
perspective is to identify those processes and develop the best possible
measures with which to track your progress.

To satisfy customers, you may have to identify entirely new internal
processes rather than focusing your efforts on the incremental improvement of existing activities. Service development and delivery, partnering
with the community, and reporting are examples of items that may be
represented in this perspective. We will examine the development of
performance measures for internal processes in greater depth during
Chapters Eight and Nine.

Learning and Growth Perspective

If you want to achieve ambitious results for internal processes, customers,
and financial stakeholders, where are these gains found? The measures in
the Learning and Growth perspective of the Balanced Scorecard are really
the enablers of the other three perspectives. In essence, they are the
foundation upon which the Balanced Scorecard is built. Once you identify
measures and related initiatives in your Customer and Internal Process
perspectives, you can be certain of discovering some gaps between your current organizational infrastructure of employee skills, information systems,
and organizational climate (e.g., culture) and the level necessary to achieve
the results you desire. The measures you design in this perspective will help
you close that gap and ensure sustainable performance for the future.

Like the other perspectives of the Scorecard, we would expect a mix of
core outcome (lag) measures and performance drivers (lead measures) to
represent the Learning and Growth perspective. Employee skills, employee
satisfaction, availability of information, and alignment could all have a place

in this perspective. Many organizations I've worked with struggle in the development of these measures. Perhaps the reason is that it is normally the last perspective to be developed, hence the teams are intellectually drained from their earlier efforts of developing new strategic measures; or they simply consider this perspective "soft stuff," best left to the human resources group. No matter how valid the rationale, this perspective cannot be overlooked in the development process. Remember, the measures you develop in the Learning and Growth perspective are really the enablers of all other measures on your Scorecard. We will return to this important topic in Chapters Eight and Nine.

Financial Perspective

Financial measures are important components of the Balanced Scorecard, in the for-profit, public, and nonprofit worlds. In the for-profit domain, the measures in this perspective tell us whether our strategy execution—which is detailed through measures chosen in the other perspectives—is leading to improved bottom-line results. In the nonprofit and public sectors, financial measures ensure we're achieving our results in an efficient manner that minimizes cost. We normally encounter classic lagging indicators in the Financial perspective. Typical examples include: revenue, profitability, and budget variances. As with the other three perspectives, we will return to have another look at financial measures in Chapters Eight and Nine.

The Balanced Scorecard as a Strategic Management System

For many organizations, the Balanced Scorecard has evolved from a measurement tool to what Kaplan and Norton have described as a "Strategic Management System."[21] While the original intent of the Scorecard system was to balance historical financial numbers with the drivers of future value for the firm, as more and more organizations experimented with the concept they found it to be a critical tool in aligning short-term actions with their strategy. Used in this way the Scorecard alleviates many of the issues of effective strategy implementation discussed earlier in the chapter. Let's revisit those barriers and examine how the Balanced Scorecard may in fact remove them.

Overcoming the Vision Barrier through the Translation of Strategy

The Balanced Scorecard is ideally created through a shared understanding and translation of the organization's strategy into objectives, measures, targets, and initiatives in each of the four Scorecard perspectives. The translation of vision and strategy forces the executive team to specifically determine what is meant by often vague and nebulous terms contained in vision and strategy statements, for example: "superior service" or "targeted customers." Through the process of developing the Scorecard, an executive group might determine that "superior service" means responding to inquiries within 24 hours. Thereafter, all employees can focus their energies and day-to-day activities on the crystal-clear goal of response times, rather than wondering about, and debating the definition of, "superior service." Using the Balanced Scorecard as a framework for translating the strategy, these organizations create a new language of measurement that serves to guide all employees' actions toward the achievement of the stated direction.

Cascading the Scorecard to Overcome the People Barrier

To successfully implement any strategy, it must be understood and acted upon by every level of the firm. Cascading the Scorecard means driving it down into the organization and giving all employees the opportunity to demonstrate how their day-to-day activities contribute to the company's strategy. All organizational levels distinguish their value-creating activities by developing Scorecards that link to the highest-level organizational objectives.

By cascading, you create a "line of sight" from the employee on the front line back to the director's office. Some organizations have taken cascading all the way down to the individual level, with employees developing personal Balanced Scorecards that define the contribution they will make to their team in helping it achieve overall objectives. In Chapter Ten we will take a closer look at the topic of cascading and discuss how you can develop aligned Scorecards throughout your organization.

Rather than linking incentives and rewards to the achievement of short-term financial targets, managers now have the opportunity to tie their team, department, or agency rewards directly to the areas in which they exert influence. All employees can then focus on the performance drivers of future value and on which decisions and actions are necessary to achieve those outcomes.

Strategic Resource Allocation to Overcome the Resource Barrier

Developing your Balanced Scorecard provides an excellent opportunity to tie resource allocation and strategy together. When you create a Balanced Scorecard, you not only think in terms of objectives, measures, and targets for each of our four perspectives, but just as critically you must consider the initiatives or action plans you will put in place to meet your Scorecard targets. If you create long-term stretch targets for your measures, you can then consider the incremental steps along the path to their achievement.

The human and financial resources necessary to achieve Scorecard targets should form the basis for the development of the annual budgeting process. No longer will departments submit budget requests that simply take last year's amount and add an arbitrary 5 percent. Instead, the necessary costs (and profits) associated with Balanced Scorecard targets are clearly articulated in their submission documents. This enhances executive learning about the strategy, as the group is now forced (unless they have unlimited means) to make tough choices and trade-offs regarding which initiatives to fund and which to defer.

The building of a Balanced Scorecard also affords you a great opportunity to critically examine the current myriad initiatives taking place in your organization. As a consultant, when I begin working with a new client, one of the laments I hear repeatedly from front-line employees is, "Oh no, another new initiative!" Many executives have pet projects and agendas they hope to advance, often with little thought of the strategic significance of such endeavors. Initiatives at every level of the organization and from every area must share one common trait: a linkage to the organization's overall strategic goals. The Balanced Scorecard provides the lens for making this examination. Once you've developed your Scorecard, you should review all the initiatives currently under way in your organization and determine which are truly critical to the fulfillment of your strategy and which are merely consuming valuable and scarce resources. Obviously, the resource savings are beneficial, but more importantly you signal to everyone in the organization the critical factors for success and the steps you are taking to achieve them. Chapter Eleven is devoted to a greater review of this topic and provides guidance on how you can link your budgets to strategy.

Strategic Learning to Overcome the Management Barrier

In rapidly changing environments, we all need more than an analysis of actual versus budget variances to make strategic decisions. Unfortunately, many management teams spend their precious time together discussing variances and looking for ways to correct these "defects." The Balanced Scorecard provides the necessary elements to move away from this paradigm to a new model in which Scorecard results become a starting point for reviewing, questioning, and learning about your strategy.

The Balanced Scorecard translates your vision and strategy into a coherent set of measures in four balanced perspectives. Immediately, you have more information to consider than merely financial data. The results of your Scorecard performance measures, when viewed as a coherent whole, represent the articulation of your strategy to that point and form the basis for questioning whether your results are leading you any closer to the achievement of that strategy.

As you will see in the next section, any strategy you pursue represents a hypothesis, or your best guess, of how to achieve success. To prove meaningful, the measures on your Scorecard must link together to tell the story of, or describe, that strategy. If, for example, you believe an investment in employee training will lead to improved quality, you need to test that hypothesis through the measures appearing on your Scorecard. If, say, employee training increases to meet your target, but quality has actually deteriorated, then perhaps that is not a valid assumption; instead, maybe you should be focusing on, for example, improving employee access to key information. It may take considerable time to gather sufficient data to test such correlations, but simply having managers begin to question the assumptions underlying the strategy is a major improvement over making decisions based purely on financial numbers.

The Balanced Scorecard as a Communication Tool

In the preceding sections I discussed the use of the Balanced Scorecard as both a pure measurement system, and its evolution into a Strategic Management System. In particular, I delved into the power of the Scorecard in translating the strategy and telling its story to all employees—what you might call *communicating*. So why am I devoting an entire section (albeit a short one) to outline why I consider the Balanced Scorecard to be a communication tool? Simply because I believe it to be the most basic and powerful attribute of the entire system. A well-constructed Scorecard eloquently describes your strategy and makes the vague and imprecise world of visions and strategies come alive through the clear and objective performance measures you've chosen.

Much has been written in recent years about knowledge management strategies within organizations, and many schools of thought on the topic exist. One common trait of all such systems may be the desire to make the implicit knowledge held within the minds of your work force explicit and open for discussion and learning. We live in the era of the knowledge worker, the employee who—unlike his or her organizational predecessors who relied on the physical assets of the company—now owns the means of production: knowledge. There may be no greater challenge facing your organization today than codifying and acting on that knowledge. In fact, Peter Drucker, widely considered the father of modern management, has called managing knowledge worker productivity one of the great management challenges of the twenty-first century.[22] Sharing Scorecard results throughout the organization gives employees the opportunity to discuss the assumptions underlying the strategy, learn from any unexpected results, and dialog on future modifications as necessary. Simply understanding the firm's strategies can unlock many hidden organizational capacities, as employees, perhaps for the first time, know where the organization is headed and how they can contribute during the journey. One organization I worked with conducted employee surveys before and after the development of the Balanced Scorecard. Prior to implementation less than 50 percent said they were aware of, and understood, the strategy. One year following a full Balanced Scorecard implementation, that number had risen to 87 percent! If you believe in openly disseminating information to your employees, practicing what some would call "open-book management" then I can think of no better tool than the Balanced Scorecard to serve as your "book."

BALANCE IN THE BALANCED SCORECARD

As you develop the Balanced Scorecard in your organization, you may encounter some resistance to the term itself. Some may feel the Balanced Scorecard represents the latest management fad sweeping executive suites around the nation, hence the mere mention of such a buzzword would preclude employees from accepting the tool regardless of its efficacy. This may represent a legitimate concern, depending on the fate of previous change initiatives within your organization. But whereas others may prefer to use other monikers for the tool—such as Performance Management System, Scoreboard, or any number of others—I believe it is important to consistently use the term Balanced Scorecard when describing this tool, because the concept of *balance* is central to this system, specifically relating to three areas:

- *Balance between financial and nonfinancial indicators of success.* The Balanced Scorecard was originally conceived to overcome the deficiencies of a reliance on financial measures of performance by balancing them with the drivers of future performance. This remains a principle tenet of the system.

- *Balance between internal and external constituents of the organization.* Financial stakeholders (funders, legislators, etc.) and customers represent the external constituents represented in the Balanced Scorecard, while employees and internal processes represent internal constituents. The Balanced Scorecard recognizes the importance of balancing the occasionally contradictory needs of all these groups in effectively implementing strategy.

- *Balance between lag and lead indicators of performance.* Lag indicators generally represent past performance. Typical examples might include customer satisfaction or revenue. While these measures are usually quite objective and accessible, they normally lack any predictive power. Lead indicators, in contrast, are the performance drivers that lead to the achievement of the lag indicators. They often include the measurement of processes and activities. Response time might represent a leading indicator for the lagging measure of customer satisfaction. While these measures are normally thought to be predictive in nature, the correlations may prove subjective and the data difficult to gather. A Scorecard should include a mix of lead and lag indicators. Lag indicators without leading measures don't communicate how you are going to achieve your targets. Conversely, leading indicators without lag measures may demonstrate short-term improvements but don't identify whether these improvements have led to improved results for customers, ultimately allowing you to achieve your mission.

SUMMARY

Many leaders feel they know what is most critical to the success of their organizations. However, it is only through the measurement of these vital indicators that they can accurately reflect their progress on an ongoing basis. The Balanced Scorecard is a powerful tool that enables any organization to pinpoint and track the vital few variables that make or break performance.

This chapter delineated the factors that have led to the increased importance and use of the Balanced Scorecard. The first is a steady climb in the number of accounting and business scandals plaguing the organizational world. While the majority of these debacles affect the for-profit world, the public and nonprofit sectors are not immune. Concerned citizens, regulatory bodies, and legislative authorities are demanding an increase in disclosure of material organizational performance. The second component of the Scorecard's rise in prominence is our almost exclusive reliance on financial measures of performance. Traditionally, the measurement of organizations has been financial; however, our dependence on financial measures of performance has come under criticism in recent years. Critics suggest financial measures are not consistent with today's environment, and that they lack predictive power, reinforce functional silos, may sacrifice long-term thinking, and are not relevant to many levels of the organization. Successfully implementing strategy is the third and final key issue facing the enterprise. Four barriers to strategy implementation exist for most organizations: a vision barrier, people barrier, resource barrier, and management barrier.

The chapter also described how the Balanced Scorecard balances the historical accuracy and integrity of financial numbers with the real drivers of future success. The framework enforces a discipline around strategy implementation by challenging executives to carefully translate their strategies into objectives, measures, targets, and initiatives in four balanced perspectives: Customer, Internal Processes, Learning and Growth, and Financial. While originally designed in 1990 as a measurement system, the Balanced Scorecard has evolved into a Strategic Management System and powerful communication tool for those organizations fully utilizing its many capabilities. Linking the Scorecard to key management processes such as budgeting, compensation, and alignment helps overcome the barriers to implementing strategy. While originally conceived with the for-profit enterprise in mind, the Balanced Scorecard has been applied with tremendous success in non-profit and governmental agencies around the world.

Finally, the chapter stressed the importance of the word "balance" in the Balanced Scorecard. It represents the balance between:

- Financial and nonfinancial indicators
- Internal and external constituents of the organization
- Lag and lead indicators

NOTES

1. Marcus Buckingham and Curt Coffman, *First Break All the Rules* (New York: Simon & Schuster, 1999).
2. Dow Jones News Service, "Johnson & Johnson Statement on Puerto Rico Lawsuit," *Dow Jones Newswire*, August 26, 2002.
3. John Harwood, "Americans Distrust Institutions in Poll," *The Wall Street Journal*, June 13, 2002, p. A4.
4. Robert G. Eccles, Robert H. Herz, E. Mary Keegan, and David M.H. Phillips, *The Value Reporting Revolution* (New York: John Wiley & Sons, Inc., 2001), p. 123.
5. Mark Frigo, "Strategy-Focused Performance Measures," *Strategic Finance*, September, 2002.
6. R.W. Dye, "Who's Minding the Store," *CMA Management Journal*, June 2002.
7. "Eye on Europe," *Business Ethics*, May/June/July, 2002.
8. Jay W. Lorsch, "Smelling Smoke: Why Boards of Directors Need the Balanced Scorecard," *Balanced Scorecard Report*, September–October, 2002, p. 9.
9. Institute of Management and Administration Controllers' Report, "20 Best Practice Insights: How Controllers Promote Faster, Better Decisions," Institute of Management and Administration, 2001.
10. Henry Mintzberg, Bruce Ahlstrand, and Joseph Lampel, *Strategy Safari* (New York: The Free Press, 1998).
11. Brian E. Becker, Mark A. Huselid, and Dave Ulrich, *The HR Scorecard* (Boston: Harvard Business School Press, 2001), p. 213.
12. R. Charan and G. Colvin, "Why CEOs Fail," *Fortune*, June 21, 1999.
13. Robert S. Kaplan and David P. Norton, "The Balanced Scorecard—Measures That Drive Performance," *Harvard Business Review*, January–February 1992: pp. 71–79.
14. Robert S. Kaplan and David P. Norton, *The Balanced Scorecard* (Boston: Harvard Business School Press, 1996).
15. Governmental Accounting Standards Board, "Performance Measurement at the State and Local Levels," 2001.
16. Peter Senge, *The Fifth Discipline: The Art and Practice of the Learning Organization* (New York: Currency Doubleday, 1990).
17. Timothy J. Galpin, *Making Strategy Work* (San Francisco, CA, Jossey-Bass, 1997).
18. Robert S. Kaplan and David P. Norton, "The Balanced Scorecard—Measures That Drive Performance," *Harvard Business Review*, January–February 1992: pp. 71–79.

19. Michael E. Porter, "Strategy and the Internet," *Harvard Business Review,* March 2001, pp. 62–78.
20. Michael Treacy and Fred Wiersema, *The Discipline of Market Leaders* (Reading, MA: Perseus Books, 1995).
21. Robert S. Kaplan and David P. Norton, "Using the Balanced Scorecard as a Strategic Management System," *Harvard Business Review,* January–February, 1996, pp. 75–85.
22. Peter F. Drucker, *Management Challenges for the 21st Century* (New York: HarperCollins, 1999).

CHAPTER 2

Adapting the Balanced Scorecard to Fit the Public and Nonprofit Sectors

Roadmap for Chapter Two Chapter One focused on the Balanced Scorecard as it was originally conceived with the for-profit world in mind. As private-sector firms around the world began to harness the power of the Balanced Scorecard, some public and nonprofit agencies, in their own quest to improve results, began looking to the Scorecard with intrigue. Intrigue soon transformed into actual use as these early adopters discovered that with some modifications the Balanced Scorecard readily adapted to their circumstances. In this chapter, we explore the nature and history of public and nonprofit performance measurement, and discover how the Balanced Scorecard can fill some voids in the measurement efforts of these organizations.

The chapter begins with a look back at performance measurement efforts in both the public and nonprofit sectors. You'll discover that both sectors have a long history of measuring performance, using a variety of techniques. We'll also look at some of the struggles that have been encountered in the pursuit of meaningful performance measurement.

Adapting the "geography" of the Scorecard to fit nonprofit and public sector enterprises is our next topic. I'll dissect the model and detail both the subtle and not so subtle changes in application to show you that what really separates the Balanced Scorecard from other performance measurement systems is the notion of cause and effect—how the measures link together to tell a strategic story. I include an example to illustrate this important detail. The chapter concludes by reviewing a sample of the many benefits you can derive from employing a Balanced Scorecard system.

PERFORMANCE MEASUREMENT IN THE PUBLIC AND NONPROFIT SECTORS

Assessing the Landscape of Public-Sector Performance Measurement

Attempts to monitor government performance are not without precedent. In 1960, Robert McNamara was appointed Secretary of Defense by newly elected President John F. Kennedy. Among McNamara's first undertakings was to centralize decision-making control within the Department of Defense. To do this, he turned to the so-called Planning, Programming, and Budgeting System (PPBS), a budgeting system and suite of analytical techniques developed by the RAND Corporation.[1]

Zero-Based Budgeting and Management by Objectives (MBO) replaced PPBS as the programs du jour of the 1970s; and the 1980s saw the rise of productivity improvement and quality management. In 1988, a President's Quality Award was established. The new program was closely aligned with the Malcolm Baldrige National Quality Award, and focused on customer-driven quality, continuous improvement and learning, and employee participation and development, among a host of criteria. Things changed again in the early 1990s, as you will see below.

Government Performance and Results Act (GPRA)

Time certainly does fly. It's been almost ten years since former President Bill Clinton signed into law the Government Performance and Results Act (GPRA) on August 3, 1993. Talk about a noble cause: The GPRA sought to effect a fundamental transformation in the way government was managed, by placing increased emphasis on what was being accomplished as opposed to what was being spent. The act required that federally funded agencies develop and implement an accountability system based on performance measurement, including setting goals and objectives and measuring progress toward achieving them.

Once President Clinton assumed control of the Oval Office in 1993, he was eager to leverage the new focus on quality with the performance improvement ethic he championed during his tenure as Arkansas governor in the 1980s. In March 1993, he appointed Vice President Al Gore to head a six-month study on what had to be done to further improve government performance. "Creating a Government That Works Better and Costs Less" was the resulting report, which eventually led to the development of the National Partnership for Reinventing Government.

All of this leads back to August 1993 and the signing of the GPRA. Under the act, all federal agencies are required to develop mission statements, overall outcome-related goals, internal performance goals and objectives, and measures to be used to evaluate progress toward those goals and objectives.[2]

The GPRA was not the only performance-related legislation passed during the early and mid-nineties. There were also the Government Reform Act of 1994 and the Information Technology Management Reform Act of 1996. They required federal agencies to strategically plan how they would deliver high-quality goods and services to their customers, and specifically measure their programs' performance in meeting those commitments.

GPRA has received mixed reviews since its enactment, and it's difficult to assess whether the goals originally espoused in the act are being consistently achieved. However, some findings have suggested very positive outcomes resulting from GPRA, including: the development of consistent mission statements, communication of strong departmental commitment, clearly stated performance objectives and accountability, and the placement of high value on customer service.[3]

State and Local Governments Turning to Performance Measurement

Results-based management certainly isn't limited to the federal sector. With increasing momentum this movement is finding its way into state and local government as well. Recent studies show that 34 percent of counties with populations over 50,000 and 38 percent of cities with populations over 25,000 use some type of performance measurement system.[4] State and local governments that voluntarily embark on performance measurement systems are probably just staying slightly ahead of the curve. Many experts believe the Governmental Accounting Standards Board (GASB) will soon require these jurisdictions to provide "service efforts and accomplishments," which are tantamount to performance measures.

Probably the best-known example of Balanced Scorecard use in the public sector comes from a local government organization. The City of Charlotte, North Carolina, was an early adopter of the Balanced Scorecard system and has been using the tool for many years. Its success story is featured in Chapter Thirteen.

Measuring Performance in Nonprofit Organizations

There are more than 1.5 million nonprofit organizations registered with the Internal Revenue Service in the United States. In total, they represent about 8 percent of the country's gross domestic product (GDP) and 7 percent of total employment. The 9.6 million people employed in the nonprofit sector generate an annual payroll of over $480 billion.[5] Perhaps upon first reading these statistics, you will be, as I was, quite surprised. However, when you pause to reflect on this sector for a moment, you will realize just how immense and broad it is. Nonprofit organizations touch every aspect of modern societies, though, typically, "charity" organizations come to mind first. In fact, so-called charity organizations represent but one of a host of diverse players in the nonprofit space. Also included are religious organizations, social service agencies, some health care organizations, membership-based associations, educational establishments, arts and culture enterprises, and many others. While each serves a different constituency, what they have in common is the trait of being mission-based.[6]

Summing up the vital work performed by organizations in this sector is difficult to do in a few sentences. Fortunately, in their book *High-Performance Nonprofit Organizations*, Christine Letts, William Ryan, and Allen Grossman provide this very compelling synthesis: "*The nonprofit sector is filled with great ideas and thoughtful, caring people. In many ways, it represents our collective best inclinations; generosity, inclusivity, and determined optimism. The nonprofit sector attempts to bridge the many gaps in our society by bringing people together, proposing alternatives, advocating for change, and implementing remedies....As one of the under-pinnings of American Society, the nonprofit sector has built an enduring legacy of community and service.*"[7]

Nonprofit agencies have been measuring their performance for many years. Here is a summary of areas addressed by performance measurement:[8]

- *Financial accountability.* The original focus of nonprofit measurement was on documenting how funds were spent. "Standards of Accounting and Financial Reporting for Voluntary Health and Welfare Organizations" provided early guidelines.

- *Program products, or outputs.* This category represents the classic measurement efforts of most nonprofit and government organizations: counting the number of products or services delivered and the number of people served.

- *Adherence to standards of quality in service delivery.* Concerns with service delivery practices led to the development of regional and national certification and accreditation groups. These agencies ensured consistent and quality delivery of products and services.

- *Participant-related measures.* The seeds of this measurement movement can be traced back to the 1980s when funders began requiring assurances that those most in need were indeed being served. Nonprofits responded by measuring client demographics and status prior to service.

- *Key performance indicators.* Often referred to in abbreviated form as KPIs, this category can serve as a repository for all areas of measurement. Originally, key performance indicators were mainly composed of ratios among various categories of performance.

- *Client satisfaction.* Measuring the satisfaction of clients served began to gain prominence in the late 1980s. Among the determinants of satisfaction that have been measured are: timeliness of the service, accessibility, and overall satisfaction.

All of the measurement efforts just chronicled are noble in cause and reflect a sincere desire to improve performance. However, most nonprofits would agree that measurement is not an area of real competence and, frankly, is not done frequently enough to demonstrate real results. In the next section we'll contemplate why this may be the case.

Nonprofits Struggle to Invest in Organizational Capacity

In their annual reports, many nonprofits feature pie charts depicting the allocation of the funds received during the previous year. From which slice of that pie do you suppose most nonprofit executives derive the bulk of their satisfaction? Usually, it's the tiny sliver that displays the proportion of their funds that went to "administration" or "overhead." Those categories are anathema to any self-respecting nonprofit executive director. At least that's the standard thinking. It's little wonder they feel this way considering the tremendous pressure exerted by influential donors who proclaim they won't tolerate any of their largess going to fund overhead. Rhonda Pherigo is the director of Consulting Services at the Center for Nonprofit Management in Dallas, Texas, whose mission is to improve the management effectiveness of the nonprofit sector as it seeks to enhance the quality of life of its community. She explains the struggle for building capacity: *"There is a tendency for private foundations to fund the heartstring stories, and we don't have a case like that. We help organizations improve their ability to do good."*[9]

Interestingly, in the for-profit world, organizational capacity is a driving force in the race for competitive success. It's not the products and services that corporations sell that ultimately determine their achievements, but their ability to constantly innovate, cleverly market, and continuously improve their offerings. In other words, it's their commitment to investing in capacity. Nonprofits appear to view this investment choice as a zero-sum game in which anything invested in capacity is considered lost to direct service.[10] Ironically, that thinking may lead to decreased service delivery and, ultimately, reduced funding. Jeffrey Bradach, a consultant to nonprofits sums it up nicely: *"Generally, they (nonprofits) are vastly undercapitalized, understaffed, and poorly managed. Most nonprofits use their limited resources to market themselves to the same donors and foundation year after year. There's little if any investment in organizational infrastructure or staff development. Compared to the for-profit sector, the nonprofit world is back in the late 1970s and early 1980s, when Japan was beating up on American businesses....It's only beginning to understand that if you want good outcomes, you have to invest in building strong organizations."*[11]

ADAPTING THE BALANCED SCORECARD

The chapter thus far has given you a look through the window of performance measurement in both the public and nonprofit sectors. Clearly, both sectors have experienced the benefit of measurement and, with varying levels of effort and success, have embarked on measurement initiatives. What has been lacking, however, is the answer to this seemingly simple question: Is what we're doing (both in the public and nonprofit sectors) making a difference—is anyone better off as a result of our efforts? To answer that question, executives, managers, and employees alike need to view performance from a broader perspective. They require a system that not only counts the inputs and outputs of the system, but one that provides an opportunity to assess progress in reaching the organization's true mission.

The Balanced Scorecard has risen to the performance measurement challenge of the private sector and is equally well equipped to facilitate a rapid and dramatic transition of twenty-first-century nonprofit and public organizations. Exhibit 2.1 displays the Balanced Scorecard model that is applicable to public and nonprofit enterprises. We can use this diagram to differentiate between private and public and nonprofit sector use of the Scorecard.

Exhibit 2.1   Balanced Scorecard for the Public and Nonprofit Sectors

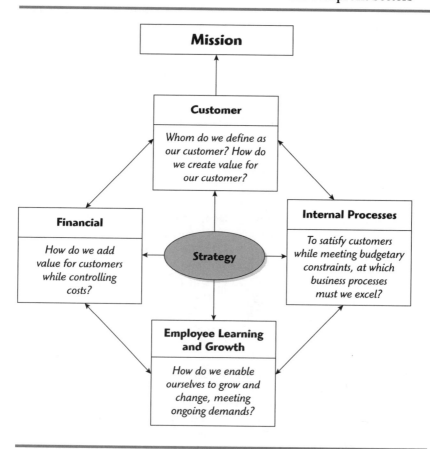

Mission Moves to the Top of the Balanced Scorecard

In the for-profit Balanced Scorecard model, all of the measures appearing on the Scorecard should lead to improved bottom-line performance. Improving shareholder value is the endgame for profit-seeking enterprises, and they are accountable to their financial stakeholders to do just that. Not so in either the public or nonprofit organization.

While you are accountable for the efficient allocation of funds (a topic we'll examine more closely in the Financial perspective), that is not your ultimate aspiration. You work to serve a higher purpose, for example: "to reduce the incidence of HIV," "to bring classical music to your community," or "to increase public safety." You may be hesitant to include such lofty objectives on your Balanced Scorecard, claiming, "We don't have total control over our mission," or "We can't influence the outcomes." However, it is only through measurement that you are able to claim any real difference in the lives or circumstances of your constituents. Of course, you won't achieve your mission overnight, and in fact may see only periodic movement. This is precisely why the other perspectives of the Balanced Scorecard are so vital. Monitoring performance, and learning from the results, in the Customer, Internal Processes, Employee Learning and Growth, and Financial perspectives will provide you with the short- to medium-term information you require to guide you ever closer to achievement of the mission.[12]

Strategy Remains at the Core of the Balanced Scorecard

Strategy remains at the core of the Scorecard system, regardless of whether it's a local theater company, city government, Fortune 500 company, or a mom-and-pop store. Nonprofit and government organizations often have a difficult time cultivating a clear and concise strategy. While many attempt to develop statements of strategy, they amount to little more than detailed lists of programs and initiatives used to secure dollars from funding bodies. Many so-called strategy documents can be upwards of 50 pages.

We'll break down the topic of strategy and strategic planning in Chapter Six. For now, suffice it to say that strategy is about those broad priorities you plan to pursue in order to achieve your mission. The priorities must be consistent with your unique situation and fit one another in an effort to respond effectively to your challenges and opportunities. Once you've developed your strategy, the Balanced Scorecard serves as the device for effective translation and implementation.

Customer Perspective Is Elevated

A clear distinction between private- and public-sector Balanced Scorecards is drawn as a result of placing mission at the top of the framework. Flowing from the mission is a view of the organization's customers, not financial stakeholders. Achieving a mission does not equate with fiscal responsibility and stewardship; instead, the organization must determine whom it aims to serve and how their requirements can best be met. Rick Pagsibigan is the chief strategy officer at the Red Cross of Philadelphia. When developing their Balanced Scorecard, placing the Customer perspective at the top of the model was a logical choice. Pagsibigan explains, *"We put the Customer perspective at the top. The message is that anything and everything we do regarding financials, revenues, and so on is there to support our customers."*[13]

In the profit-seeking world, companies are accountable to their capital providers (shareholders) for results, and they monitor this accountability through the results attained in the Financial perspective of the Scorecard. Again, this is not the case in the nonprofit and public sectors. Here the focus is on customers, and serving their needs in order to accomplish the mission. But the question of "who is the customer" is one of the most perplexing issues that nonprofit and government Scorecard adopters face. In these sectors, unlike the for-profit world, different groups design the service, pay for the service, and ultimately benefit from the service. This web of relationships makes determining the customer a formidable challenge. Establishing the real customer in many ways depends on your perspective. In the public sector, the legislative body that provides funding is a logical choice, as is the group you serve. However, think about that group you "serve." Would law enforcement agencies consider the criminals they arrest their customers? You could probably make a case for that. Conversely, many would argue that constituents are the ultimate beneficiaries of policing activities and are therefore the real customers.

Fortunately, the Balanced Scorecard doesn't force you to make this difficult decision. Including all customers is permissible and possible using the public-sector Scorecard framework. Not only is it possible, it's desirable since meeting the mission will most likely entail satisfying disparate customer groups, each of which figures in your success. Each group of customers identified will likely result in different measures appearing in the other three perspectives of the Scorecard. Once nonprofit and public-sector executives and managers have made their way through this tangled maze, the job of choosing performance measures in all perspectives becomes much simpler.

No Balanced Scorecard Is Complete without a Financial Perspective

No organization, regardless of its status, can successfully operate and meet customer requirements without financial resources. Financial measures in the public and nonprofit sector Scorecard model can best be seen as either enablers of customer success or constraints within which the group must operate. Many will argue, with merit, that it's difficult to put a financial price on the work they perform. Consider a nonprofit agency attempting to provide prenatal care to disadvantaged expectant mothers. Its prized outcome is the birth of a healthy baby, which is as far from financial concerns as you can stray. Nevertheless, the agency in this case must persuade reluctant managers that financial measures aren't inconsistent with quality service delivery and achieving the mission. In fact, when services are performed at least cost, or with great efficiency, the program will likely attract more attention and warrant even greater investment from funders. A win for everyone.

Identifying Internal Processes That Drive Value for Customers

When developing objectives and measures for this perspective, it is necessary to ask, "What are the key internal processes we must excel at in order to drive value for our customers?" Every organization from the smallest local service agency to the largest departments of the federal government will have documented processes for establishing their goals. Small organizations may have dozens, while larger entities may have processes numbering in the hundreds.

The key to Balanced Scorecard success lies in selecting, and measuring, just those processes that lead to improved outcomes for customers, and ultimately allow you to work toward your mission. The processes you choose to focus on will normally flow directly from the objectives and measures chosen in the Customer perspective. It's not uncommon for the Internal Processes perspective to house the greatest number of objectives and measures on the Balanced Scorecard.

Employee Learning and Growth Perspective Provides the Foundation for a Well-Constructed Balanced Scorecard

Operating as mission-based organizations, nonprofit and public-sector agencies rely heavily on the skills, dedication, and alignment of their staff to achieve their socially important goals. Employees and organizational infrastructure represent the thread that weaves through the rest of the Balanced Scorecard. Success in driving process improvements, operating in a fiscally responsible way, and meeting the needs of all customer groups depends to a great extent on the ability of employees and the tools they use in support of your mission.

As crucial as the objectives and measures of the Employee Learning and Growth perspective are, they're often overlooked. Considered "soft stuff" or "pure overhead," many organizations will ignore these base ingredients to building a successful Balanced Scorecard. They do so at their peril. Motivated employees with the right mix of skills and tools operating in an organizational climate designed for sustaining improvements are the key ingredients in driving process improvements, working within financial limitations, and ultimately driving customer and mission success.

Three areas are particularly relevant to capture in this perspective. First, employee skills and competencies: Do you have the right mix of skills to meet your challenges (and opportunities) on an ongoing basis? Second, the flow of information, or what is sometimes termed "information capital": Do employees have the tools and information they require to make effective decisions that impact customer outcomes? Finally, the organizational climate should be addressed. This typically consists of elements such as alignment and motivation. We'll examine each of these in more detail in chapters Eight and Nine.

IMPORTANCE OF CAUSE AND EFFECT

Now that you've been introduced to the Balanced Scorecard and have seen how it can be easily adapted to fit your organization, no doubt you're thinking about what you currently measure. You may be thinking, "We measure customer outcomes, we look at our quality, and we try to monitor our training; I guess we're close to having a Balanced Scorecard already." On the road maybe, but you've got a ways to go before you can claim to have a real Balanced Scorecard.

Many organizations do have a mix of financial and nonfinancial indicators, and they dutifully monitor them on a monthly or quarterly basis. However, this ad hoc collection of indicators does little to provide them with a guide for learning about and executing their strategy. Let's say, for example, you measure your investment in training and you find that employees have received an average of eight hours of training per month, exceeding your target of five hours. You're also measuring quality, and have found that quality of services provided is dropping. What action would you take based on those results? Would you increase or decrease the amount of training you're currently supplying to your staff? The answer depends on your assumption regarding the relationship of training to quality. The true value of performance measures is derived from examining the results in light of the assumptions you make about the relationships among the indicators. If you believed an investment in training would be positively correlated with training, but results have suggested otherwise, now you have information upon which to act and make decisions.

Remember, the Balanced Scorecard is first and foremost a tool for translating your strategy and helping you work toward your mission. The best strategy ever conceived is simply a hypothesis developed by its authors. It represents their best guess as to an appropriate course of action, given their knowledge of information concerning the environment, competencies, and so on. For most organizations, strategy is a new destination, somewhere they haven't traveled to before. What is needed is a method to document and test the assumptions inherent in the strategy. The Balanced Scorecard allows you to do just that.

A well-designed Balanced Scorecard should describe your strategy through the objectives and measures you have chosen. These measures should link together in a chain of cause-and-effect relationships from the performance drivers in the Employee Learning and Growth perspective all the way through to improved customer outcomes as reflected in the Customer perspective. We are attempting to document our strategy through measurement, making the relationships between the measures explicit so they can be monitored, managed, and validated. Only then can we begin learning about, and successfully implementing, our strategy.

Exhibit 2.2 provides an example of cause and effect that can be used to demonstrate this concept. Let's say you're the executive director of a local performing arts organization. You consider the community in which you operate to be a customer of the theater; therefore, you include the objective of "Build community support" in the Customer perspective of the Scorecard. But how do you build community support? At which processes must you excel? You hypothesize that community support is a function of the number of new and innovative performances you stage. As a result, you decide to add the objective, "Develop new and innovative performances" in your Internal Processes perspective.

Exhibit 2.2   Telling Your Strategic Story through Cause-and-Effect Linkages

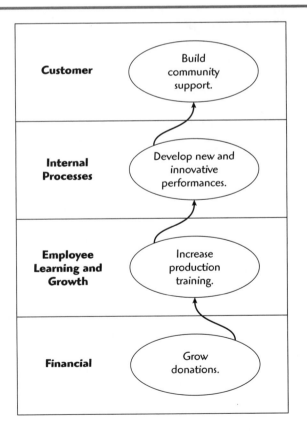

Now you move to the Employee Learning and Growth perspective. What, from an employee perspective, will allow you to stage unique performances? You believe that providing employees with training on the latest staging techniques will lead to more innovative performances. Thus, "Increase production training" is an appropriate objective. Finally, you realize that you live in a world of budgetary constraints and won't be able to achieve any of your objectives unless you run a tight financial ship. More donations would be tremendously helpful, so you add "Grow donations" as an objective in the Financial perspective. You've now created a series of linked objectives that run through the Scorecard, telling your strategic story.

The linkage of measures throughout the Balanced Scorecard is constructed with a series of if-then statements: If we grow our donations, then we'll have the resources to increase training. If we increase training, then we believe production innovation will increase. If innovation increases, then support from the community will rise.

Developing tight cause-and-effect linkages is a challenge for any organization. Going through the mental gymnastics required to build a seamless integration of objectives and measures is difficult and draining work. The degree of difficulty is compounded in the nonprofit and public sectors. The myriad influences surrounding your work are major contributing factors to the difficulty. Nevertheless, I encourage you to attempt this task when developing your Balanced Scorecard. Once you've made an initial set of hypotheses about your performance, you're in a great position to begin learning about which levers really drive your success. You may not get all the answers, but I guarantee you'll be generating better questions. And as the great management guru Peter Drucker reminds us, *"The most common source of mistakes in management decisions is the emphasis on finding the right answer rather than the right question."*[14] Our work with strategy maps in Chapter Eight will revisit the topic of cause and effect.

BENEFITS OF USING A BALANCED SCORECARD

Many organizations struggle with performance measurement and management. In fact, 80 percent of respondents in one recent study reported making changes in their Performance Management system during the last three years. The same study reported that for 33 percent of those organizations, the change was described as a "major overhaul."[15] The Balanced Scorecard has emerged as a proven tool in the battle to provide meaningful performance information. Organizations around the globe are taking notice and turning to the Balanced Scorecard. Here in the United States, about 50 percent of the Fortune 1000 are using the Balanced Scorecard.[16]

Of course, the Scorecard isn't just for large corporations. Small and medium-sized enterprises have embraced the concept as well. All cite the Scorecard's elegant simplicity, focus on strategy, and ability to drive alignment as key benefits of the framework. What about nonprofit and government agencies? What benefits might they expect from investing in the Scorecard? Listed below are some of the most commonly mentioned benefits users from your sectors have received.

Demonstrate Accountability and Generate Results

President George W. Bush has said, *"Government likes to begin things, to declare grand new programs and causes. But good beginnings are not the measure of success. What matters in the end is completion. Performance. Results. Not just making promises, but making good on promises."*[17] Never before have results mattered so much to government and nonprofit organizations.

Chapter One recapped some of the sensational corporate scandals that have recently spread like a virus through the for-profit world. Accountability has become almost a universal slogan. Public-sector and nonprofit organizations are not immune to these cries for change. Look at the world of philanthropy. Over the past 11 years, charitable donations by individuals have grown by 50 percent, from $110 billion in 1990 to $164 billion in 2001. But this new philanthropy demands results. *"The new philanthropists attach a lot of strings. Recipients are often required to meet milestone goals, to invite foundation members onto their boards, and to produce measurable results or risk losing their funding."*[18] The task of monitoring results has created a virtual industry of its own, with many organizations and Web sites set up to track your local government's or favorite nonprofit's performance.[19] Rick Pagsibigan of the Philadelphia Red Cross sums up the current environment very nicely: *"It used to be that people gave because it felt good; now they give to feel good, and look at their return on investment. To show them the outcomes we first have to measure."*[20]

That's where the Balanced Scorecard comes in. To be accountable and demonstrate results, you need to accurately measure the true performance of your organization. Simply counting people served or dollars spent won't cut it in today's environment. You need to demonstrate advancement on the high-level, mission-based objectives that your constituents are requiring you to provide. The Balanced Scorecard with its focus on mission and strategy and broad view of performance allows you to do just that. Legendary New York City Mayor Rudy Giuliani understands the bond between measurement and accountability: *"Objective, measurable indicators of success allow governments to be accountable, and I relentlessly pursued that idea."*[21]

Attract Scarce Resources (Funding and Employees)

California Governor Gray Davis recently had the very unenviable task of reporting the state's deficit for the upcoming fiscal year. The final tally? A whopping $34.8 billion dollars![22] It's hard to even fathom a number of that magnitude, but for the thousands of agencies counting on money from Sacramento, the pain will be all too real. Competition for money and talent has never been more demanding. In the nonprofit sector, the race for donor dollars is increasingly intense, with competition coming from some very surprising places. The next time you're online, try typing "e-panhandling" into the search box on Yahoo! You'll find that it has its own category, and at the time of this writing, there are more than 50 Web sites exclusively dedicated to soliciting personal handouts. My favorite is "Make me richer than Bill Gates." At a buck a pop, this person is going to be waiting a while!

While the Balanced Scorecard may not make your organization richer than Bill Gates, it can help you attract scarce resources. By developing a Balanced Scorecard, reporting progress on achieving your strategic objectives, and proving your efficiency and effectiveness, you can ensure the migration of scarce resources to your organization, department, or agency. The Broad Foundation of Los Angeles, California, recently awarded a $195,000 grant to Detroit Public Schools District. Part of the rationale for the behest was the fact that Detroit Public Schools will be using the Balanced Scorecard. *"The Detroit Public Schools are among the first K-12 districts to adopt the Balanced Scorecard process,"* said Executive Director Geri Markley, Office of Continuous Improvement. *"The Scorecard provides a balanced view of districtwide performance from four perspectives: students, funders, internal systems, and employees."*[23]

Create a Focus on Strategy

Translating your strategy into action is the true purpose of the Balanced Scorecard. While many organizations measure, they frequently lose sight of the fact that measurement should be about achieving strategy, not "counting widgets." Regarding this "measurement gap," Bill Ryan, a consultant to nonprofit organizations and co-author of *High Performance Nonprofit Organizations*, offers: *"People are measuring performance, financial performance, programmatic performance, certain narrow indicators of organizational performance—maybe board diversity or composition, for instance—they're measuring lots of different aspects of performance at the behest of lots of different stakeholders— usually multiple funders. And yet none of those performance measurement systems actually correspond to their own values, their own objectives, their own really fundamental goals and social missions....So something like a Balanced Scorecard can help people integrate all those fragmented performance measurement systems into something coherent, that's aligned with their real fundamental purpose."*[24]

Simply put, the Balanced Scorecard allows you to focus on what really matters, the few critical drivers of success that power your strategy and lead to the achievement of your mission. The Safer Foundation is a Chicago-based organization that assists ex-offenders in becoming productive, law-abiding members of the community. Executive Director Diane Williams says using the Balanced Scorecard "allows us to focus on our strategy."[25] To achieve demonstrated results, attract resources, and prove your accountability, you absolutely must keep your eyes on your strategy at all times.

Produce Information, Not Data

Have you ever noticed that there are unintended consequences produced by every so-called innovation? Consider the great boon of technology. Back in the 1950s, pundits suggested that the proliferation of labor-saving devices would mean shorter workweeks and more time for leisure. Well, technology has definitely improved productivity but I don't know about that promise of reduced workweeks. The fact is, we're working longer and harder than ever.

Technology has also produced a Grand Canyon-sized gap between data and information. We're awash in data these days. Every office I go into features binder-filled walls that seem to be creeping ever closer to the inhabitants. Those same binders are chock full of data, but they tend to be lacking in a supply of real information. Health care consultant James Lifton has seen the problem first hand: *"What we're really talking about is information....Voluntary trustees can get a lot of data and not understand what they mean or not have time to review them all. I've seen boards get a three-ring binder or a large packet, and sometimes they don't know what to make of it, or they're unwilling or unable to take the time to go through it."*[26] The Balanced Scorecard resides exclusively in the information domain. It does so by measuring only the critical few drivers of organizational success. A Balanced Scorecard that contains 50 or 60 measures probably has abundant data, but I'll take a Scorecard that has 10 or 12 measures for real information value.

Self-Preservation

Did you know that nearly half of all federal employees perform tasks that are readily available in the commercial marketplace?[27] It's true: activities such as data collection, administrative support, and payroll services. Having your function outsourced to a third-party (private-sector) provider is definitely an option these days, as taxpayers and funders continue to scrutinize how their dollars are being spent and what results are coming of those investments. For those of you in the public sector, there is even scrutiny from within! For the first time ever, the Office of Management and Budget (OMB) recently bid out the process of printing the federal budget. Since the 1860s, Congress had mandated that all executive branch agencies give their printing business to the Government Printing Office (GPO). OMB director Mitch Daniels felt a monopoly of over 140 years was enough. In the end, the GPO won the work, but its fee was reduced from $505,000 to $387,000.[28] Amazing what a little competition will do.

The Balanced Scorecard allows you to demonstrate quality results at efficient prices—that is, if you're not afraid to cast a bright light on your current processes. The Scorecard also helps you do that by pinpointing the vital few processes that really drive customer outcomes.

Drive Change

Charles Darwin once noted, "The survivors of any species are not necessarily the strongest. And they are not necessarily the most intelligent. They are those who are most responsive to change." This quote can be aptly applied to any modern organization as well. Only the change-ready survive! Measurements from a Balanced Scorecard can help drive the change you need to meet your desired outcomes. Shelley Metzenbaum, the director of the Performance Management Project at the Kennedy School of Government at Harvard University, tells the story of the Charles River in Massachusetts. The goal of the "Clean Charles 2005" initiative was to make the Charles River swimmable in 10 years. In just five years, the river went from being swimmable mere 19 percent of the time to 65 percent of the time. Metzenbaum notes it was a monthly measurement system, establishing water quality every few miles along the river, that provided the information needed to drive the change.

Inspire Trust

I've already discussed how the Balanced Scorecard can help you demonstrate accountability and attract scarce resources to your organization. The driver of both those outcomes is enhanced trust: trust from the community, trust from your funders, and trust from your employees. The benefits of increased levels of trust are by no means limited to the intangible. Research has demonstrated, "*Those who have high confidence in charities, as well as believe in their honesty and ethics, give an average annual contribution of about $1,800. This is about 50 percent greater than the amount given by those sharing neither opinion, who average just over $1,200 in annual household contributions to charity, once again underscoring the strong connection between public trust and giving.*"[29]

These are just a sampling of the many benefits conferred by the application of a Balanced Scorecard. You'll also see that creative links from the Scorecard to your key management processes such as budgeting and planning will make your entire organization even stronger. As with most things in life, the more effort and focus you put into the Balanced Scorecard, the more you'll get out of it. Here's an open invitation: Once you've started using the Balanced Scorecard, I encourage you to contact me and let me know how it has benefited you. Who knows, maybe I'll be writing about you in a future edition of this book.

SUMMARY

"*Adapt or perish, now as ever, is nature's inexorable imperative.*" So said English author and historian H.G. Wells many years ago. Applying this powerful language to the Balanced Scorecard suggests that if you expect to achieve success with this tool, you must adapt it to fit your organization. Outlining that process was the subject of this chapter.

It began by examining past and present measurement efforts in both the public and nonprofit sectors. The public sector has been measuring performance for many years, and has employed a wide variety of tools to accomplish the task. In the 1960s, the Performance Planning and Budgeting System was utilized. It was followed by zero-based budgeting, management by objectives, and total quality initiatives. Then, in 1993, the Government Performance and Results Act (GPRA) was passed into law, requiring that federally funded agencies develop and implement an accountability system based on performance measurement, including setting goals and objectives and measuring progress toward achieving them. At the state and local levels, the Governmental Accounting Standards Board (GASB) has advocated the use of "service efforts and accomplishments."

The nonprofit sector has also experimented with performance measurement, adopting indicators of financial accountability and participant-related metrics among a variety of areas. Many nonprofits have struggled with the notion of performance measurement, possibly because of a general unwillingness to invest in organizational capacity. Many agencies fear that every dollar spent on initiatives such as performance measurement take that sum from the achievement of their mission. Many pundits now suggest that a strong and capable infrastructure is a prerequisite of nonprofits in their pursuit of mission objectives.

The Balanced Scorecard has been widely accepted in the for-profit world, with over half the Fortune 1000 employing the system. This chapter examined the differences between the for-profit model and that utilized by public and nonprofit sectors, pointing out that while strategy remains at the core of the Scorecard, mission objectives are elevated to the top of the framework. Customer objectives also rise in prominence on Scorecards designed for public and nonprofit agencies. Financial objectives and measures are critical to any organization and often serve as enablers or constraints. Both the Internal Processes perspective and Employee Learning and Growth perspectives remain on the public and nonprofit Scorecards.

Later the chapter addressed the fact that many organizations have a mix of financial and nonfinancial indicators, and they dutifully monitor them on a monthly or quarterly basis. However, this ad hoc collection of indicators does little to provide them with a guide for learning about and executing their strategies. What separates the Scorecard from other systems is the focus on cause and effect. The objectives and measures chosen for your Balanced Scorecard should weave together through the four perspectives to tell your strategic story.

This chapter concluded by examining some of the many benefits you can derive from the Balanced Scorecard system. They included: demonstrating accountability and generating results, attracting scarce resources, creating a focus on strategy, producing information (as opposed to data), self-preservation, driving change, and inspiring trust.

NOTES

1. Andrea Gabor, *The Capitalist Philosophers* (New York: Times Business, 2000), p. 143.
2. Carl G. Thor, "The Evolution of Performance Measurement in Government," *Journal of Cost Management,* May/June 2000.
3. Ron Carlson, "A Look at GPRA Practices: How Far Have We Traveled?" *The Public Manager,* Fall 2000, pp. 25–29.
4. Evan Berman and Xiao Hu Wang, "Performance Measurement in U.S. Counties: Capacity for Reform," *Public Administration Review,* September/October, 2000.
5. Independent Sector, "The New Nonprofit Almanac in Brief," 2001.
6. Adapted from an e-mail to the author from Donald Golob, September 4, 2002.
7. Christine W. Letts, William P. Ryan, and Allen Grossman, *High-Performance Nonprofit Organizations* (New York: John Wiley & Sons, Inc., 1999), p. 1.
8. Margaret C. Plantz, Martha Taylor Greenway, and Michael Hendricks, "Outcome Measurement: Showing Results in the Nonprofit Sector," *New Directions for Evaluation,* Fall 1997.
9. From interview with Rhonda Pherigo, July 23, 2002.
10. Christine W. Letts, William P. Ryan, and Allen Grossman, *High-Performance Nonprofit Organizations* (New York: John Wiley & Sons, Inc., 1999), p. 32.
11. John A. Byrne, "The New Face of Philanthropy," *BusinessWeek,* December 2, 2002, pp. 82–94.
12. Robert S. Kaplan, "The Balanced Scorecard and Nonprofit Organizations," *Balanced Scorecard Report,* November–December, 2002, pp. 1–4.
13. From interview with Rick Pagsibigan, September 19, 2002.
14. Bob Frost, *Crafting Strategy* (Dallas, TX: Measurement International, 2000), p. 12.
15. Mark L. Frigo, "The State of Strategic Performance Measurement: The IMA 2001 Survey," *Balanced Scorecard Report,* November–December, 2001, pp. 13–14.
16. Robert S. Kaplan and David P. Norton, "On Balance," *CFO Magazine,* February 2001, p. 74.
17. George W. Bush, "The President's Management Agenda," from www .whitehouse.gov/omb/budget/fy2002/mgmt.pdf.
18. John A. Byrne, "The New Face of Philanthropy," *BusinessWeek,* December 2, 2002, pp. 82–94.
19. See, for example, www.guidestar.org or www.charitynavigator.com.
20. From interview with Rick Pagsibigan, September 19, 2002.
21. Rudolph W. Giuliani, *Leadership* (New York: Hyperion, 2002).
22. "California's Gray Hole," *The Wall Street Journal* online, December 20, 2002.
23. U.S. Newswire, "Detroit Public Schools Awarded Grant by The Broad Foundation," December 10, 2002.
24. From interview with Bill Ryan, September 17, 2002.
25. From interview with Diane Williams, October 3, 2002.
26. Michelle Bitoun, "Show Them the Data," *Trustee,* September, 2002, p. 18.
27. From the President's Management Agenda at www.whitehouse.gov/omb/budget/fy2002/mgmt.pdf, p. 17.
28. George Will, "Why Privatization Will Work," *Washington Post,* December 22, 2002.
29. Independent Sector, "Keeping the Faith: Confidence in Charitable Organizations in an Age of Security," 2002.

PART TWO

Pouring the Foundation for Balanced Scorecard Success

CHAPTER 3

Before You Begin

Roadmap for Chapter Three It was Christian Bovee who observed, *"The method of the enterprising is to plan with audacity and execute with vigor."* This chapter is devoted to the first half of Bovee's inspirational wisdom. Planning is crucial in virtually every initiative we undertake, whether it's building a house, writing a report, or developing a Balanced Scorecard. A number of elements of the project must be considered long before any nails can be driven, pens lifted, or metrics debated and decided upon. In this chapter we'll take a careful look at each of the building blocks of a successful Balanced Scorecard project.

The chapter begins by posing the question: Why do we need the Balanced Scorecard? It then challenges you to develop specific objectives for using the Scorecard in your organization. No project of this magnitude can be completed without the allocation of human and financial resources, and we'll review each of these elements. Next, once you've determined your objectives and have gathered resources, you must decide where to build your first Scorecard. I'll provide a number of criteria to help you make this important decision. We'll then transition to the human element of the Balanced Scorecard, beginning with a review of the vital nature of executive sponsorship. A close look at your Balanced Scorecard team will follow; we'll consider the size of the team, skills necessary, and roles and responsibilities of all members. The chapter concludes with a development plan for your Balanced Scorecard implementation.

DEVELOPING OBJECTIVES FOR YOUR BALANCED SCORECARD

The philosopher Plato once suggested, "The beginning is the most important part of the work." Many years later, another oft-quoted sage remarked, "You've got to be careful if you don't know where you're going 'cause you might not get there." Those, of course, are the inimitable words of Yogi Berra. I'm inclined to agree with both of these statements and believe they apply very well to our discussion of objectives for your Balanced Scorecard program.

The Balanced Scorecard has distinguished itself over the last decade as a truly transformational business tool. However, even the most elegantly conceived and skillfully constructed Balanced Scorecard will not instantly transform your organization. To harness the powerful benefits of this framework, you must first determine specifically why it is you need to change your organization and how the Scorecard will aid you in your efforts. As Jeff Celentano from the City of North Bay, Ontario, told me, *"This is what I think is needed to succeed when you are trying to implement a Balanced Scorecard: understanding by your management team. And I don't just mean your ability to connect the dots; I mean understanding why we are doing this. If you don't have a burning issue, what is the need to get into this? What is the value for us?"*[1] In other words, what is your "burning platform" for change?

The term "burning platform" has been a mainstay in the business lexicon for many years. For those of you not familiar with its origin, the story goes something like this: A man working on an oil platform in the North Sea was awakened suddenly one night by an explosion. Amidst the chaos, he made his way to the edge of the platform. As a plume of fire billowed behind him, he decided to jump from the burning platform even though he had been trained to never consider this as an option for the following reasons: It was a 150-foot drop from the platform to the water, and there was often debris and burning oil on the surface; and if the jump into the 40°F water didn't kill you, you would die of exposure within 15 minutes. Luckily, the man survived the jump and was hauled aboard a rescue boat shortly thereafter. When asked why he jumped, he replied, "Better probable death than certain death."[2] The point is, the literally "burning" platform caused this man to radically change his behavior. You may not be running for your life, but you undoubtedly face changes every day that threaten your organization's success. Those issues, and the Scorecard's ability to solve them, will form the basis of your objectives for using the Balanced Scorecard.

If all this talk about jumping from oil rigs seems a tad dramatic for you, consider that most people will change only when *"survival anxiety is greater than learning anxiety."*[3] Learning anxieties are the basis for resistance to change and represent apprehensions of trying something new for fear that it will be too difficult or we'll look stupid while attempting it. Survival anxieties, in contrast, are those painful realizations that in order to succeed, we have to change.[4] The oil worker who took the perilous North Sea plunge clearly had greater survival anxiety than learning anxiety. Your challenge is to introduce survival anxiety while also lessening learning anxiety, thereby creating a safe environment in which true learning can occur. The objectives you develop for your Balanced Scorecard will introduce your survival anxieties to employees. They will describe why you must change in order to succeed. Additionally, the use of the Scorecard will provide a safe environment for learning, and therefore simultaneously lessen learning anxiety—a real win-win situation.

Exhibit 3.1 provides a number of possible reasons for launching a Balanced Scorecard program. While all of these are valid, you should not consider this a "pick and choose" exercise of selecting objectives that sound good to you. In order to realize real benefits from the Balanced Scorecard, you must determine your specific rationale for launching this implementation. Nancy Foltz of the Michigan Department of Transportation describes their objectives for using the Balanced Scorecard. "*The Balanced Scorecard was selected as a tool to identify the commonalities of strategy, expand our focus and understanding of customer needs, and align systems and structures to meet customer needs.*"[5] These are all excellent objectives for launching a Scorecard effort. The City of North Bay, Ontario, also felt the Scorecard would assist them in meeting the many challenges facing their organization. Jeff Celentano describes the key objective. "*There was an increased desire both politically and administratively for improved accountability.*"[6] This is an objective that will most likely motivate many public and nonprofit organizations.

Let me give you an example of a problem that can occur when you don't have clear objectives. One client I worked with was totally committed to the concept of the Balanced Scorecard, and was very eager to get it up and running quickly; as a result, we failed to develop clear objectives for the Scorecard at the start of the implementation. The implementation team went to work and built a great Balanced Scorecard that told the story of the firm's strategy in about 30 objectives. When the CEO saw this, he was clearly disappointed. Although he was impressed with the work that had gone into the Scorecard, it turned out that his main objective was to use the system primarily as a communication tool; therefore, he wanted a dozen measures or fewer. The team had to go back to work and pare down the objectives to meet the CEO's wishes. Valuable time and some positive energy were lost in the process.

Exhibit 3.1   Rationale for Using a Balanced Scorecard

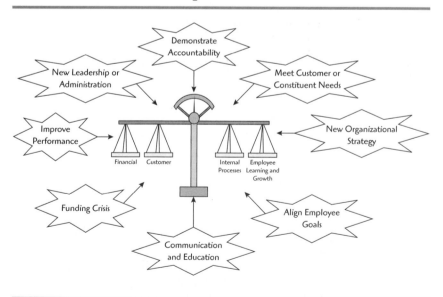

Adapted from material presented in *Balanced Scorecard Step-by-Step: Maximizing Performance and Maintaining Results*, by Paul R. Niven (New York: John Wiley & Sons, Inc., 2002).

In my first book, *Balanced Scorecard Step-by-Step: Maximizing Performance and Maintaining Results* (John Wiley & Sons, Inc., 2002), I chronicled the Scorecard efforts of the Texas State Auditor's Office (TSAO). This team of 237 dedicated individuals supports the Texas legislature and is responsible for auditing the executive branch agencies entrusted with state funds for the provision of services to the state's 20 million citizens. They understand the temptation of simply measuring results. Deborah Kerr of the TSAO explains. *"It is easy to get caught up in the creation of measures and targets and lose sight of your purpose. While measures are important, remembering why you want to measure performance will keep you focused on the outcomes."*[7]

A well-articulated, widely understood, and ceaselessly communicated rationale for the Balanced Scorecard will prove to be a major asset in your efforts. The simple act of developing your objectives will force the establishment of consensus among all team members. Building that consensus will greatly assist your communication and education efforts, as everyone will truly be on the same page. Objectives are also critical at those inevitable moments when your project loses some of its momentum. The focal point of your guiding objectives can serve as a rallying cry to reenergize and refocus the efforts of your team, reminding everyone exactly why you chose to develop a Scorecard. Author and consultant to nonprofits Bill Ryan sums it up nicely: *"Organizations must really understand their motivation in doing this [Balanced Scorecard] work. Because with these systems there will come daunting stretches, there will come times when people are wondering, why are we doing this? What will get organizations over those humps is understanding the relevance of these tools to the social vision they have. More attention to the rationale is really useful and important."*[8]

HUMAN AND FINANCIAL RESOURCES NECESSARY FOR THE BALANCED SCORECARD

Even if you're fortunate enough to enjoy complete support from the senior leaders within your organization, you can be sure that at some point, someone will ask, "What is this going to cost?" You should be prepared to answer that question, so in this section we'll look at both the human and financial resources required when developing and using a Balanced Scorecard system. Later in the chapter we'll examine the critical role of executive sponsorship in a successful Scorecard initiative.

A caveat at the outset: You won't find an exact Scorecard budget in this section or at any point in this book. I've already touted the Balanced Scorecard's wide applicability as a strong attribute of the system. Given the fact that virtually any organization can enjoy the benefits offered by the Scorecard, it's difficult to pin down exact resource requirements. Every organization will have differing levels of comfort expending both human and financial resources, and every organization will have different limitations. Therefore, the purpose of this section is to provide a guide to the general classifications of resources required.

No Balanced Scorecard can be built in isolation. The best Scorecards represent the collective inspiration and knowledge from a team of organizational experts. That means you'll need a group of people devoted to your Scorecard initiative. In my consulting work I've seen Balanced Scorecard teams ranging in size from 3 to 30 people. Later in this chapter I'll outline who should have a seat at your Scorecard table and the specific roles and responsibilities each will play.

The Scorecard also comes with a financial price tag. The good news is you don't have to break the bank in order to develop a highly successful and sustainable Balanced Scorecard program. Here are a number of items you may wish to consider when building a budget for your Balanced Scorecard:

- *Employee time.* There is a salary cost associated with the time committed to the Balanced Scorecard. This cost will be skewed toward the front end of the project as your team works together building the Balanced Scorecard. Once initiated and operating, resource requirements in this category should diminish.

- *Consulting.* A highly qualified and skilled consultant can mean the difference between a well-developed Scorecard embraced by all employees and one that languishes in a binder on your office shelf.

- *Software.* When I began working with the Balanced Scorecard many years ago, Microsoft Excel charts were considered the vanguard of Scorecard reporting. Since that time, Scorecard reporting systems have proliferated almost exponentially. Today there are literally dozens of choices available, with price tags ranging from a few hundred to several hundred-thousand dollars. Chapter Twelve provides an in-depth look at Balanced Scorecard reporting options.

- *Educational Materials.* I consider training and education a key differentiator in successful Balanced Scorecard implementations. There is absolutely no substitute for training. Your investment in education can range from a few copies of a book to sending your entire team to one of the many Scorecard conferences held around the world. We'll revisit the topic of training and education in Chapter Four.

- *Logistical expenses.* Many organizations will do much of their initial Scorecard development off-site. I strongly advocate this approach. Concentration on the task at hand is definitely enhanced when participants aren't distracted by ringing phones, assistants passing urgent notes, and a screen full of attention-demanding e-mail messages. Your costs here may include rental fees, supplies, and meals.

WHERE TO BUILD THE BALANCED SCORECARD?

This chapter opened with a review of objectives for your Balanced Scorecard program. I emphasized the importance of developing a solid foundation for the Scorecard before embarking on the actual work of building performance objectives and measures. Simply put, it's critical to get off to a good start and generate instant momentum for the Scorecard. Determining where to build your first Balanced Scorecard is the next step in the initial momentum-building phase.

The size of your organization will, to a great degree, dictate where your first Scorecard is developed. Those of you working in larger organizations will be faced with the most choices. You could decide to develop a high-level organizational Scorecard or choose a "pilot" location for your first development efforts. Departments within the organization, or even support groups such as from finance or human resources, could launch the Balanced Scorecard.

For many organizations, starting at the top and building a high-level Balanced Scorecard for the entire enterprise is often the best choice for a number of reasons. First, the objectives and measures on this Scorecard can be widely communicated to all employees, ensuring that everyone is aware of the critical drivers of success for your organization. Second, this set of measures will provide focus for all groups and promote collaboration among departments in an effort to implement the strategy and work toward the mission. Finally, starting at the top greatly assists your cascading efforts. "Cascading" the Balanced Scorecard represents the process of driving the Scorecard to lower levels of the organization, giving all employees the opportunity to demonstrate how their day-to-day actions contribute to long-term goals. The objectives and measures on the highest-level Scorecard will serve as the starting point for cascaded Balanced Scorecards.

As just detailed, starting at the top has its advantages, but it's clearly not for everyone. Many organizations will choose to pilot the Balanced Scorecard at the department or agency level in the hope of achieving success there that can later be duplicated elsewhere. The Community Services Group of the County of San Diego, California, made such a choice recently. This group houses a number of disparate services provided to county residents, including: Library, Housing and Community Development, Animal Control, Registrar of Voters, and General Services. It would be difficult to draft a high-level Scorecard broad enough to initially capture the interests of these varied groups. Therefore, the group chose to pilot the Balanced Scorecard in the Animal Control service, chosen primarily for two key reasons: First, the service has a relatively simple structure with one head office and two branch offices. Second, as Staff Officer John Ramont suggests, "*Animal Control has a relatively straightforward mandate; everyone knows what they do.*"[9] The department's Strategy Map of performance objectives is shown in Exhibit 3.2.

Exhibit 3.2 San Diego County Department of Animal Control Strategy Map

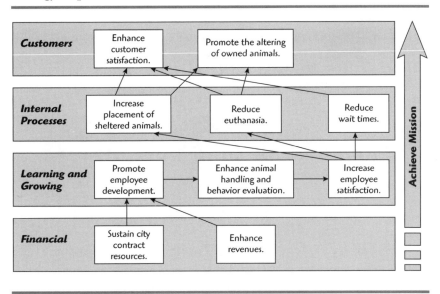

Criteria for Choosing an Appropriate Organizational Unit

To help you make the important decision of where to develop your first Balanced Scorecard, I've developed a number of criteria you should consider. They are presented in Exhibit 3.3. Let's review these and determine how they might impact your Scorecard development decision.

Mission and Strategy

Chapter Two reviewed the new "geography" of the nonprofit and public-sector Balanced Scorecard. You learned that mission is elevated to the top of the Scorecard since you do not have a profit or shareholder imperative. Your organizations are chartered with the obligation of serving customers to fulfill a social, business, or societal need. Therefore, any group you select for your first Scorecard should possess a mission for its existence.

A strategy is also critical since at its core the Balanced Scorecard is a tool designed to assist you in translating strategy into action. Without a strategic stake in the ground, you're very likely to end up with an ad hoc collection of financial and nonfinancial measures that do not link together to tell the story of your strategy. Without this linkage of cause-and-effect relationships

Exhibit 3.3   Seven Criteria for Choosing Where to Begin Your Balanced Scorecard

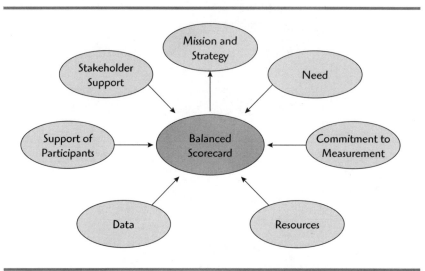

Adapted from material presented in *Balanced Scorecard Step-by-Step: Maximizing Performance and Maintaining Results*, by Paul R. Niven (New York: John Wiley & Sons, Inc., 2002).

articulated to describe your strategy, it will be difficult to determine whether improvements in one area of the Scorecard are producing the desired effects on other key indicators. In fact, detrimental effects may occur as you pursue a series of conflicting initiatives not linked to a clear strategy.

Having said this, the lack of a clearly defined strategy certainly doesn't preclude you from building a Balanced Scorecard. It does mean you will construct a different *type* of Scorecard, one most likely focused on either key performance indicators or critical stakeholders.[10] Chapter Six is devoted exclusively to the topic of strategy and strategic planning.

Stakeholder Support

Public and nonprofit enterprises have a large number of internal and external stakeholder relationships. Employees, customers, boards of directors, legislators, funding bodies, and regulatory oversight agencies are but some of the many stakeholders to which you are frequently accountable. Of course, you also have senior leaders who are critical to the success of any new initiatives, including the Balanced Scorecard. While it is most likely not practical or possible to garner the full support of every stakeholder group, you must determine who the critical influencers are within your organizational sphere. In the next section we'll examine the vital importance of executive sponsorship.

Need for a Balanced Scorecard

Any unit you choose should have a clear and compelling need to adopt a Balanced Scorecard system—its own "burning platform" for change. Exhibit 3.4 provides an assessment guide you can review with potential groups to determine the need for a Balanced Scorecard effort. To complete the exercise, read each statement and consider how much you agree with what is stated. The more you agree, the higher the score you assign. For example, if you fully agree, assign a score of 5 points.

Support of Participants

There is no doubt that stakeholder and executive support is critical for a Balanced Scorecard implementation to succeed. However, while executives may use Scorecard information to make strategic decisions, you will also depend heavily on managers and first-line supervisors using the tool in their jobs. When the Scorecard is driven down to all levels through a process of cascading, the alignment and focus derived across the organization can lead to real breakthroughs in performance.

Managers and supervisors make this happen with their understanding, acceptance, support, and usage of the Balanced Scorecard. Not all members of these groups will demonstrate such a willingness to participate, however. While open criticism of new senior management initiatives is fairly rare, these managers and supervisors will often remain silent or demonstrate only mild enthusiasm, which workers quickly interpret as a questionable show of support for the program.[11] When choosing your organizational unit for the Balanced Scorecard, make an honest evaluation of the management team and supervisors you'll be relying on for participation and support.[12] Later in this chapter we'll take a closer look at midmanager support.

Commitment to Measurement

The Balanced Scorecard represents a new way of assessing performance, one that introduces significant accountability for results. Making the transition to this new environment is as much a philosophical and cultural transformation as a business adaptation. Therefore, you must ensure that any group you choose is committed to using this new system to clearly demonstrate its results.

Exhibit 3.4   Assessing the Need for a Balanced Scorecard

1 2 3 4 5	1. Our organization has invested in Total Quality Management (TQM) and other improvement initiatives but we have not seen a corresponding increase in customer results.
1 2 3 4 5	2. If we did not produce our current Performance Reports for a month, nobody would notice.
1 2 3 4 5	3. We create significant value from intangible assets such as employee knowledge and innovation, customer relationships, and a strong culture.
1 2 3 4 5	4. We have a strategy (or have had strategies in the past) but have a hard time successfully implementing it.
1 2 3 4 5	5. We rarely review our performance measures and make suggestions for new and innovative indicators.
1 2 3 4 5	6. Our senior management team spends the majority of their time together discussing variances from plan and other operational issues.
1 2 3 4 5	7. Budgeting at our organization is very political and based largely on historical trends.
1 2 3 4 5	8. Our employees *do not* have a solid understanding of our mission, vision, and strategy.
1 2 3 4 5	9. Our employees *do not* know how their day-to-day actions contribute to the organization's success.
1 2 3 4 5	10. Nobody owns the performance measurement process at our organization.
1 2 3 4 5	11. We have numerous initiatives taking place at our organization, and it's possible that not all are truly strategic in nature.
1 2 3 4 5	12. There is little accountability in our organization for the things we agree as a group to do.
1 2 3 4 5	13. People tend to stay within their "silos," and as a result we have little collaboration among departments.
1 2 3 4 5	14. Our employees have difficulty accessing the critical information they need to serve customers.
1 2 3 4 5	15. Priorities at our organization are often dictated by current necessity or "firefighting."
1 2 3 4 5	16. The environment in which we operate is changing, and in order to succeed we too must change.
1 2 3 4 5	17. We face increased pressure from stakeholders to demonstrate results.
1 2 3 4 5	18. We *do not* have clearly defined performance targets for both financial and nonfinancial indicators.
1 2 3 4 5	19. We cannot clearly articulate our strategy in a one-page document or "map."
1 2 3 4 5	20. We sometimes make decisions that are beneficial in the short term, but may harm long-term value creation.

Scoring Key:

20–30	If your score fell in this range you most likely have a strong performance measurement discipline in place. The program has been cascaded throughout your organization, to ensure all employees are contributing to your success, and is linked to key management processes.
31–60	You may have a performance measurement system in place but are not experiencing the benefits you anticipated or need to succeed. Using the Balanced Scorecard as a Strategic Management System would be of benefit to you.
61–100	Scores in this range suggest difficulty in successfully executing your strategy and meeting the needs of your customers and other stakeholders. A Balanced Scorecard system is strongly recommended to help you focus on the implementation of strategy and align your organization with overall goals.

Data

This criterion raises two questions: First, does this unit support a culture of measurement—that is, would they be amenable to managing by a balanced set of performance measures? While every group within a modern organization should rely on performance measures, for your first attempt, you may wish to choose a unit with a history of reliance on performance measures. Second, will the unit be able to supply data for the chosen performance measures? This may be difficult to assess initially, since at least some of the measures on your Balanced Scorecard may be new, with data sources as yet unidentified. However, if the unit has difficulty gathering data for current performance measures, they may be reluctant or unable to source the data you'll ultimately require for your Balanced Scorecard.[13]

Resources

Earlier in the chapter we reviewed the human and financial resources necessary to build a Balanced Scorecard. The group you choose must be willing and able to ante up appropriate resources of both varieties.

In Exhibit 3.5, I have created a sample worksheet you can use to determine the right organizational unit for your initial Balanced Scorecard effort. In this example, the Finance department is being considered for a Scorecard implementation:

- Plotted along the left-hand side of the table are the seven criteria just discussed.

- In the second column, I have assigned a score out of 10 for this unit against each of the criteria.

Exhibit 3.5 Sample Worksheet for Choosing Your Organizational Unit

BALANCED SCORECARD PROJECT
ORGANIZATIONAL UNIT ASSESSMENT
Finance Department

Criteria	Score (Out of 10)	Weight	Total Points	Rationale
Mission and Strategy	10	30%	3	The Finance team recently completed a retreat, during which they developed a new mission and strategy.
Stakeholder Support	9	30%	2.7	The Finance director has polled all key stakeholders and is confident of their support in this effort.
Need	10	15%	1.5	Finance has been plagued with errors and as a result has poor customer satisfaction.
Support of Participants	7	10%	0.7	This young, energetic management group is willing to experiment with new approaches.
Commitment	8	5%	0.4	The team members realize they must change in order to improve and are ready to embrace the accountability of the BSC.
Data	10	5%	0.5	Finance has ready access to anticipated Scorecard data requirements.
Resources	4	5%	0.2	The unit is understaffed and will have difficulty finding resources for this project.
Total		**100%**	**9.0**	

Overall Assessment

The Finance department seems to be an excellent candidate for the development of a Balanced Scorecard. It scored 9 out of a possible 10 points. The staffing issue, while significant, should be mitigated by the fact that the group is motivated to use the Scorecard system and is clearly in need of a new performance measurement system.

Adapted from material presented in *Balanced Scorecard Step-by-Step: Maximizing Performance and Maintaining Results*, by Paul R. Niven (New York: John Wiley & Sons, Inc., 2002).

- The third column represents weights for each of the seven dimensions based on my judgment and experience. You may feel more comfortable assigning equal weights to each of the seven items, but clearly some areas, such as mission and strategy and stakeholder support are imperative to success and should be weighted accordingly.

- The fourth column contains the score for the unit within each criterion. Under Mission and Strategy, it was assigned a score of 10, which, when multiplied by the weight for that category, yields 3 total points.

- In the final column, I've provided a rationale for the scores assigned based on an assessment of the unit in the context of that specific criterion. (It's important to document your decision-making process in order to validate it with others responsible for choosing the Balanced Scorecard organizational unit.)

- Finally, a total score is calculated and an overall assessment provided.

The overall assessment provides worksheet participants with the opportunity to discuss potential strengths and weaknesses of the unit, mitigate significant risks, and offer opinions on the viability of this group for the Balanced Scorecard project.[14]

EXECUTIVE SUPPORT: A CRITICAL ELEMENT OF YOUR BALANCED SCORECARD

Legendary General Electric CEO Jack Welch once commented, *"To make initiatives work, it took passionate, all-consuming commitment from the top...every leadership action must demonstrate total commitment to the initiative."*[15] I don't agree with everything uttered by this iconoclastic leader, but his words on executive sponsorship are 100 percent correct. More than a measures initiative, the Balanced Scorecard represents a change in project. A change in how you measure, in the way you manage, and the way you demonstrate accountability. To facilitate this dramatic transformation, you absolutely must have the support of executives and stakeholders.

Senior managers and executives set the tone for any organization. If these leaders provide only shallow and casual support for the Balanced Scorecard, this demonstration will be rapidly translated by all employees as a sign the project probably isn't worth their time and effort. Employees *"watch what the boss watches"*[16] and know which projects are likely to merit their attention.[17] The only thing potentially worse than a lack of support is the "lip-service" support offered by an executive who demonstrates none in deeds and actions. This "behavioral integrity" has been proven in the for-profit world to have a significant impact on profits. In one study of 6,500 hotel workers, researchers discovered that a 12 percent improvement in a hotel's score on leadership integrity (following through on promises and demonstrating values they preached) resulted in increased profits of $250,000 per year.[18]

Securing Sponsorship for Your Balanced Scorecard

Some organizations are extremely fortunate to enjoy executive sponsorship and have noted the tremendous benefit it confers. Bridgeport Hospital and Healthcare Services of Bridgeport Connecticut is one such organization. *"Though the Scorecard is continually being refined and changed, one thing that hasn't changed over the three years is top management's commitment. From the start, senior management endorsed and has driven the card with support from all relevant stakeholders plus buy-in from the Board of Directors. Its enthusiasm for the Balanced Scorecard has spread to its parent organization. The Yale New Haven Health System now uses a Balanced Scorecard of performance metrics. "*[19]

I'm sure you've witnessed the power and importance of executive sponsorship for change initiatives during your career. I'm equally convinced that many of you know the maddening frustration that results from seeing a potentially beneficial change vanish almost instantly because your leader or leaders could not be convinced of its importance, relevance, or worth. Assuming you don't want the Balanced Scorecard to suffer this ignominious fate, let's examine a number of techniques you can use to convince even the most skeptical senior executive of the Balanced Scorecard's worth.

- *Demonstrate accountability.* Former Mayor of New York City, Rudy Giuliani, has noted, *"In government...the temptation to cover shortfalls by increasing taxes can make political leaders lazy. Worse, the 'customers' of government—the citizens—can and will eventually do just what any dissatisfied customer does—go elsewhere, and eventually vote elsewhere too. "*[20] In the public sector, your senior leaders are accountable to elected officials. Those elected to public office normally wish to remain in office, and thus need to demonstrate results, lest they be voted out. Advise your executives that a Balanced Scorecard system can be used to demonstrate accountability and show real results.

- *Attract resources.* Nonprofit agencies rely heavily on funders to provide the financial resources they require to serve targeted customers. If agencies do not effectively measure performance, funders receive meaningless data or must acknowledge that they are supporting ineffective programs.[21] Using the Balanced Scorecard demonstrates to funders a willingness on the part of the nonprofit to provide meaningful information that can be used in future resource decisions.

- *Defend your performance.* Here's a quiz: If you were to conduct an online search on how often the word "greed" appeared within seven words of "CEO" or "executive," how many hits do you think you'd generate? One researcher did just that and found only 23 hits in all of 2000. For 2001, the number actually decreased to 20. However, in the scandal-plagued year of 2002, he received 102 hits in just the first eight months alone.[22] Public-sector and nonprofit salaries aren't in the same league as for-profit executives, but they are escalating. Thomas Lofton, chairman of the Lilly Endowment was paid $775,000 in 2001. Joseph Volpe, general manager of the Metropolitan Opera Association of New York earned a very respectable $725,000 for his efforts.[23] Citizens and stakeholders are demanding results for this level of remuneration. As previously noted, the Balanced Scorecard is designed to help you demonstrate your results.

- *Show progress.* Administrations and boards of directors change, but that doesn't mean you necessarily have to shift your priorities with every reshuffling of the deck. Nancy Foltz of the Michigan Department of Transportation explains how they plan to use the Balanced Score-card to aid in the transition to a new administration. *"Our governor is term-limited and so he will be leaving the end of this year...and we'll have a new governor in January so the likelihood is very high that we'll have a new director. The new executives that are here very much would like to have a scorecard in place and functional so that when the new director is in we can say, Here is a tool we use to guide us and measure us, and let's build on that."*[24]

- *Look for a good fit.* You need to identify senior executives who believe in the value, and indeed necessity, of balanced performance measurement and management. Senior managers who have gone through a strategic planning process designed to help them focus their efforts and define their objectives will also be more amenable to the Balanced Scorecard approach. Find the senior manager who fits this profile and make sure their door is the first stop on your sponsorship tour.

- *Recognize the power of peer pressure.* Outline the many achievements of other organizations pursuing a Balanced Scorecard approach. Success stories of Balanced Scorecard implementations abound in the business literature and at conference venues around the world. Testimonials from other senior executives are also very convincing, like this one from Charlotte, North Carolina, Mayor Pat McCrory: *"The Balanced Scorecard has helped me to communicate a strategic vision for the city to my constituents, the citizens, and to prospective businesses that are considering locating here. It helps the city manager focus on things that will have the biggest impact on the city."*[25]

- *Read what the "survey says."* Everyone wants to feel needed, and you can make your senior management feel very needed in the Balanced Scorecard process by sharing a couple of key statistics on the implementations of other organizations. A Best Practices LLC study found that half of benchmark participants' CEOs took part in the process.[26] In a study conducted for the Balanced Scorecard Report, respondents reported that CEOs, more than any other individuals, were the sponsors of the Balanced Scorecard. Thirty-one percent of the organizations stated the CEO was their sponsor.[27]

- *Educate.* In order to engage employees, you must first provide training. Before you train your employees, however, you must ensure that your senior leaders understand this tool and the value it presents. Exhibit 3.6 outlines a potential agenda for such a training session, and Chapter Four focuses on the importance of Scorecard training and communication planning.

Let me give you an example of executive sponsorship in action. Recall from the discussion on objectives for your Balanced Scorecard that I told you about a CEO who was disappointed with the large number of objectives the implementation team had placed on their organization's Balanced Scorecard. He wanted the Balanced Scorecard to serve as a communication tool and therefore was looking for just a few key objectives. Rather than criticize the team, he called them together, thanked them for their excellent work—he was amazed at how much they had accomplished in such a short period of time—and then reiterated his personal commitment to the Scorecard and explained that their very comprehensive work had forced him to carefully evaluate why he wanted the Balanced Scorecard. He then clearly explained his vision for the program and challenged them to develop a small number of truly crucial drivers for the organization. That's real commitment and sponsorship in action: It's empathy, it's commitment, it's vision, and it's challenge.

As a consultant and writer, I have the unique opportunity to learn from organizations around the world. Over the past several years I've consulted with dozens of organizations, have spoken at and attended conferences around the world, and have read stacks of case studies on organizational change. The theme of executive sponsorship is the one unifying element running through every encounter I've had. One statistic dramatically demonstrates the importance of sponsorship. In "Driving Corporate Culture for Business Success," the researchers found that a massive 98.7 percent of respondents stated that role modeling by senior executives of new behaviors and changes is key to enabling change.[28] Somewhat less dramatic, but equally valid, is what Nicole Alejandre from the County of San Diego, California, told me about executive sponsorship. *"If you don't have executive sponsorship, you're in limbo, and if your team doesn't feel comfortable working in that environment of ambiguity, it's difficult to move forward."*[29]

Exhibit 3.6   Agenda for a Training Session

Prior to the session you should consider distributing Balanced Scorecard literature to your executive team. Copies of books (like this one!), or good articles on the subject will help your audience prepare for the presentation to come. Regarding the session itself, if possible I would suggest holding it at an offsite location. Keeping distractions to a minimum will prove beneficial for all involved. To have an administrative assistant knock on the door and shuttle an engaged executive out of the room at a pivotal moment can be disastrous to your momentum.

Consider using an outside consultant to deliver the actual material or at least participate in the event. There are a number of reasons I take this position. First, a well-trained consultant will have delivered countless presentations of this nature and will use time tested material. Second, and unfortunately, many times an outside voice will carry more weight with, and be assumed to have more credibility by, executives than will an internal one. This is a sad but true reality of modern organizational life. Finally, and perhaps most importantly, you're holding this event because you want to win the support of your executive team. An experienced consultant will have faced similar crowds many times and be well-prepared to answer all queries and objections raised by the audience. And believe me, cogent and articulate responses here can translate to real support down the road.

Regarding the actual agenda, I suggest a two- or three-hour event structured as follows: 30 minutes on your organization and why a change is necessary (defining your "burning platform"), and 90 minutes on performance management and the Balanced Scorecard. Topics covered should include background information, a detailed review of the methodology, case studies, and success stories. Spend the final 30 to 60 minutes answering questions, and soliciting support for the implementation. Oh, and one final thing, don't forget to feed them. I say that only half jokingly. If your culture is one in which food is present at all meetings, don't leave those sandwiches and cookies out of this session!

Paul Niven leads a Balanced Scorecard training session

YOUR BALANCED SCORECARD TEAM

Teams have become a very popular concept in today's organizational world. Enterprises around the globe are realizing that in an economy dominated largely by intangible assets, it's collaboration among employees spanning the entire organization that drives results. The Balanced Scorecard is very well suited to a team approach. No one person in your organization possesses the requisite knowledge to build a Scorecard that tells your strategic story. The best Scorecards represent the collective know-how and experience of people from across the enterprise. Therefore, in the following sections of the chapter, we'll consider the key aspects of your Balanced Scorecard team, and look at the roles and responsibilities of team members.

How Many People Should Be on Your Balanced Scorecard Team?

The literature on teams often suggests they can range in size from 3 to 30. Studies of Balanced Scorecard implementations have demonstrated that a majority of organizations use 10 or more people in the Scorecard building process.[30] This number seems a bit high to me; in my experience, the most effective teams are limited to fewer than 10 participants, regardless of the size of the organization. Any more than 10 people in a room makes for a major facilitation challenge. Just try getting 10 people to agree on what to eat for lunch, let alone what the key performance measures are for your organization!

The key in choosing the appropriate number of people for your team lies in representing all the areas of your organization that you expect to be using the Scorecard. If, for example, you're creating a high-level Balanced Scorecard, you should strive for representation from each of your departments or groups. Should you have more than 10 departments, you may require a larger Balanced Scorecard team than I normally advise. If your Scorecard effort is beginning at the department level, then key representatives within the unit should have a presence on the team. Remember my earlier admonition: No one person has all the knowledge of strategy, stakeholder needs, and competencies to build an effective Scorecard. The knowledge you need to build an effective Balanced Scorecard resides in the minds of your colleagues spanning the entire organization.

Involving a number of people in the process increases the likelihood they will act as ambassadors of the Scorecard within their group, thereby increasing knowledge and enthusiasm for the tool. Bridgeport Hospital provides an excellent example of wide involvement in the development process. *"The leadership of the hospital, the board of directors, the medical staff, and clinical leadership came together to map the course to attain the...goals. Senior medical staff chairs worked in parallel with administrative staff to define clinical priorities, and junior physicians also helped refine and establish clinical priorities."*[31] From this description, it's clear that Bridgeport used senior staff, middle management, and front-line personnel in the Scorecard building process. Senior staff provide overall insight into strategic directions. Middle management involvement is important since it is often the group that is tasked with translating strategies and policies into action. Finally, front-line employees comprise the group that is most likely to be immediately affected by changes, and thus should definitely be included in any change-related initiative. They are also likely to be the most knowledgeable about the organization's day-to-day operations, and as a result can offer valuable and practical insights on the Scorecard discussion.

Which Skill Sets Should Team Members Possess?

"Mix it up" could be the tag line for this discussion. Any team will thrive on a mix of complementary skills. As a prerequisite, all members of the team should be experts in their individual areas, while also possessing a solid understanding of the entire organization. Beyond functional skills, you should attempt to fill the team with a mix of *visionaries* (people who see what the organization can be, and can rally people around that vision) and *actionaries* (people who will ensure that the goals and tasks of the project are realistic and are accomplished).[32] Expect heated debates and exchanges as the visionaries passionately depict a bold future while the actionaries attempt to articulate current realities.

Depending on the size of your organization, the chance exists that at least some team members will not have met previously. This was the case with a client team I worked with recently. At first I saw this as a disadvantage, fearing it would take extra time for the team to "gel." While there was definitely a period of growing pains for the team, in the end, the lack of personal relationships strengthened the level of debate around the Scorecard. There were no preconceived notions among the members, and everyone felt comfortable defending their positions.

Team Member Roles and Responsibilities

Many academics and consultants suggest a Balanced Scorecard should be the exclusive domain of the executive team. In other words, for the Scorecard to prove successful, it must be crafted solely by your senior leaders. My experience says otherwise. While full executive involvement would undoubtedly be beneficial, it's simply not practical to expect this to occur. The vast majority of Scorecard implementations of which I've been a part have featured an executive sponsor leading a team of individuals spanning the organizational hierarchy. Let's look specifically at typical roles and responsibilities that should be present on your Balanced Scorecard team.

Executive Sponsor

In *The Heart of Change,* authors Dan Cohen and John Kotter observe, *"Many change initiatives flounder because they're headed up by people who lack the time or the clout to accomplish what's necessary."*[33] The Balanced Scorecard can easily suffer this fate without a strong executive sponsor skillfully orchestrating the process. Using the knowledge he or she has accumulated, the sponsor will provide invaluable insights into mission and strategy. He or she will also be relied upon to maintain constant communication with key stakeholder groups such as boards of directors and elected officials. As the senior member of the Balanced Scorecard team, the sponsor should also ensure the team receives the human and financial resources necessary for a successful implementation.

Perhaps most important, the sponsor must prove to be a tireless advocate and enthusiastic ambassador of the Balanced Scorecard. As previously discussed, people watch what the boss watches, and will be carefully evaluating both the words and actions of your executive sponsor. To accomplish all of this and still have time for a day job, the sponsor must possess ample credibility within the organization. *"Credibility derives from organizational achievements, trust, and the visible support of other top executives. Every time he's been asked to perform, he has always delivered."*[34] The executive sponsor is not expected to provide full-time support to the Scorecard effort. However, attendance at Scorecard meetings and an "open door policy" for the Scorecard team should be considered mandatory.

Balanced Scorecard Champion (or Team Leader)

Balanced Scorecard co-developer David Norton believes many Scorecard success stories share a common trait. Virtually every senior executive sponsor had a partner, *"a change agent who played the lead role in introducing the Balanced Scorecard."*[35] I would call this change agent the Balanced Scorecard *champion,* and suggest this role is perhaps the most vital ingredient of Scorecard success. If the executive sponsor paves the way for success, it's the champion who ensures the smooth flow of traffic on the Scorecard freeway. This individual will guide the Scorecard process, both philosophically (providing thought leadership and best practices) and logistically (scheduling meetings, ensuring tasks are completed, etc.).

The role is a challenging one and demands a skilled communicator and facilitator. While the champion is fully expected to contribute to Scorecard development, he or she also has the often challenging tasks of team building and conflict resolution. As with the executive sponsor, the champion should enjoy widespread credibility throughout the organization. However, the source of credibility does not necessarily need to emanate from a long history within the organization. Some very skilled champions are recruited from outside the ranks of current employees based on their Scorecard knowledge and expertise. This confers credibility of another sort: expert credibility, which is often in short supply at the outset of a Scorecard implementation. Your champion should provide full-time support to the project, and as I will discuss in Chapter Fourteen, "Sustaining Balanced Scorecard Success," should be in a position to support the Scorecard's development and linkage to management processes on an ongoing basis. While the role is permanent, you can expect some variations in the key tasks over time. At various times, the champion will act as missionary, consultant, point person to fighting resistance, and chief of staff or general manger.[36]

Balanced Scorecard Team Members

Your executive sponsor and Balanced Scorecard champion will provide background, context for the Scorecard implementation, and subject matter expertise. The job of the Scorecard team members is to translate that material into a working Scorecard that effectively tells the story of your strategy. You'll rely on your team members to bring specialized knowledge of their functional area, and to liaise closely with their own senior leaders. Building support and momentum is a never-ending task of any Scorecard implementation. Team members must constantly communicate with their leaders; building support, sniffing out any possible resistance, and providing feedback to the larger Scorecard team. They should also identify resources within the organization that will prove valuable as the Scorecard development continues, for example, noting who controls key performance data.

During the implementation phase of the project, expect your team members to devote at least 50 percent of their time to this effort. Any potential team member who can offer only 10 to 20 percent of their time must be viewed with caution. While they may carry valuable knowledge of their particular area, this knowledge must be weighed against the very negative impact that lack of participation will have on the effort. Some teams inaugurate the process by making the formation of a "team charter" their first order of business. The charter may include key milestones, group values, and important resources. I'm all for a team charter, but with this caveat: Don't let this ostensibly helpful step turn into a debilitating headache. One nonprofit I worked with spent about two weeks deliberating feverishly over the team's name! That is not a valuable use of anyone's time.

Organizational Change Resource

It has been said the Balanced Scorecard is more than a metrics project. At the core, it's a change process, a change in the way you measure, which has implications for how you manage, and ultimately how people are held accountable for results. Scorecard implementations in any setting will introduce their share of change issues. In the public and nonprofit sectors, however, the change issues are elevated substantially. Here is what Dennis Feit of the Minnesota Department of Transportation told me about launching a Scorecard effort. "*When you've got a lot of dedicated and talented people, and when you come in and say I want to measure your performance, there's an initial shock and almost hurt and pain about that—'What, you don't trust me? I've been working so hard....' So there's a delicate art I'm trying to learn: How do you approach someone who's dedicated and has been performing well, and say, 'Now I want to measure you...? How do you get past the initial shock—'Why would you do that, I'm so busy, and besides the process of measuring is going to make my performance go down because I don't have time to measure.'"*[37] These are all extremely valid points. An organizational change resource working with your team can help you identify many of these issues, and provide solutions to address them. The resource is not a full-time requirement, but should consult to the team on an as-needed basis.

Exhibit 3.7 summarizes the roles and responsibilities of your Balanced Scorecard team.

YOUR BALANCED SCORECARD DEVELOPMENT PLAN

In many ways this entire book is your Balanced Scorecard development plan. Each chapter lays out in detail the steps necessary to develop a powerful Balanced Scorecard system. This section will serve as a primer of what's to come, as well as provide you with input you can use right now to develop your own Scorecard plan.

This chapter has given you everything you need to place a solid Scorecard stake in the ground as you begin your efforts. Chapter Four will build on this foundation and provide two additionally essential elements: training and communication. To summarize, the tasks you may consider part of your "planning phase" of Scorecard development are:

- Developing your rationale for using the Balanced Scorecard.
- Determining resource requirements and availability.
- Deciding where to build your first Scorecard.
- Gaining senior leadership support and sponsorship.
- Forming your Balanced Scorecard team.
- Providing training to your team and other key stakeholders.
- Developing a communication plan for your Balanced Scorecard implementation.

Exhibit 3.7 Balanced Scorecard Team Roles and Responsibilities

Role	Responsibilities
Executive Sponsor	• Assumes ownership for the Balanced Scorecard project. • Provides background information to the team on mission, strategy, and methodology. • Maintains communication with internal and external stakeholders. • Commits resources (both human and financial) to the team. • Provides support and enthusiasm for the Balanced Scorecard throughout the organization.
Balanced Scorecard Champion	• Coordinates meetings; plans, tracks, and reports team results to all audiences. • Provides thought leadership on the Balanced Scorecard methodology to the team. • Ensures all relevant background material is available to the team. • Provides feedback to the executive sponsor and senior management. • Facilitates the development of an effective team through coaching and support.
Team Members	• Provide expert knowledge of functional areas. • Inform and influence their respective senior leaders. • Act as Balanced Scorecard ambassadors within their unit or department. • Act in the best interests of the organization as a whole.
Organizational Change Expert	• Increases awareness of organizational change issues. • Investigates change-related issues affecting the Balanced Scorecard project. • Works with the team to produce solutions mitigating change-related risks.

Adapted from material presented in *Balanced Scorecard Step-by-Step: Maximizing Performance and Maintaining Results*, Paul R. Niven.

It's often tempting to dive right in to the Scorecard waters and begin developing measures without laying the foundation described. Trust me, you'll find the water very chilly if you do. Without objectives for your Scorecard, you'll have a difficult time determining whether you should develop 10, 20, or 50 measures. A lack of sponsorship will see your Scorecard fade away at the first sign of crisis and conflicting demands.

Without Scorecard training, you'll likely develop an ad hoc mix of financial and nonfinancial measures that add little value above and beyond your current measurement solution. Take the necessary time to complete each of the tasks listed. When your Scorecard journey faces challenges, as it inevitably will, this list will ensure you have a steady compass by which to steer the tool's future development.

Steps in Developing the Balanced Scorecard

Listed next are the key steps involved in developing a Balanced Scorecard. The corresponding chapters of the book in which you'll learn more about the topic are shown in parentheses.

1. Develop or confirm your mission, values, vision, and strategy (5 and 6).
2. Confirm the role of the Balanced Scorecard in your Performance Management framework (7).
3. Select your Scorecard perspectives (8).
4. Review relevant background materials (8).
5. Conduct executive interviews (8).
6. Create your strategy map (8).
7. Gather feedback (8).
8. Develop performance measures (9).
9. Develop targets and initiatives (9).
10. Develop the ongoing implementation plan (covered in the remaining chapters of the book).

The time it will take you to complete the steps outlined depends on a number of factors, including: the sense of urgency to create a Balanced Scorecard, amount of resources dedicated to the implementation, knowledge of key staff, and of course, executive support. Strategy maps are literally drawn in a day at some organizations, while others will labor over the task for weeks. The Scorecard is not something to be "picked away at" as time permits. As with any change related project, sustaining momentum is critical. Exhibit 3.9 presents a proposed development plan lasting 16 weeks. With focused effort and support, the vast majority of organizations should be able to craft a Scorecard within this time frame. A "Planning Review Worksheet" is presented in Exhibit 3.8 to help you record your readiness as you begin the Balanced Scorecard implementation process.

Exhibit 3.8 Checklist to Begin Your Balanced Scorecard

City of Cape Sydney
Balanced Scorecard Implementation
Planning Review Worksheet

Item	Yes/No	Comments	
Have we determined objectives for our Balanced Scorecard implementation?	Yes	Our city has been subject to funding cuts for a third consecutive year. We've developed a new strategic plan that will mitigate the effects of future cuts. The Balanced Scorecard will be used to translate the strategy into operational terms and align all departments with overall city goals.	
Have specific resources been allocated to the implementation?	Yes	**Human**	**Financial**
		We have received approval from managers and leaders to have selected individuals serve on our BSC team.	We have developed a project budget of $XXX for year 1. Included in this amount are consulting fees, software, seminar expenses, and materials
Have we determined where to build our first Scorecard, and why?	Yes	As noted above, we have recently completed a citywide strategic planning effort. As a result, we will develop a high-level Balanced Scorecard for the city. With that in place we will cascade to all departments and support groups within the city.	
Do we have executive support for this process?	Yes	We have conferred with all key stakeholder groups and have received strong support for the Balanced Scorecard. Both the mayor and city council strongly endorse the Scorecard. The city manager and all department heads have received Scorecard education briefings and also fully support the initiative.	
Have we finalized our Balanced Scorecard team, including: an executive sponsor, Balanced Scorecard champion, team members, and an organizational change resource?	Yes	**Executive Sponsor:** K. Chiasson, the city manager, will act as our executive sponsor. Chiasson has been an ardent supporter of the Scorecard and has seen it work in other cities. **Balanced Scorecard Champion:** G. Garfinkel has been appointed the Scorecard champion. He has been with the city for 10 years and has the trust and respect of all managers. He has also been instrumental in the success of past change efforts. **Team Members:** Our Scorecard team is comprised of: M. Siddall (Fire Dept.), S. Trew (Police), H. Crooks (Planning & Building), A. MacDonald (Finance), B. Pottle (Transportation), R. Nicholls (Recreation), S. Munro (Library). **Organizational Change Resource:** D. Barnhart, Manager, Organizational Development, will assist the team on as-needed basis with organizational change issues. For more information on the team, please see the attached team charter.	
Have we finalized our development plan?	Yes	Our goal is to complete the city's Balanced Scorecard within 12 weeks. A workplan for specific milestones and deliverables has been developed.	

Exhibit 3.9   A Balanced Scorecard Development Plan

Week	1	2	3	4	5	6	7	8	9	10	11	12	13	14	15	16	17	18	19	20
Planning Phase																				
1. Developing your rationale for the Scorecard	▮																			
2. Determining resource requirements and availability		▮																		
3. Deciding where to build your first Scorecard		▮																		
4. Gaining senior leadership support and sponsorship			▮▮																	
5. Forming your Balanced Scorecard team			▮▮																	
6. Providing training					▮															
7. Developing a Communication Plan					▮▮															
Development Phase																				
1. Develop or confirm mission, values, vision, and strategy								▮												
2. Confirm the role of the Scorecard in your Performance Management Framework									▮											
3. Select your Scorecard perspectives									▮											
4. Review relevant background materials								▮▮												
5. Conduct executive interviews										▮										
6. Build your strategy map											▮▮									
7. Gather feedback													▮							
8. Develop performance measures														▮▮						
9. Develop targets and initiatives																▮				
10. Develop ongoing implementation plan																	→			→

72

SUMMARY

Cardinal Richard Cushing reminds us to *"Plan ahead: It wasn't raining when Noah built the ark."* I want you to be "warm and dry" when you begin developing your Scorecard, hence, my purpose in this chapter was to help you pour a very solid foundation for your Balanced Scorecard development efforts to follow. I began by introducing the "burning platform for change." I challenged you to determine specifically which issues are plaguing your organization and how the Balanced Scorecard can alleviate them and lead you toward the fulfillment of your mission. You learned that clear objectives help you build consensus among team members, ensure a common focus for your development efforts, and sustain Scorecard momentum.

It's difficult to identify with precision the financial resources necessary to develop a Balanced Scorecard. There are a number of variables, including: size of the organization, current resources, and ongoing obligations. The chapter reviewed many of the typical expenses that should be considered when embarking upon a Scorecard initiative. It also discussed the human resources required to craft an effective Balanced Scorecard.

With objectives and resources in place, an organization must decide where to build its first Scorecard. Many assume starting at the top with a high-level organizational Scorecard represents the best option. This is often the case, but every organization is different, and some may benefit from "piloting" the Scorecard in a lower-level department or function. Seven criteria for helping you make the "where to build" decision were identified: presence of mission and strategy, stakeholder support, need for a Scorecard, support of all participants, commitment to measurement, presence of data, and resources.

In my experience, the one truism of any organizational initiative is this: Without senior leadership support, it will wither and quickly fade from view! Leaders set the tone for organizations, and employees tend to take their cues from the actions they see modeled every day. If your leaders are providing only casual support for the Scorecard, their apathy will be manifested in a product that is weakly embraced and rarely used. To ensure executive support, I listed a number of techniques you can apply. They included: demonstrating accountability, showing progress, and looking for a good fit.

I define a team as "a small number of people with complementary skills who are committed to a common purpose, performance goals, and approach for which they hold themselves mutually accountable."[38] I broke this definition down to its component parts in the context of the Balanced Scorecard. A productive Balanced Scorecard team must include an executive sponsor, champion, team members, and possibly an organizational change resource. All roles are critical and carry with them specific responsibilities.

Developing the Balanced Scorecard consists of two phases: planning and development. With commitment and the dedication of resources, most organizations should be able to develop a Balanced Scorecard within 16 weeks.

NOTES

1. From interview with Jeff Celentano, June, 2002.
2. From www.qualitydigest.com.
3. Diane L. Coutu, "The HBR Interview: The Anxiety of Learning," *Harvard Business Review*, March 2002, pp. 100–106.
4. Ibid.
5. From interview with Nancy Foltz, September 19, 2002.
6. From interview with Jeff Celentano, June 2002.
7. Deborah L. Kerr, "The Balanced Scorecard in the Public Sector," *Perform Magazine*, Vol. I, No. 8, pp. 4–9.
8. From interview with Bill Ryan, September 17, 2002.
9. From interview with John Ramont, December 6, 2002.
10. Paul R. Niven, *Balanced Scorecard Step-by-Step: Maximizing Performance and Maintaining Results* (New York: John Wiley & Sons, Inc., 2002), p. 43.
11. Janice A. Klein, "Why Supervisors Resist Employee Involvement," *Harvard Business Review*, September–October 1984, pp. 87–96.
12. Paul R. Niven, *Balanced Scorecard Step-by-Step: Maximizing Performance and Maintaining Results* (New York: John Wiley & Sons, Inc., 2002), p. 44.
13. Ibid., p. 45.
14. Ibid., p. 46.
15. Jack Welch and John Byrne, *Jack: Straight from the Gut* (New York: Warner Business Books, 2001).
16. Robert Simons and Antonio Davila, "How High Is Your Return on Management?" *Harvard Business Review*, January–February 1998, p. 70.
17. Paul R. Niven, *Balanced Scorecard Step-by-Step: Maximizing Performance and Maintaining Results* (New York: John Wiley & Sons, Inc., 2002), p. 48.
18. Tony Simons, "The High Cost of Lost Trust," *Harvard Business Review*, September 2002, p. 18.
19. Andra Gumbus, Bridget Lyons, and Dorothy E. Bellhouse, "How Bridgeport Hospital Is Using the Balanced Scorecard to Map Its Course," *Strategic Finance*, August 2002, p. 46.
20. Rudolph W. Giuliani, *Leadership* (New York: Hyperion, 2002).
21. Margaret C. Plantz, Martha Taylor Greenway, and Michael Hendricks, "Outcome Measurement: Showing Results in the Nonprofit Sector," *New Directions for Evaluation*, Fall 1997.
22. Geoffrey Nunberg, "Straight Talk," *Harvard Business Review*, December 2002, p. 18.
23. Kimberly Weisul, "Up Front," *BusinessWeek*, December 2, 2002, p. 6.
24. From interview with Nancy Foltz, September 19, 2002.
25. Pamela A. Syfert and Lisa B. Schumacher, "Putting Strategy First in Performance Management," *Journal of Cost Management*, November–December 2000, pp. 32–38.

26. Best Practices Benchmarking Report, *Developing the Balanced Scorecard* (Chapel Hill, NC: Best Practices, LLC, 1999).

27. Laura Downing, "Progress Report on the Balanced Scorecard: A Global Users Survey," *Balanced Scorecard Report,* November–December 2000, pp. 7–9.

28. Business Intelligence, "Driving Corporate Culture for Business Success," 1999.

29. From interview with Nicole Alejandre, September 25, 2002.

30. Best Practices Benchmarking Report, *Developing the Balanced Scorecard* (Chapel Hill, NC: Best Practices, LLC, 1999).

31. Andra Gumbus, Bridget Lyons, and Dorothy E. Bellhouse, "How Bridgeport Hospital Is Using the Balanced Scorecard to Map Its Course," *Strategic Finance,* August 2002, p. 46.

32. Michael Allison and Jude Kaye, *Strategic Planning for Nonprofit Organizations* (New York: John Wiley & Sons, Inc., 1997), p. 35.

33. Dan S. Cohen and John P. Kotter, *The Heart of Change* (Boston: Harvard Business School Press, 2002).

34. Nick Wreden, "Executive Champions: Vital Links between Strategy and Implementation," *Harvard Management Update,* September 2002, pp. 3–5.

35. David P. Norton, "Change Agents: The Silent Heroes of the Balanced Scorecard Movement," *Balanced Scorecard Report,* May–June 2002. pp. 1–4.

36. Ibid.

37. From interview with Dennis Feit, October 4, 2002.

38. John R. Katzenbach and Douglas K. Smith, *The Wisdom of Teams* (Boston: Harvard Business School Press, 1993).

CHAPTER 4

Training and Communication Planning for Balanced Scorecard Success

Roadmap for Chapter Four Scorecard creators Kaplan and Norton have sometimes referred to the concept as "simple" but not "simplistic." Unfortunately, a lot of organizations that choose to develop Scorecards hear the reference to "simple", but somehow manage to tune out the words "not simplistic." If the Balanced Scorecard is simple, they reason, it probably doesn't require a huge investment in training. Sadly, this is simply not the case. While the Scorecard concept itself is relatively straightforward, the tool has many subtleties and hidden complexities. It is the exploitation of these subtle elements such as cause-and-effect linkages, lag and lead indicators, and so on, that will drive the breakthrough results for which the Scorecard has become famous. Training has the capability to unlock the power of the Scorecard by placing everyone involved in its development on a level playing field of knowledge. This chapter will provide you with everything needed to design and deliver a comprehensive Scorecard training program.

Without a proper base of Scorecard training, your employees may not have the understanding necessary to take full advantage of this concept. Equally as detrimental is a lack of communication. Missed opportunities, inconsistent expectations, and confusion may all occur should you not actively and effectively communicate your Scorecard initiative. Many change initiatives fail to deliver on their promised results. This is a sad, and reluctantly accepted, reality of organizational life. While the causes are many, lack of communication is consistently cited as a surefire way to short-circuit any change program. In the second half of this chapter, we'll explore the role of communication planning in Balanced Scorecard success. We'll determine precisely why communication is so critical, consider the role of communication objectives, outline the elements of any productive communication plan, and discuss how you can evaluate your success.

TRAINING IS CRITICAL FOR BALANCED SCORECARD SUCCESS

Let me share with you a situation I encounter from time to time at organizations wishing to pursue the development of a Balanced Scorecard. Someone reads an article or hears about the Balanced Scorecard from a colleague. This individual then does some cursory research and learns that the Balanced Scorecard is a relatively straightforward and common-sense solution. Given that, and the need for improvement within his or her organization, the person suggests the development of a Balanced Scorecard.

With the decision to construct a Scorecard completed, a team is then put together. The members read the same article, maybe even a book, after which they are still convinced it's a simple concept. Awareness sessions are held during which the Scorecard is trumpeted as a measurement system featuring financial and nonfinancial measures, but little is offered regarding the many subtleties and complexities of the model. Then the team begins the difficult work of translating strategy, developing objectives and measures, and hypothesizing about cause and effect, and they realize it's not that simple! However, at this point they're into the implementation stage and don't want to slow their momentum with training. The cost of this decision will frequently manifest itself in poorly designed Scorecards, lack of use, and weak alignment within the organization. The resulting Scorecard will most likely contain an ad hoc group of financial and nonfinancial measures but in no way tells the story of the organization's strategy.

It's often the deceptive simplicity of the Scorecard that makes people very susceptible to the false notion that in-depth training is not required. Feeling the Scorecard can be simply mastered, the organization will sponsor one-time, high-level training and then trust their employees' business instincts to kick in and fuel the development of powerful new performance measures.

This chapter will provide you with the materials you need to ensure your organization doesn't suffer the misfortune that often results from a lack of Scorecard training.

Training Generates Tangible Benefits

Well-known management guru Tom Peters is famous for his "pull no punches" style and simple, practical advice. Here is his not-so-subtle message for organizations that don't invest in regular employee training: "*Companies that don't encourage employee education of all kinds are dumb!*"[1] I told you he didn't pull any punches. While "dumb" is a subjective evaluation, many researchers have objectively confirmed that training not only leads to a better-educated and motivated workforce, but can also produce dramatic improvements in bottom-line results. In one recent study conducted by the Governmental

Accounting Standards Board (GASB) "*Training for management and staff about performance measurement development and selection*" was cited by a majority of respondents as an important aspect of a successful Performance Management system.[2]

For those of you brave enough to dabble in the stock market—and I realize your numbers could be plummeting after the disastrous market performance of 2002—you may be interested to know that investments in employee training have been positively correlated with financial results. Knowledge Asset Management (KAM), an investment firm in Bethesda, Maryland, tracks organizations that make large investments in training and education. The combined performance of companies in KAM's research portfolio consistently outperformed the Standard & Poor's 500 index.[3]

There are many stories in organizational folklore regarding the benefits of training. A favorite of mine concerns Dow Chemical founder, Dr. Herbert H. Dow. One day while riding his bike to work, Dr. Dow was stopped by a company supervisor who presented him with a classic good news-bad news scenario. The bad news was that a spill had occurred, which would cost the company $50,000. The good news, remarked the supervisor, was that he had fired the employee who caused the spill. Upon hearing the news, Dr. Dow remarked, "You better get him back here, because I just spent $50,000 to train him."[4]

DESIGNING YOUR BALANCED SCORECARD TRAINING PROGRAM

Most training professionals, and more importantly most training participants, would probably agree that a training event is considered successful when three conditions are met: the training is *effective*, *efficient*, and *engaging*.[5] Effective implies accomplishing relevant objectives that lead to participant success. Making the best use of participant's time and energy characterizes efficiency. Finally, engaging training sessions and workshops draw the participants into the event and ensure their unique experiences are part of the process. The sections that follow outline the key steps in designing Balanced Scorecard training sessions that ensure effectiveness, efficiency, and engagement.

Working with Adult Learners

The unique characteristics of adult learners cannot be overestimated when designing a training event. Materials, training flow, and activities must reflect the broad spectrum of learning styles and individual experiences each learner brings to the event. Milano and Ullius have produced six key principles related to adult learning.[6] I have outlined them here:

- *Experience is the richest resource for adult learning, therefore, the core methodology of adult education is the analysis of experience.* Adults bring a lifetime of experiences to the learning event and learn best when they're able to draw on their past events. Training design must contain activities that allow the adult learner to analyze the new material in the context of their individual experience. For many, this will entail examining past measurement efforts and discussing them in light of Balanced Scorecard and strategic measurement.

- *Adults are motivated to learn as they experience needs and interests that learning will satisfy.* Most adult learners will see learning as a means to an end of meeting a current need. The more immediate the need, the greater the motivation to learn. As a result, the training session's goals and activities should directly relate to a legitimate need of the participants. Always begin with the end in mind. What is the need that must be satisfied, and how does this event do so? What does your team need to be able to do in order to take advantage of Balanced Scorecard opportunities?

- *Adults have a deep need to be self-directing, therefore, the role of the facilitator is to engage in a process of mutual inquiry with them rather than to transmit his or her knowledge to them and then evaluate their conformity to it.* Adult learners may value the trainer's opinions, but ultimately they will decide on the value of what is being discussed. The design should acknowledge this analysis and encourage it by including activities that encourage participants to openly analyze what they are learning and make an evaluation. Rather than stifling the potential conflict that may arise, facilitators should welcome it and encourage frank discussion, which often leads to breakthroughs. For example, participants may feel there are better or more established ways to measure performance than the Balanced Scorecard. Facilitators should draw this out and be ready to discuss the differences between the Scorecard and other methods, and the benefits conferred by using the Scorecard.

- *If the environment does not feel safe to the learner, personal energy will be directed toward self-protection, leaving little for inquiry, analysis, and learning.* The challenge is to create an environment that encourages honest dialogue while protecting the self-esteem of the adult learner. Training sessions must be designed with this in mind, for example, by ensuring appropriate content for the audience, activities that encourage an exchange of ideas, and clarification when one "right answer" is appropriate.

- *Adults have clear expectations about training (based on past experiences), and these expectations will largely determine participants' behavior.* Therefore, the design must manage the expectations of those in attendance. Facilitators should attempt to determine expectations of participants in advance, perhaps by including some participants in the training design process. Goals and objectives of the event should be written from the perspective of the learners and their needs, rather than from the viewpoint of the facilitator. And, finally, participant needs must be acknowledged and built into the session. When developing new training sessions, the design team should analyze the specific needs of the participants and any issues they may have. These needs and issues must form the basis for the event.

- *Adults learn in a variety of ways and have preferences in learning styles.* All adults have preferred ways of learning new information based on their past experiences, hereditary makeup, and current environment. Training sessions must be designed to balance the many preferred learning styles participants bring to the event. For example, content should have a mix of "how" and "why," and materials should engage all learners by including an appropriate mix of text and graphics. Designers must be cognizant of their own learning preferences to ensure all activities are not simply those reflecting personal appeal and comfort.

Conducting a Training Needs Assessment

In order to improve in any subject, you must first determine where gaps exist between current and desired levels of performance. The needs assessment asks questions (and provides answers) that help you determine skill gaps that must be filled during the training event.

Here is a list of questions you should consider regarding the skill level of Scorecard training session participants:

- What skills and knowledge do participants possess regarding Balanced Scorecard and, more specifically, developing performance measures?
- What new skills and knowledge are necessary for participants to be able to develop Balanced Scorecard performance measures that will help you execute your strategy?
- Will any existing skills or knowledge of participants need to be modified or enhanced for them to develop Balanced Scorecard performance measures?

You should also conduct a more general analysis of the groups attending your training sessions. Here are a number of items to consider[7]:

- *Number of participants attending each session.* This will ensure you design appropriate activities for the audience size.
- *Level of expertise.* As discussed previously.
- *Positions/titles/reporting relationships.* Open discussions can sometimes be hampered if individuals are attending the session with their superiors.
- *Diversity (age, gender, culture, etc.).* Many organizations have a diverse employee base, and training design should respect this diversity.

- *Politics.* Two issues here: First, are there potential politics or conflicts between individuals attending the session? Second, are there political "hot buttons" that should not be pushed during the workshop?
- *Anticipated participant response.* Are attendees likely to welcome the event or be resistant to what is being offered?

The needs assessment allows you to draw a portrait of the participants attending your event. Having defined their needs, and considering the gap you must close, you can now develop goals, objectives, and key topics for your training session.

Developing Objectives for Your Balanced Scorecard Training

Chapter Three discussed the importance of developing overall objectives for your Balanced Scorecard program. Objectives, too, are critical to training design, as they provide the foundation for all other elements of the session. Everything that is designed subsequently, including materials, handouts, and evaluation tools, must align with the objectives of the training session.

The objective of your training session answers the question: "Why are we conducting this training?" An obvious response might be, "To increase knowledge of the Balanced Scorecard." Though certainly true, it is also quite broad and vague. After reviewing the outcomes of your needs assessment, you should attempt to develop a goal statement that more accurately captures the spirit of your specific event. For example, it could be, "To provide our core team with the skills and knowledge necessary to develop our high-level organizational Scorecard within 12 weeks."

Agenda for Your Training Session

At this point we are ready to construct the flow of the training event, including the selection and sequencing of agenda items to support your objectives. The topics you choose to present should be engaging, inviting learners to participate actively in the event. Participants should interact with one another, with the facilitators, and with the content itself. The following are a number of criteria for selecting effective and engaging agenda items.[8]

- *Support objectives.* The activities chosen must directly relate to the overall aims of the session.

- *Offer variety.* Avoid repetition of similar activities.
- *Respect various adult learning styles.* The activities should fit with a variety of learning styles, balancing a use of both text and graphics, for example.
- *Transfer learning.* The activities should mirror as closely as possible the real world of the participants. Even though the session may be introducing new material, the learners will bring past experiences that are similar and can be drawn upon to support the learning. Always attempt to build on or enhance what participants already bring to the event. Always use examples and cases to which most participants will easily and comfortably relate.
- *Reflect the number of participants.* The size of the group will dictate not only the type of activity chosen but also the amount of time allotted.

Sample Balanced Scorecard Training Agenda

As noted, the agenda and activities you develop for Scorecard training should reflect your unique needs and objectives. For many public and non-profit organizations, the following items would most likely form part of a typical Balanced Scorecard training session:

- *Begin with an introductory activity.* We've all heard the old adage, "you never have a second chance to make a first impression." So it goes with your Scorecard training session. It's very important to get off to a good start. Design an opening activity that relates to the topic, supports the objectives, and "grabs" the attention of participants. This could be anything from constructing a building with nothing but playing cards to sharing a powerful story. I frequently start my training sessions by sharing with participants a clever riddle that challenges their assumptions about performance measurement. Whatever you choose to do, this short activity can help create a need to know, assess the knowledge of the Scorecard currently possessed by participants, and start them thinking about how the Balanced Scorecard relates to them.
- *Describe your "burning platform."* Which specific issues do you face (or opportunities do you have) that require you to change, and change now? In this portion of the training event, you will articulate the challenges inherent in your current environment and discuss why change is imperative if you hope to ultimately achieve your mission. You may also wish to include more "macro" considerations; for example: the scandal-plagued business environment and how that affects you, demographic swings, and changing economic prospects.

- *Give background on the Balanced Scorecard.* Provide participants with the history of the Balanced Scorecard and explain how it has evolved over the past 12 years to become a universally accepted business tool.

- *Define Balanced Scorecard fundamentals.* In this component of the event, you should review the specifics of the Scorecard methodology. Begin with the model as originally conceived for the for-profit world and describe how it can be easily adapted to fit the nonprofit or public sectors. Each of the four perspectives should be discussed in some detail, with particular emphasis placed on what is typically measured in each area. And don't forget to have some fun with your presentation. Do whatever it takes to make it relevant and enjoyable for your audience. The San Marcos campus of the California State University system has been working with the Balanced Scorecard since 2001, and keeping the Scorecard training light has been an important ingredient of its success. Abbi Stone and Katy Rees told me they, *"[T]ook a lot of the theory out, and basically said, 'Hey we've got these issues facing our university, our division, and here's a tool we think can help us align our organization to the strategy.' We used some comical examples to get the point across."*[9] Exhibit 4.1 displays their witty depiction of what can happen when you fail to meet your customers' needs!

- *Answer: "How does the Balanced Scorecard benefit us?"* Once participants have learned about the Scorecard system, it's time to return to the issues plaguing your organization. Facilitate an open discussion of how the Scorecard can prove beneficial in assisting you to meet the challenges you face.

- *Share success stories.* I could talk until I'm blue in the face (and believe me I can!) about the value of the Balanced Scorecard. But for most people it all comes down to this: Who else in our sector has used the Scorecard successfully? Spend some time discussing Scorecard use in other public and nonprofit organizations. To generate examples, use some of the organizations discussed in this book, speak with colleagues, or conduct your own research. You'll probably find more examples than you expect!

- *Use a case study.* There is no substitute for learning by doing. Nothing accelerates learning like a case study that forces participants to begin grappling with the Balanced Scorecard concept and applying its core principles. Though it's important to devise a case study that will be meaningful to your audience, it's not necessary to base the case on your own situation. (I frequently use subjects everyone has experience with, such as banking.) To facilitate the case study, break your audience into teams and have each develop Scorecard objectives in the four perspectives for your fictional case. Then give each team the opportunity to present its Scorecard to the rest of the group.

Exhibit 4.1   Importance of Determining Customer Needs

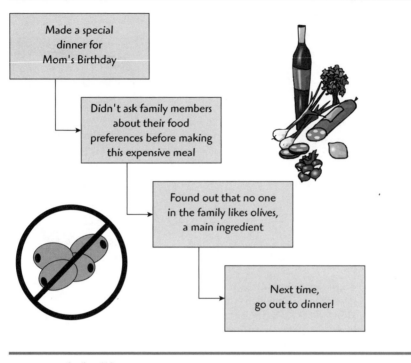

www.csusm.edu/bsc/10

Plan on spending a half-day conducting your training session. Assuming that equates to an event of three hours, I suggest you allot at least one of those hours to the case study. The discussion and learning generated from a well-designed case study is unparalleled by other agenda items. A case study is also a terrific way to satisfy a number of adult learning styles. The case should include a narrative outlining the mock organization. This will appeal to those participants whose preferences run toward learning through text presentations. The group will of course draw their Scorecard on a flip chart, which should prove enticing to those who prefer visual learning. Finally, the group will share their output, which will be attractive to members who enjoy verbal learning opportunities. Exhibit 4.2 provides a number of other options for learning materials you might want to use in your training session.

Exhibit 4.2   Choosing Materials for Your Balanced Scorecard Training Sessions

The materials chosen for the Balanced Scorecard training session are the tangible, physical items needed for the learning event. Participant materials could include any combination of the following:

- Prework assignments
- Reading materials: books, articles, etc.
- Participant workbooks
- Worksheets for skills practice
- Case studies
- Directions for activities
- Forms for note taking
- Job aids
- Bibliographies

Learning Aids:
- Wall Charts
- Guest Lecturers
- Presentations
- Flip Charts
- Videos
- Audiotapes
- Music
- Pictures

In designing the materials, the following points should be considered:
- Consider organizational culture: Some organizations, for example, prefer simple black-and-white text with little graphics. You should always adhere to the organizational norms.
- Adult learning. Remember to balance text with graphics, how and why, etc., to ensure all learning styles are accommodated.
- Ensure the amount of written materials is consistent with what is being presented. Don't overwhelm the participants with written material they may not use and could find intimidating.

Based on material presented in *Designing Powerful Training,* by Michael Milano and Diane Ullius (San Francisco: Jossey-Bass, 1998).

Unless you currently have an in-house Scorecard expert in your midst, I strongly suggest using an outside facilitator or consultant to lead at least your initial training session. A good consultant will be able to spark group thinking and apply proven concepts to ensure you achieve your objectives. He or she will also deliver that most critical of currencies—credibility—to your Scorecard project at this most important of junctures.

Evaluating the Success of Your Training Session

Training evaluation is often an afterthought consisting of a simple form distributed at the end of the event as participants are on their way out the door. Taking a more strategic approach to training evaluation can lead to insights regarding actual transfer of knowledge and application of skills learned. Four levels of evaluation may be considered[10]:

- *Reaction.* At this level you seek to evaluate participants' feelings, thoughts, and perceptions about the training session itself. There are a number of specific factors on which you can solicit reactions: perceived usefulness of what was learned, the physical environment, participant materials, learning aids, activities used, the trainer, times, and content.

- *Learning.* Here you are attempting to gauge what participants have actually learned during the event. Comparing behaviors demonstrated during the training with the learning objectives will help you determine whether the event has been successful. "Tests" conducted at the end of the event will help demonstrate whether the participants have developed new skills. Additionally, focus groups or interviews after the event may be used to evaluate learning.

- *Behavior.* Here you are attempting to measure whether the new skills are being applied on the job or on the team. The challenge of course is isolating the relationship between the workshop learning and on-the-job performance. Also, timing is important since this evaluation is necessarily done after the training event.

- *Results.* Here you attempt to determine the impact of the training on organizational objectives. Essentially you are evaluating the workshop's "return on investment."

Typically, the simplest level to capture in evaluation forms is the first one, reaction. Unfortunately, most of us tend to solicit reactions after the training event has ended. This, of course, provides great feedback for future sessions, but does little to quell issues raised by the current group. Consider tracking reactions throughout the event. For example, at a break, do a "spot check" of participants to gauge their reactions to the session. Or have participants write their comments on index cards and hand them in as they leave for a break. Making "course corrections" and showing your ability and willingness to adapt to meet learners' needs is a great way to win their trust and support.

Other Training Options

Hands-on, classroom training is a great way, but only one way, to share Scorecard techniques and generate questions and discussion about this tool; other options are also available. The field of Balanced Scorecard is quite mature, and a rich and abundant supply of literature is available. To begin, I suggest you share with your team the three seminal articles written by Kaplan and Norton appearing in the *Harvard Business Review* from 1992 to 1996. To supplement those, choose some of the literally hundreds of other articles and white papers available; narrow your search by including any documents that specifically reference the public and nonprofit sectors. A number of good books have been published on these subjects as well, and you should consider providing at least one to each of your team members. Your team will also benefit from attending one of the many excellent conferences on Performance Management and the Balanced Scorecard. Here, too, you have the opportunity to tailor training with implementation by choosing an event focused on your sector or implementation plan. These conferences provide a very valuable exchange of ideas, challenges, and solutions.[11]

Another great way to start your team thinking about Scorecard concepts is to have them develop a Balanced Scorecard specifically for your implementation. Building a Scorecard for the project gives your team the opportunity to deliberate on just the sort of issues they'll be applying to the whole organization very shortly. For example, have them answer questions such as: Who are our customers? How do we best meet their needs? To do so, at which processes must we excel? Which competencies and skills do we require? What financial constraints are present and must be monitored?

And don't forget that the Scorecard is a powerful measurement, management, and communication tool. The metrics crafted by your team will help them stay focused on the task at hand and gauge the progress they're making during the implementation phase. In Exhibit 4.3, I've constructed a sample project team Balanced Scorecard.

Final Thoughts on Balanced Scorecard Training

It's important to remember that for the majority of employees within your organization, the team you assemble will be the embodiment of the Balanced Scorecard. If the members don't come across as knowledgeable and credible sources of information, you can be certain that skepticism for the initiative will increase. Some team members may come to the project with a background in Performance Management and Balanced Scorecard concepts, while others may be experiencing their first exposure to these topics. Either way, to ensure a level playing field for the entire team, you have to invest heavily in up-front training. Fairfax County, Virginia, is one organization that takes the subject of training very seriously. Its efforts are chronicled in Exhibit 4.4.

Exhibit 4. 3   Sample Balanced Scorecard for Your Implementation Team

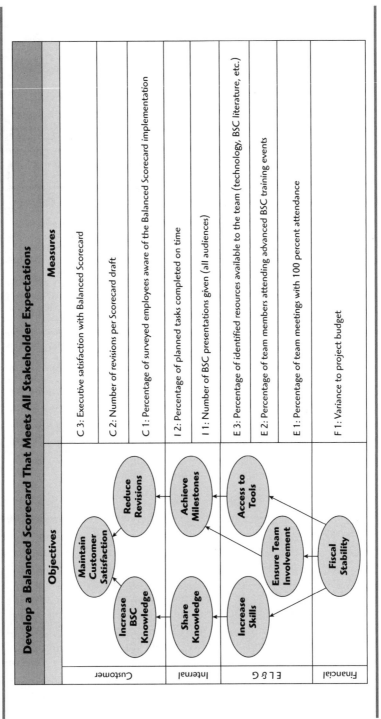

Develop a Balanced Scorecard That Meets All Stakeholder Expectations		
	Objectives	**Measures**
Customer	Maintain Customer Satisfaction / Reduce Revisions / Increase BSC Knowledge	C 3: Executive satisfaction with Balanced Scorecard
		C 2: Number of revisions per Scorecard draft
		C 1: Percentage of surveyed employees aware of the Balanced Scorecard implementation
Internal	Achieve Milestones / Share Knowledge	I 2: Percentage of planned tasks completed on time
		I 1: Number of BSC presentations given (all audiences)
EL&G	Access to Tools / Ensure Team Involvement / Increase Skills	E 3: Percentage of identified resources available to the team (technology, BSC literature, etc.)
		E 2: Percentage of team members attending advanced BSC training events
		E 1: Percentage of team meetings with 100 percent attendance
Financial	Fiscal Stability	F 1: Variance to project budget

From *Balanced Scorecard Step-by-Step: Maximizing Performance and Maintaining Results*, Paul R. Niven (John Wiley & Sons, Inc., 2002).

Exhibit 4.4   Fairfax County Trains for Measurement Success

Located in northern Virginia, Fairfax County is home to more than 1 million people. The county employs over 11,000 and has been recognized as "one of the best-managed jurisdictions in America" according to Governing Magazine and the Government Performance Project. This notable achievement is based on results in a number of areas, one of which is termed *"Managing for Results."* Fairfax County received an "A-", one of only three awarded in this category which looked at strategic planning and performance measurement.

The County began their performance measurement initiative by researching other jurisdictions. They quickly learned that many of those using performance measurement systems had invested in cursory training efforts and, as a result, achieved only limited results from their systems. Fairfax County vowed to make a significant investment in training their core team, and later, all employees.

Training of team members focused on both basic performance measurement techniques and concepts, and also on how these concepts affected the County. The curriculum contained sections on measurement basics, data collection, surveying for customer satisfaction, and managing for results. To ensure the training was relevant, facilitators guided team members through exercises which encouraged them to consider how they would actually measure performance in a number of specific county departments. This "hands-on" application was an excellent complement to the new language of

performance measurement being introduced to the team.

Once the core team was well versed in performance measurement tools they took their show on the road. The team offered to help agencies throughout the County develop their own strategic performance measures. It was later discovered that those agencies who requested help early and often developed better measure than those who attempted to "go it alone."*[i]*

Fairfax County's training initiative has evolved in step with changes to their performance measurement system. For example, recognizing that not all employees can fit formal training sessions into their schedules, the performance measurement team is in the process of developing online courses which can be accessed at the convenience of learners. One thing that hasn't changed over the years is the County's commitment to training. Performance Measurement Program Coordinator Barbara Emerson explains the importance of training for performance success. *"The better agency staff understand performance measurement concepts and tools, the more likely they will be to develop measures that will lead to improvements in service delivery."[ii]*

[i] Barbara Emerson, "Training for Performance Measurement Success," *Government Finance Review*, April, 2002. pp. 22-25.
[ii] Ibid

From www.co.Fairfax.va.us/.

One of the most important aspects of training is the questions it raises. When I work with a client and conduct my training sessions, the participants are not only thinking about the Scorecard in an academic sense, but, practically, they're thinking about what it will mean at their organization. This specific logic path leads them to consider just how they might cascade the Scorecard, how they'll define their terms, and why they even want to use a Balanced Scorecard system. These are all important questions that must be answered before a successful implementation can take place.

Finally, just as your Balanced Scorecard grows and evolves, so too should your training curriculum. The steps described so far in the chapter will help you get off to a solid start, but continuous training is a core ingredient of your Scorecard implementation that must never be neglected. Be sure to add new "modules" that correspond to the maturing nature of your implementation. Courses on cascading the Scorecard, budget and management reporting linkages, and of course technology (should you choose a software reporting solution) will all pay dividends in greater understanding and use of the system.

DEVELOPING A COMMUNICATION PLAN TO SUPPORT YOUR BALANCED SCORECARD INITIATIVE

Communication: A Vital Link to Success

How do you feel about the communication that takes place within your organization? What's your opinion on the effort that's expended on communication? Any better? Most organizations feel they do a decent job of the latter, exerting effort on communication, but they aren't pleased with the overall results. Needless to say, this is a huge problem since information is the lifeblood of today's organizational success, and information is a direct product of effective communication. In fact, Peter Drucker has said that the most important thing a nonprofit organization can do is "*to build itself around information and communication instead of around hierarchy.*"[12]

Why Communication Is Critical to Your Balanced Scorecard

Quick quiz: The Balanced Scorecard is...? I'm sure you recall—without referring back to Chapter One—that a Scorecard is three things: a measurement system, strategic management system, and a communication tool. All of these represent big changes in how the organization gauges its success. Hence, the Balanced Scorecard more than anything else is a *change initiative.* And we all know change is tough, really tough, especially when you're introducing something that is potentially threatening. For those affected, change can be unsettling, frightening, confusing, and painful—in other words, something to generally be avoided at all costs.

Change efforts struggle for many reasons, but fundamentally the vast majority of organizations struggle with change because of their inability to answer these five questions on the part of those undergoing the change:

1. What do you want me to do?
2. What's in it for me?
3. How will this change affect me?
4. What will you do to help me make the change?
5. How am I doing?

Communication planning holds the key to unlocking some of the answers. A well-conceived, designed, and delivered communication strategy and plan gives you the opportunity to proactively shape your message, ultimately making change if not pleasant, at least palatable. This is the chance to sell your message of change, improvement, and success to all your stakeholders. Jack Welch, former CEO of General Electric, is someone who knows a thing or two about what it takes to make change happen within organizations. He suggests—no, bellows: "*I learned that for any big idea, you had to sell, sell, and sell to move the needle at all.*"[13]

Objectives for Your Communication Plan

By now you may be getting the impression that I take the idea of setting objectives pretty seriously: objectives for your Balanced Scorecard program, objectives for your training sessions, and now objectives for your communication plan. Whatever you're doing, the first step should always be a careful and critical prodding of why you're engaging in the activity in the first place. What is the purpose and what are your objectives? This is especially critical for communication planning since this process centers on the delivery of key messages and information that can literally make or break the success of your implementation.

The objectives you select for your communication plan should of course represent your unique situation. However, the next list contains a number of common objectives[14]:

- Build awareness of the Balanced Scorecard at all levels of the organization.
- Provide education on key Balanced Scorecard concepts to all audiences.
- Generate the engagement and commitment of key stakeholders in the project.
- Encourage participation in the process.
- Generate enthusiasm for the Balanced Scorecard.
- Ensure team results are disseminated rapidly and effectively.

The Michigan Department of Transportation (MDOT) considered the following as its objectives for communication planning: "The purpose and focus of the communication strategy will be the explanation of the Scorecard and its value to MDOT, its linkage to our business plan and current goals, its incorporation of existing measurements, and its application and value in the future."[15] Notice the inclusion of the words, "its value to MDOT": A specific reference of this nature ensures the team never loses sight of one of the key communication-related questions I posed at the outset of this section: What's in it for me? They will ensure their communications clearly articulate why this change is taking place and why it's valuable for employees, and thus worthy of their time and attention.

Setting objectives for the communication plan will often lead you to the establishment of a theme or metaphor you can use to creatively "trademark" your implementation. Some people like slogans and themes, others think they're hokey and convey little if any value. Whatever your opinion, there is little doubt that themes are colorful, and often memorable. And memorability is a powerful weapon in the arsenal of communication. For Bridgeport Hospital, the communication theme was "Destination to Journey 2005," using the analogy of a bus trip to the future. Highways represented the hospital's five strategic imperatives, landmarks represented the objectives, and mile markers represented the performance measures.[16] Whatever theme you choose should reflect your organization, your culture, and your aspirations.

Key Elements of a Communication Plan

One simple and effective method of designing your communication plan is to take advantage of the "W5" approach—who, what, when, where, and why. Each is discussed here in the context of communication planning.

Who: The Target Audiences

The size of your organization and scope of your implementation will help you define the specific audiences for your communication plan. In general, you should consider each of the following groups: senior leaders, management (those with direct reports), all employees, the project team, a steering committee (if you use one), boards of directors, and elected officials.

Who: The Communicator

Once you've determined your target audiences, you can match them with appropriate message providers. Each group will have different needs and require specific messaging. A board of directors, for example, would likely receive more formal communications consisting of presentation material and oral updates, typically delivered by senior leaders. In contrast, a newsletter written for the employee body might connote a more casual attitude and be written by a member of the project team.

What and Why: Defining the Key Messages

Every communication plan will contain a number of key messages, which are translated from your plan objectives, and should of course be aimed at your target audiences. Let's revisit the MDOT's communication plan objectives and consider how they might be translated into key messages. *"The purpose and focus of the communication strategy will be the explanation of the Scorecard and its value to MDOT, its linkage to our business plan and current goals, its incorporation of existing measurements, and its application and value in the future."* Based on these objectives, we would expect messaging around how the Scorecard can help solve current issues facing MDOT, how it builds on current measures at the departments, and how it will prove beneficial both now and in the future as conditions change.

When: Frequency of Communication

All effective communication shares one common trait: targeting specific needs. The frequency of your communication will vary depending on the needs of your target audiences. For example, you'll want to keep your senior leaders well informed on a frequent basis. Your project team also requires up-to-date information. However, you could meet the information needs of a board of directors with less frequent communiqués. Having said all that, I remind you of what one leading change expert has said about communication. *"Without credible communication, and a lot of it, employees' hearts and minds are never captured."*[17] Those are the words of change guru John Kotter. Heed this advice and, if anything, err on the side of too much, rather than too little, communication.

Where and How: Communication Vehicles

Ahh, now the fun part: the communication vehicles! Have you ever opened a birthday card and been greeted with a song or other musical accompaniment? A friend once told me the computer power offered in that tiny card would have matched the output of the world's greatest computers of just 50 years ago. Urban myth perhaps? In any event, the point is, we've made tremendous technological advances in the past few decades. Today, with even the humblest of office software packages, you possess a plethora of graphical and communication options. Add to the mix some good old-fashioned creativity and imagination, and you're off to the communication races.

Despite the technological leaps I've just touted, face-to-face communication remains the most reliable form of interchange among us humans. Getting out and speaking directly to your target audiences represents your best chance of truly influencing attitudes and stacking the deck of change in your favor. But, if you're going to get on your Scorecard soapbox, you've got to be prepared to answer the tough questions you're sure to get from a sometimes skeptical, and typically apprehensive, audience. Honesty is, of course, the best policy, and you should answer all queries to the best of your current ability. It's also very helpful to develop your key messages, thereby ensuring the responses you're broadcasting are consistent across time and audience groups.

Two increasingly popular communication vehicles are the Internet and the organizational intranet. Both are reliable, relatively inexpensive, and for those with Web access, very easy to use. The Finance and Administrative

Services department at the San Marcos campus of California State University has used the Internet to provide all interested parties with the latest updates on its Balanced Scorecard efforts. Its home page is featured in Exhibit 4.5.

Exhibit 4.5   Balanced Scorecard Home Page from Cal State San Marcos

Finance & Administrative Services
Balanced Scorecard

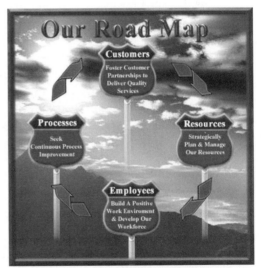

Points Of Interest

Guiding Principles

Strategy Map & Glossary

Leadership Team & Core Team

Balanced Scorecard Basics

Presentations

Links

Feedback Form

Newsletter

The Finance & Administrative Services Division Has Begun Our Balanced Scorecard Journey To...

- Improve our Division's effectiveness
- Focus efforts across the Division towards a single strategy
- Improve the culture and climate of our division
- Help us prioritize daily activities
- Assist us with making choices while continuing to deliver services to the campus community
- Measure our progress towards improvement in these areas

From www.csusm.edu/bsc.

The U.S. Army Medical Department (AMEDD) chose its intranet as the best source of disseminating Scorecard information. AMEDD conducts medical research and training, while also serving more than 3 million active-duty military personnel, retirees, and their families. The Balanced Scorecard page on its intranet includes[18]:

- Video clip introduction from the Surgeon General
- Implementation plan
- "Getting Started" section
- AMEDD's strategy map of Scorecard performance objectives
- Balanced Scorecard deployment schedule
- Communications plan
- Reporting system
- Key contacts and a list of those trained in Scorecard development
- Frequently Asked Questions (FAQs)
- Information links to third-party sources
- Lessons learned

Not all organizations will possess the technical or financial resources necessary to develop a sophisticated intranet, but, fortunately, alternative communication vehicles abound; it's simply a matter of finding what works best for your audiences, given cultural preferences, demographics, and so on. Consider any or all of the following as possibilities: group presentations, project plans, newsletters, workshops, brown-bag lunches, video presentations, message kits, e-mails, news bulletins, raffles and contests, pay-stub messages, demonstrations, road shows, and town-hall meetings.

Recall from our discussion of training earlier in the chapter that adults tend to have different learning proclivities. Keep that in mind as you design your communication vehicles, and attempt to provide a balance of media, ensuring you make a connection with everyone in your target audience. Rick Pagsibigan of the Red Cross of Philadelphia understands the importance of using a variety of communication channels. He explains,

> Different people learn in different ways. Some like to read, some like to hear, some like to feel and touch, some prefer to see practical applications, some enjoy conceptual or theoretical constructs. Essentially what I was trying to do was to appeal to as many audiences as possible. We did that by using a variety of channels. One method is our Change Management group. The task of this group was to understand the strategic plan and the Balanced Scorecard, and communicate them to the rest of the organization in a way that makes sense. They used a series of meetings, handouts, presentations, and so on.
>
> A second way is through e-mails, informing staff of what's happening with strategic planning and the Balanced Scorecard process. I use the CEO to deliver the message to staff on our latest developments. Another channel is the board of

directors. We had our board present the strategic plan and Balanced Scorecard. To do so they needed to understand it in order to effectively communicate it to their peers.[19]

Evaluating the Effectiveness of Your Communication Efforts

Earlier in the chapter I reviewed the process of evaluating training efforts. I described the process as one that is "often an afterthought." When it comes to evaluating the outcomes of communication plans, "often an afterthought" would probably be a charitable declaration. "Don't even consider it" is probably more reflective of what really takes place. But the good news is, even anecdotal evidence can help you gauge the effectiveness of your communication efforts. For example: Are groups completing their Scorecard tasks on time? Are you receiving questions about the Scorecard? Have requests been made for Scorecard presentations? These are all indications that your messages are probably reaching a receptive ear.

For those that have the means and the inclination, a formal survey of audiences is recommended. Using survey data you can assess your efforts on the following criteria[20]:

- *No contact.* Has not heard of the Balanced Scorecard project.
- *Awareness.* Has heard about the project, but doesn't know what it is.
- *Conceptual understanding.* Understands the Balanced Scorecard and any individual effects.
- *Tactical understanding.* Understands both the personal and organizational effects of the Balanced Scorecard.
- *Acceptance.* Will support the Balanced Scorecard and the changes it will bring.

A simplified communication plan is shown in Exhibit 4.6.

Final Thoughts on Communication Planning

Writer and aviator Anne Morrow Lindbergh once remarked that, *"Good communication is as stimulating as black coffee and just as hard to sleep after."* In today's hectic world we are literally awash in communication. But how much of what passes for communication would meet Lindbergh's standard of "good?" Your challenge is to cut through the clutter that can surround a new initiative such as the Balanced Scorecard and focus on delivering the right message to the target audience, at the right time, in the appropriate manner.

Let me conclude this section with the following quote, which sums up the importance of communication in a performance measurement effort: *"Communication is a critical component of every measurement-related activity. Without the ability to transfer information from one person to another, alignment would be improbable if not impossible."*[21]

Exhibit 4.6 Simplified Communication Plan for Your Balanced Scorecard Project

Audience	Purposes	Frequency	Delivery Vehicle	Communicator
Senior Leadership	· Gain commitment · Remove obstacles · Report progress · Prevent surprises	Bi-weekly	Direct contact	Executive Sponsor
Elected Officials	· Gain commitment · Remove obstacles · Report progress	Monthly	Direct contact	Executive Sponsor
Management	· Convey purpose · Explain concepts · Report progress · Gain commitment	Bi-weekly	· E-mail · Management Meetings · Articles · Intranet	Champion/Team Members
All Employees	· Convey purpose · Introduce concepts · Eliminate misconceptions · Report progress	Monthly	· E-mail · Newsletters · Town-hall meetings · Intranet	Project Team Members
Project Team	· Track progress · Assign tasks · Review expectations	Weekly	· Team meeting · Status memos · Intranet	Champion

Adapted from material presented in *Balanced Scorecard Step-by-Step: Maximizing Performance and Maintaining Results*, Paul R. Niven (New York: John Wiley & Sons, Inc., 2002).

SUMMARY

Believing the Balanced Scorecard to be a tool that can be quickly and easily
mastered, many organizations will proceed directly to Scorecard development, bypassing any training efforts. Poorly designed Scorecards that are
quickly ignored by leaders and employees alike often result from this decision. Effective and ongoing communication of the Scorecard process is also
frequently neglected by Scorecard adopting organizations. This chapter
explored each of these topics in depth and offered practical solutions for
developing training and communication plans that deliver real results.

We began the chapter by suggesting all training programs must share
three traits. The training must be effective, efficient, and engaging. *Effective*
implies accomplishing relevant objectives that lead to participant success.
Making the best use of participants' time and energy characterizes *efficiency*.
Finally, *engaging* training sessions and workshops draw the participant into
the event and ensure their unique experiences are part of the process.

Since you'll be delivering your Scorecard training to adults, the chapter
also examined the unique characteristics of adult learners, identifying six key
principles that apply: experience is the richest source of learning for adults;
adults are motivated to learn in order to fill needs; adults are self-directing;
a safe environment must be established to facilitate adult learning; behavior
is driven by expectations; and everyone has preferred learning styles.

A training needs assessment prompts you to determine the gap between
current skill levels and the standard you require. To that end, a number of
questions were provided to help you assess your training needs. Training
objectives are designed to help overcome the gaps identified in the needs
assessment.

Though the agenda for your Scorecard training event will be a function of
your individual needs and objectives, the following elements will typically be
found in most training sessions: an introductory activity, a description of your
"burning platform for change," background on the Scorecard concept, fundamentals of the tool, a discussion of how the Scorecard will benefit you, success stories, and a case study. An evaluation should follow every training event.

While hands-on classroom training provides an excellent opportunity for
open dialog and discussion of your Scorecard project, other training options
do exist. They include journal articles, books, conferences, and seminars.

The Balanced Scorecard is a powerful communication tool, signaling to
everyone in the organization the key landmarks along your journey to
success. But before you can use the Scorecard to communicate your results,
you must develop a plan to communicate exactly why you've embarked on
the Scorecard effort and how this process will enable you to reach your
goals. Your Scorecard communication plan serves this purpose.

Objectives for your communication can be many and varied; however,
most organizations will choose from among these goals: building awareness
of the Balanced Scorecard at all levels of the organization, providing
education on key Balanced Scorecard concepts to all audiences, generating

the engagement and commitment of key stakeholders in the project, encouraging participation in the process, generating enthusiasm for the Balanced Scorecard, and ensuring that team results are disseminated rapidly and effectively.

Communication plans can be effectively structured using the "W5" approach: who, what, when, where, and why. "Who" supplies both the communicator and the target audience. "What" and "why" comprise the plan's key messages. "When" defines the frequency of communications. "Where" and "how" describe the multitude of communication vehicles you'll employ to get your message across.

NOTES

1. Bob Nelson, *1001 Ways to Energize Employees* (New York, NY: Workman Publishing), p. 181.
2. Governmental Accounting Standards Board, "Performance Measurement at the State and Local Levels: A Summary of Survey Results," 2001.
3. Martin Delahoussaye, Kristine Ellis, and Matt Bolch, "Measuring Corporate Smarts," *Training*, August 2002.
4. Ibid.
5. Michael Milano and Diane Ullius, *Designing Powerful Training* (San Francisco: Jossey-Bass, 1998).
6. Ibid., p. 24.
7. Ibid., p. 67.
8. Ibid., p. 159.
9. From interview with Abbi Stone and Katy Rees, September 18, 2002.
10. Donald Kirkpatrick, *Evaluating Training Programs* (San Francisco: Berrett-Koehler, 1994).
11. Paul R. Niven, *Balanced Scorecard Step-by-Step: Maximizing Performance and Maintaining Results* (New York: John Wiley & Sons, Inc., 2001).
12. Peter F. Drucker, *Managing the Non-Profit Organization* (New York: HarperCollins, 1990).
13. Jack Welch and John Byrne, *Jack: Straight from the Gut* (New York: Warner Business Books, 2001).
14. Paul R. Niven, *Balanced Scorecard Step-by-Step: Maximizing Performance and Maintaining Results* (New York: John Wiley & Sons, Inc., 2002), p. 65.
15. From interview with Nancy Foltz, September 19, 2002.
16. Andra Gumbus, Bridget Lyons, and Dorothy E. Bellhouse, "Journey to Destination 2005," *Strategic Finance*, August 2002.
17. John P. Kotter, *Leading Change* (Boston: Harvard Business School Press, 1996).
18. Patricia Bush and Diane Koziel, "How and Why to Build an Internal Marketing Campaign," *Balanced Scorecard Report*, May–June 2002, pp. 7–10.
19. From interview with Rick Pagsibigan, September 19, 2002.
20. Paul R. Niven, *Balanced Scorecard Step-by-Step: Maximizing Performance and Maintaining Results* (New York: John Wiley & Sons, Inc., 2002), p: 67.
21. William Fonvielle and Lawrence P. Carr, "Gaining Strategic Alignment: Making Scorecards Work," *Management Accounting*, Fall 2001.

CHAPTER 5

Mission, Values, and Vision

Roadmap for Chapter Five Thousands of organizations around the world have used the Balanced Scorecard to successfully implement their strategies. But before a strategy is implemented, even before it's formulated, the organization must contemplate its mission, values, and vision (see Exhibit 5.1). These concepts are at the core of any effective organization—inspiring all stakeholders, guiding decisions, and aligning the actions of every employee. The Balanced Scorecard will ultimately translate the mission, values, vision, and strategy into performance metrics you can use to gauge your success in meeting your overall aims.

In this chapter we'll examine each of these building blocks in detail; we'll consider what they are and how to determine their effectiveness, review tips on developing them, and identify their vital linkage to the Balanced Scorecard. As a Scorecard practitioner you'll need to determine if the Balanced Scorecard you've developed is truly aligned with your mission, values, and vision. This chapter equips you with the tools to make that critical determination.

Exhibit 5.1 The Balanced Scorecard Translates Mission, Values, Vision, and Strategy

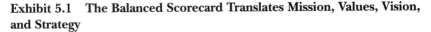

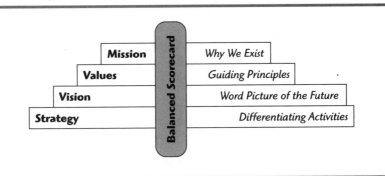

MISSION

What Is a Mission Statement and Why Is It So Important?

Anyone encountering your organization, whether it's a customer, funder, potential employee, or partner, will undoubtedly have a number of questions in mind. Who are you as an organization? Whom do you serve? Why do you exist? It is the mission of your organization that provides the answers to these vital questions.[1]

A mission statement defines the core purpose of the organization, its *raison d'etre*—that is, why it exists. The mission also reflects employees' motivations for engaging in the company's work. In the for-profit world, which is dominated almost exclusively by shareholder concerns, a mission should provide the rationale for a company's existence beyond generating stockholder wealth. Interestingly, corporate charters of the nineteenth century were regarded as a privilege, and with that privilege came the corporate obligation to serve the public interest. Even in today's shareholder-oriented markets, the mission statement should describe how an organization is indeed serving the public interest—the true responsibility of any organization, be it private, public, or nonprofit in structure.

Nonprofit and governments of course do not share the profit imperative. This has always been a world dominated by the quest of service provision. A mission statement clarifies the true purpose of these organizations and clearly articulates it to all stakeholders. The mission isn't just window dressing; in fact, the very success of public and nonprofit enterprises is often dependent, at least in part, on the development of a crystallizing mission. Researchers from the Independent Sector found that, *"a clear, agreed-upon mission statement is one of the four primary characteristics of successful nonprofit organizations."*[2] The evidence is clear that public sector organizations also benefit from the declaration of a distinctive mission, as David Osborne and Ted Gaebler reported in *Reinventing Government*: *"The experience of hashing out the fundamental purpose of an organization—debating all the different assumptions and views held by its members and agreeing on one basic mission—can be a powerful one. When it is done right, a mission statement can drive an entire organization from top to bottom."*[3]

Whichever field of endeavor we choose, one thing is clear: We all strive to make a contribution. Purpose and fulfillment in life are not gained from the collection of a paycheck, but rather are derived from contributing to something greater than ourselves, doing something of value. The organization's mission is the collective embodiment of this most basic of human desires. Hewlett-Packard co-founder David Packard held this belief deeply and made it the cornerstone of his management philosophy. This is how he described mission in a 1960 speech that is as relevant today as it was 43 years ago: *"A group of people get together and exist as an institution that we call a company so they are able to accomplish something collectively that they could not accomplish separately—they make a contribution to society,…do something which is of value."*[4] The best of our organizations offer us the opportunity to attain true meaning and fulfillment through work.

Unlike strategies and goals, which may be achieved over time, you never really fulfill your mission. It acts as a beacon for your work, constantly pursued but never quite reached. Consider your mission to be the compass by which you guide your organization. And just as a compass can lead you to safety when you're lost in unfamiliar terrain, a powerful mission can serve as your guide in times of organizational uncertainty. Consider the case of Bon Secours Health System: In the late 1980s, this health care provider, which has existed since 1824, was considering the purchase of a group of nursing homes. The deal looked good on paper, but some additional research on the acquisition revealed a troubling source of the potential good fortune. Low pay and inadequate employee benefits were the true driving force of the nursing home company's profits. Bon Secours reconsidered the acquisition in light of its mission statement. In addition to providing a caring environment for patients, the mission also stressed the same treatment for employees. Investing in the nursing homes would clearly have violated this component of Bon Secours' mission, thus the deal was rejected.[5]

Effective Mission Statements

Now that we know what they are, let's look at some of the attributes that make for an effective and enduring mission statement:

- *Simple and clear.* Peter Drucker has said one of the greatest mistakes organizations make is to turn their missions into "*hero sandwiches of good intentions.*"[6] This is a truly great metaphor that conjures up layer upon layer of societal good to be accomplished by the organization. As admirable as such intentions may be, they aren't practical. You can't be all things to all people and still expect to maintain the focus necessary to accomplish specific goals. The mission should mirror your chosen field of endeavor.

- *But not too simple.* While it's unwise to write a mission proclaiming your desire to do everything, you should also avoid overly restricting yourself. For example, consider the ramifications of this mission statement from a small community mental health organization: "to provide counseling to youth 13 to 18 years of age." Very clear indeed, but does it speak to the true purpose of the organization? How will employees, funders, and volunteers view the organization in light of this mission? Undoubtedly they'll see an organization with a very limited scope of activities. Broadening the mission to "enhancing the mental health of youth in our county," is also clear and simple, but significantly expands the organization's options.[7]

- *Inspire change.* While your mission doesn't change, it should inspire great change within your organization. Since the mission can never be fully realized it should propel your organization forward, stimulating change and positive growth. Consider the mission of Partners for a Drug-Free America: *To help kids and teens reject substance abuse by influencing attitudes through persuasive information.* As drug use habits and preferences change, this mission will remain relevant and motivate the group to direct its resources toward attitudinal adjustments of teenagers.

- *Long-term in nature.* Mission statements should be written to last a hundred years or more. While strategies and plans will surely change during that time period, the mission should remain the bedrock of the organization, serving as the stake in the ground for all future decisions. The mission of the Internal Revenue Service is to provide America's taxpayers with top-quality service by helping them understand and meet their tax responsibilities and by applying the tax law with integrity and fairness to all. This would be as appropriate 10 decades from now as it is today.

- *Easy to understand and communicate.* Nobody would argue that our modern organizational community is one awash in jargon. Buzzwords abound in offices around the world as we invent new and curious words and phrases to describe the world around us. While many people react negatively to buzzwords, some say they simply represent a sign of *"words in action and a culture on the move."*[8] Regardless of your opinion on the role of buzzwords in our modern life, they really have no place in a mission statement. Your mission should be written in plain language, which is easily understood by all readers. A compelling and memorable mission is one that reaches people on a visceral level, speaks to them and motivates them to serve the organization's purpose. You can actually consider your mission a valuable recruiting aid in attracting like-minded individuals to take up your cause.

Developing Your Mission Statement

"The first question is always, what's the mission? Ask yourself what you'd like to achieve—not day to day, but your overarching goal."[9] This is the advice offered by Rudy Giuliani. But how do we answer that question—how do we develop the mission? In the sections that follow, I'll provide you with a number of options for creating your own mission statement.

As you'll see, most exercises designed to help you develop a mission center on posing a number of key questions. When creatively combined, your thoughtful answers to these questions will lead to a powerful mission statement.

The "5 Whys"

A very effective method for developing your mission is based on a concept known as the "5 Whys" developed by James Collins and Jerry Porras.[10] Start with a descriptive statement such as, "We make X products or deliver Y services." Then ask, "Why is this important?" five times. A few "whys" into this exercise and you'll begin to see your true mission emerging. This process works for virtually any product or service organization. A waste management organization could easily move from "We pick up trash" to "We contribute to a stronger environment by creatively solving waste management issues" after just a couple of rounds. A market research organization might transition from "Provide the best market research data" to "Contribute to customers' success by helping them understand their markets."

You'll notice that with each round of "why" you'll move closer and closer to your true reason for being an organization, to the value or contribution you strive to create or make. This process is so powerful because it builds on the notion of *abstraction*, which I define as moving to a different level, leaving characteristics out. We humans are great abstractors; just ask anyone about him- or herself and chances are the first thing you'll hear is, "I'm an accountant" or "I work in high-tech." We tend to let these descriptions or abstractions define us, and we perceive the world around us through that particular lens. Why not move down the abstraction ladder a bit and see yourself as a husband or wife, neighbor, churchgoer, baseball fan, and so on. Doing so opens up a world of possibility in our lives.

Similarly, most organizations focus intently on the micro details of their operations, failing to see the bigger issues that underlie their purpose. The "5 Whys" force us to abstract to different levels, thereby leaving behind the myriad specific characteristics of our organizational being and discovering our true meaning.

Six-Question Mode for Developing Your Mission

Let's move from the "5 Whys" to the following six questions. Your responses to these queries will help you frame the fundamentals of your mission[11]:

1. *Who are we?* The answer to this seemingly simple question should provide stakeholder opinion on what makes the organization different and why it will endure. When answering this query it's important to keep in mind my earlier admonition against creating a mission that is unduly limiting. Don't restrict yourself to what is written on your organization's stationery; instead, focus on the central themes that define you.

2. *What basic social or political needs or problems do we exist to meet?* The answer to this question will provide justification for your existence.

3. *How do we recognize, anticipate, and respond to these problems or needs?* Answering this question will force the organization to look outside itself and consider the wider environment of which it is a part. Liaising with other organizations, conducting research, sharing best practice information—all of these activities are geared toward an external orientation that enable the organization to stay in constant touch with developments in the field.

4. *How should we respond to our key stakeholders?* Satisfying stakeholder needs is central to the success of public and nonprofit organizations. When contemplating this question, consider all of your stakeholders, their varied needs, and how you propose to respond to these needs.

5. *What is our guiding philosophy and culture?* Once you've developed a mission, values, and vision, a strategy will follow. To successfully implement the strategy, it should be consistent with your guiding philosophy and culture. Therefore, it's important to consider these items now and clearly articulate them in your statement of core purpose—the mission.

6. *What makes us distinctive or unique?* Competition is shaping our global economy and it has had a tremendous impact not only on the private sector, but the public and nonprofit arena as well. Any nonprofit that is unable to demonstrate unique competencies or advantages will soon be overlooked as irrelevant. Of course, in the public sector, the cry of "privatization" of services is an all too familiar refrain. Organizations must determine exactly what elevates them from others willing and able to provide similar services, in order to truly distinguish themselves in the eyes of stakeholders.

Gast's Laws

The late business professor Walter Gast formulated a series of principles in the 1940s and 1950s that suggested organizational success was more than a function of simply generating profitable returns, but was in fact something deeper. His principles have been adapted and used to help many organizations develop mission statements. Here are the six questions based on Gast's Laws[12]:

1. What "want-satisfying" service do we provide and constantly seek to improve?

2. How do we increase the quality of life for our customers and stakeholders?

3. How do we provide opportunities to productively employ people?

4. How do we create a high-quality work experience for our employees?
5. How do we live up to the obligation to provide just wages?
6. How do we fulfill the obligation of providing a return on the financial and human resources we expend?

A Simpler Approach

Each of the techniques outlined has significant merit and will undoubtedly lead to the creation of an inspiring mission. In keeping with the old 80/20 rule (80 percent of the value with 20 percent of the effort), Exhibit 5.2 provides a simple template that can help you get the mission ball rolling within your organization.

Exhibit 5.2   Simplified Mission Statement Template

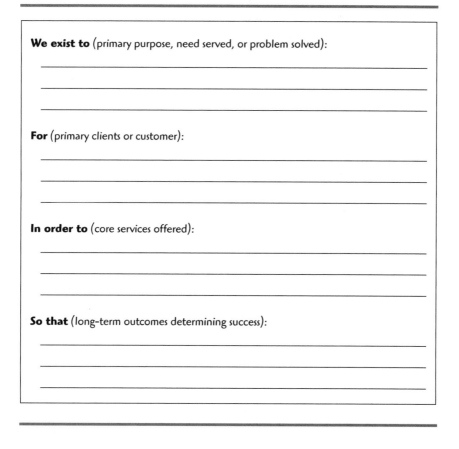

We exist to (primary purpose, need served, or problem solved):

For (primary clients or customer):

In order to (core services offered):

So that (long-term outcomes determining success):

Who Writes the Mission Statement?

An important consideration when writing your mission statement is who should be involved in the process? There are different schools of thought on this subject. Some argue the mission should be crafted by the senior leader or some other executive, sent out for comments and revisions, and finalized without any meetings or committee involvement. Others believe the mission statement, with its inherent focus on capturing the hearts and minds of all employees, cannot possibly be drafted without employee involvement. Being the good fence-sitting consultant I am, I'll come down somewhere on the middle in this debate.

Mission statements require the broad and high-level thinking of an executive to consider the many possibilities available to the organization. Charismatic leaders often possess the enviable ability of crystalizing the organization's place and future goals in compelling terms to be shared with all employees. Don't deny yourself the opportunity of gleaning your executives' wisdom and foresight. At the same time, you should also involve as many people as possible in *reviewing* the draft mission statement. Let employees at every level of the organization have the chance to "kick the tires" of this most important of documents. The mission must serve to galvanize everyone toward an exciting future, and without involvement in the process, commitment will be difficult if not impossible to acquire.

If You Already Have a Mission

As mission-driven organizations, many of you probably already have mission statements. Some might be proudly adorning office walls throughout the organization, while others may be gathering dust on a shelf or tucked out of sight in a desk drawer somewhere. If yours falls into the latter category—that is, you haven't seen or heard much about your mission for a while—that's probably a good sign it is time to reexamine it.

Start by evaluating your mission in the context of the attributes presented earlier in the chapter. Does your statement contain all of these attributes? Here are some additional questions to ask if you're uncertain about the efficacy of your current mission[13]:

- *Is the mission up to date?* Does it reflect what the organization actually does and is all about?
- *Is the mission relevant to your clients and constituents?* Does a compelling reason for your existence present itself from a review of your mission?
- *Who is being served?* Should you rewrite the mission to more accurately reflect your current customer base?

Exhibit 5.3 contains sample mission statements from a diverse group of organizations.

Exhibit 5.3   Sample Mission Statements

The City of Charlotte: The mission of the City of Charlotte is to ensure the delivery of quality public services that promote safety, health, and quality of life of its citizens. We will identify and respond to community needs and focus on the customer through:

> · Creating and maintaining effective partnerships

> · Attracting and retaining skilled, motivated employees

> · Using strategic business planning

Canine Companions for Independence: Canine Companions for Independence is a nonprofit organization that enhances the lives of people with disabilities by providing highly trained assistance dogs and ongoing support to ensure quality partnerships.

Internal Revenue Service: The mission of the Internal Revenue Service is to provide America's taxpayers with top-quality service by helping them understand and meet their tax responsibilities and by applying the tax law with integrity and fairness to all.

American Institute of Certified Public Accountants (AICPA): Provide members with the resources, information, and leadership that enable them to provide valuable services in the highest professional manner to benefit the public as well as employees and clients.

Police Bureau of Portland, Oregon: The mission of the Police Bureau of Portland, Oregon, is to maintain and improve community livability by working with all citizens to preserve life, maintain human rights, protect property, and promote individual responsibility and community commitment.

Goodwill Industries of Southern California: The mission of Goodwill Industries of Southern California is to enhance the quality of the lives of people who have disabilities and other vocational disadvantages by assisting them to become productive and self-sufficient through education, training, and job opportunities.

Public Radio International: Public Radio International's mission is to serve audiences with distinctive programming that provides information, insights, and cultural experiences essential to understanding a diverse, interdependent world.

3M: To solve unsolved problems innovatively.

American Cancer Society: The American Cancer Society is the nationwide community-based voluntary health organization dedicated to eliminating cancer as a major health problem by preventing cancer, saving lives, and diminishing suffering from cancer through research, education, advocacy, and service.

Wal-Mart: To give ordinary folk the chance to buy the same things as rich people.

Walt Disney: To make people happy.

Why Mission Is "Mission-Critical" to the Balanced Scorecard

The Balanced Scorecard was not designed to act as an isolated management tool; rather, it is part of an integrated approach to examining your organization and providing you with a means to evaluate your overall success. Above all, the Scorecard is a tool designed to offer faithful translation. What does it translate? The Scorecard decodes your mission, values, vision, and strategy into performance objectives and measures in each of the four Scorecard perspectives. Translating this "DNA" of your organization with the Balanced Scorecard ensures all employees are aligned with, and working toward, the mission. This represents one of the great values of the Scorecard system. The mission is where you begin your translating efforts. A well-developed Balanced Scorecard ensures the measures you track are consistent with your ultimate aspirations, and it guides the hearts and minds of employees in making the right choices.

When developing objectives and measures, you must critically examine them in the context of the mission you've written for the organization, to be certain they are consistent with that purpose. Let me give you an example: I'm sure many of you shop, as I do, at Wal-Mart. Its very simple and cogent mission is "*to give ordinary folk the chance to buy the same things as rich people.*" Would a measure of "market share of the richest 1 percent of Americans" make sense in light of Wal-Mart's mission? Probably not; in fact, it would reflect a fundamental shift in purpose. While Wal-Mart welcomes all shoppers (I'm sure many price-conscious wealthy people shop there, too), it relies on a strategy of low prices to attract those who aren't "rich."

The Balanced Scorecard is *descriptive*, not *prescriptive;* in other words, there are no hard-and-fast rules. So you could build and implement a Balanced Scorecard without a mission statement for your organization. It would still contain a mix of financial and nonfinancial measures linked together through a series of cause-and-effect relationships. But consider for a moment the tremendous value and alignment you create when developing a Scorecard that accurately translates your mission. Now you have a tool that can truly be your compass and guide the actions of you and your entire employee team. If you do have a mission, make certain the Balanced Scorecard you develop is true to the core essence reflected in the document. If you don't have a mission statement, I strongly encourage you to develop one and see for yourself the focus and alignment you create when translating your mission into a Balanced Scorecard framework.

VALUES

What Are Values?

Modern organizations have a multitude of ways in which to reach their goals. You may use a method of truly innovative service delivery to distinguish yourself. Or perhaps the customer service ethic at your shop is legendary, and propels you toward success. For some organizations, it's the way they behave that makes the difference and provides their source of strength. We've all experienced situations that demonstrate this: For example, perhaps a hotel employee provided you, a business traveler, with an essential item you forgot to put in your travel bag; or an amusement park worker showed up to help you, a frazzled parent, at the exact moment before the combination of stress and joy (that only an amusement park can bring) became too much for you to bear. Chances are these acts didn't result from reading the latest management guru's book or from a desire to get a promotion. No, they simply represent the way things get done at that organization—in other words, its *values.*

Values are the timeless principles that guide an organization. They represent the deeply held beliefs within the organization and are demonstrated through the day-to-day behaviors of all employees. An organization's values make an open proclamation about how it expects everyone to behave. These genuinely held values can prove to be dramatically galvanizing in times of prosperity and crisis alike. Take the case of the United Parcel Service (UPS). You may recall the agonizing strike that nearly paralyzed the company back in 1997. "Brown," as they are now known in their ubiquitous ads, survived that calamity, and Chief Executive Mike Eskew believes their values had a lot to do with it: *"It was a hugely difficult time, like a family feud. Everyone had close friends on both sides of the fence, and it was tough for us to pick sides. But what saved us was our noble purpose. Whatever side people were on, they all shared a common set of values. Those values are core to us. "*[14] Notice Eskew uses the words "core to us." In the following section, we'll examine why it's critical that the values you hold are truly representative of your organization.

Values Must Represent Your Unique Organization

What would you think of an organization that listed the following as its corporate values: communication, respect, and integrity. They sound pretty good, don't they? All simple yet powerful words that seem to suggest an organization in touch with what is necessary to achieve success. Perhaps you can see your own organization in these distinguished terms. Well, if you can, be careful. These are the values proudly espoused by Enron! Of course, Enron is not alone in using values like respect and integrity; in fact, 55 percent of Fortune 100 companies proclaim integrity as a core value.[15] As high as this percentage appears, it is undoubtedly much higher at public and nonprofit organizations for which these terms are often a way of life.

There is absolutely nothing wrong with holding respect, communication, integrity, and many of the other "greatest hits of the values collection" as part of your culture. The danger is in publicly stating these values while, in practice, following a different rulebook to guide your actions. Research has suggested that employees will quickly brand as a hypocrite any leader whose actions are not consistent with publicly stated values. Potentially more troubling for today's leaders is the fact that it's not just their actions that matter, but their *perceived actions* that really drive employee sentiment.[16] As a result, it's critical that all leaders undertake a campaign to ensure organizational values are well understood from the boardroom to the front lines. Allowing employees to develop their own perceived meanings is, at least, a recipe for confusion and, at worst, for all-out insurrection.

Management consultant Patrick Lencioni suggests an organization's values should be "aggressively authentic."[17] "Authentic" in this context means developing values that are consistent with your organizational objectives, not writing something that would be well suited for the inside of a greeting card. He cites Siebel Systems, a Silicon Valley-based developer of Customer Relationship Management Software. Siebel distinguishes itself from many of its Northern California peers by listing professionalism as its top value. This is in stark contrast to many technology companies, where basketball courts, cluttered corridors, and T-shirts are the norm. At Siebel, employees are not permitted to eat at their desks or decorate their walls with more than one or two photographs. This sends a clear message to all Siebel associates of what is necessary (and expected) to succeed.

In *Built to Last*, authors James Collins and Jerry Porras suggest that visionary organizations decide for themselves which values to hold, independent of the current environment, competitive requirements, or management fads. They quote Johnson & Johnson CEO Ralph Larsen on values: *"The core values embodied in our credo might be a competitive advantage, but that is not why we have them. We have them because they define for us what we stand for, and we would hold them even if they became a competitive disadvantage in certain situations."*[18] "What we stand for" is an important part of the quote. As discussed previously, no universal set of right or wrong values exist; instead, each organization must determine or discover the core values that comprise its essence and hold importance to those within it. Organizations tend to have a small number of core values that truly reflect their very essence. A large number may indicate confusion between values and practices. While practices, processes, and strategies should change over time in answer to the many challenges that come our way, we expect values to remain the same, providing an enduring source of strength and wisdom.

In many organizations, the core values represent the strong personal beliefs of the founder or senior leader, for example, Walt Disney's belief in imagination and wholesomeness. Just as we would expect parents to exert great influence over the developing values of their children, it is the organization's leaders who set the tone for values within an organization. Therefore, leaders must constantly strive not only to develop appropriate values, but more importantly they must consistently mirror the values in their words and actions. As the Swiss philosopher Henri-Frederic Amiel once said, *"Every man's conduct is an unspoken sermon that is forever preaching to others."*[19] One leader who does a great job of living the company's values is Herb Kelleher of Southwest Airlines, which has been consistently named among the best companies to work for in America by *Fortune* magazine. The values of maintaining a sense of humor and having fun at your job are two that are deemed critical by the CEO, and he ensures these values are shared by the entire workforce through careful recruiting efforts.

Establishing Values

I considered titling this section in question format: "Can we establish values?" After all, every organization has a set of values that are demonstrated every day; the question is, do they reflect the true essence of the organization or simply the thinking at the top of its current regime? I've noted previously that an organization's core values should not change, but should act as the guiding principles for the organization as it reacts to the world around it. In addition, we must also recognize that, like virtually everything else, some values within an organization will remain long after they cease to provide any benefit, and in fact may become a hindrance to the ongoing success of the company. Some values may even prove unethical or unacceptable in the larger societal context. This doesn't imply a wholesale change of values every few years to suit the current competitive landscape; it simply suggests an honest evaluation of your organization and the recognition of which values truly represent the essence of your organization and are the keys to your enduring success.

The key to changing values and the underlying culture of an organization lies in open and honest identification of the current value systems that exist and are rewarded in the organization. One tool to help you in this endeavor, developed by author and consultant Richard Barrett, is known as the "corporate value audit instrument."[20] Individuals in the organization use three templates of values/behaviors: the 10 values that best represent who they are (*personal values*), the 10 values that best describe how their organization/team operates (*organizational values*), and the 10 values they believe are most critical for a high-performance organization/team (*ideal organizational values*). This very illuminating diagnostic tool is used to evaluate the strengths and weaknesses of existing values and culture. Organizations are able to assess the degree of alignment between personal values, existing, and ideal organizational values, and identify the changes that are necessary to develop a successful and enduring value system.

For additional assistance in identifying values, try to answer these questions developed by author and consultant Jim Collins[21]:

- What core values do you bring to work—values you hold to be so fundamental that you would hold them regardless of whether or not they were rewarded?
- How would you describe to your loved ones the core values you stand for in your work and that you hope they stand for in their working lives?

- If you awoke tomorrow morning with enough money to retire for the rest of your life, would you continue to hold on to these core values?
- Perhaps most important, can you envision these values being as valid 100 years from now as they are today?
- Would you want the organization to continue to hold these values even, if at some point, one or more of them became a competitive disadvantage?
- If you were to start a new organization tomorrow in a different line of work, what core values would you build into the new organization regardless of its activities?

One final caveat regarding values: While the topic exudes a "warm and fuzzy" feeling, you should not feel compelled to involve your entire employee body in the creation of values. Remember that values should support your mission and help you achieve your organizational objectives. This process is not a matter of polling the entire organization and taking the top five values suggested. Rather, it's the very demanding work of critically examining your organization and determining which behaviors you need to see demonstrated on a day-to-day basis to drive the results you desire.

Values and the Balanced Scorecard

The preceding section addressed the possibility of changing the values of an organization and the mechanisms for achieving this result. The Balanced Scorecard represents the best solution for broadcasting your values, reviewing them over time, and creating alignment from top to bottom in the organization. The real key is *alignment*, enabling all employees to see how their day-to-day actions are consistent with the values of the company and how living those values is contributing to overall success.

In Chapter Ten I'll discuss the concept of cascading the Balanced Scorecard, driving it down to lower levels of the organization while ensuring alignment throughout. When we cascade, we allow employees at all levels to develop objectives and measures that represent how they influence overall agency goals. The measures selected must be consistent with the values of the organization to ensure everyone is headed in the same overall direction. Reviewing, or "auditing," the measures on lower-level Scorecards provides a great opportunity to determine if the values you espouse are really those held by your employees up and down the organizational hierarchy. If you value collaboration, for example, but your departments have no performance measures tracking collaboration, then perhaps they don't truly value it as a guiding principle of their operations. Conversely, if all lower-level Scorecards contain measures relating to customer service, but this value is not captured on the high-level organizational Scorecard, then perhaps you've missed a core value that is important to all of your employees.

Pragmatically, the Balanced Scorecard may also be used to track the extent to which your organization really "lives" its values. For organizations undergoing changes to values, or suffering from turmoil, metrics that gauge adherence to stated values may be of great benefit. That said, developing meaningful value-based metrics may prove challenging to even the most creative Scorecard builders. You could use "mystery shopper" or casual observation techniques to determine whether employees are behaving in accordance with your values. Calculating the percentage of employees who can recite your core values without prompting could also be used, but this would prove very difficult to track and might raise the ire of those being asked to spontaneously list the company's values. Another possibility is to identify behaviors consistent with your values and base at least part of the annual performance appraisal on the demonstration of these behaviors by employees.

A final thought on values in the organization comes from Tom Morris. In his book *If Aristotle Ran General Motors*, Morris has this to say about the importance of values at work. *"People who are personally reassessing their lives in light of their deepest values will not find it easy to settle for less than a work environment that respects and encourages those values. They will certainly not be able to flourish, to be and do their best, in conditions that have not been wisely developed with sensitivity to what deeply moves people and what most fundamentally matters to us all."*[22]

VISION

The Role of Vision through History

Human history has been marked by momentous events that have forever changed the way we think, act, or live. Assume, for example, that time travel is possible, and that you suddenly have the chance to take a front-row seat at any of these history-altering occasions. Which would you choose? Lincoln's Gettysburg address perhaps? Or maybe the downing of the Berlin Wall? I could list literally hundreds. If I had the opportunity, there are two legendary addresses I would like to have heard in person. The first is Martin Luther King Jr.'s "I Have a Dream" speech delivered on the steps of the Lincoln Memorial on August 28, 1963. Here is a small portion of that stirring oratory:

> I say to you today, my friends, that in spite of the difficulties and frustrations of the moment, I still have a dream. It is a dream deeply rooted in the American dream.
>
> I have a dream that one day this nation will rise up and live out the true meaning of its creed: "We hold these truths to be self-evident: that all men are created equal."
>
> I have a dream that one day on the red hills of Georgia the sons of former slaves and the sons of former slave owners will be able to sit down together at a table of brotherhood.

> I have a dream that my four children will one day live in a nation where they will not be judged by the color of their skin but by the content of their character.
>
> I have a dream today.

In my opinion, it's virtually impossible to read these words, conceived with clarity and delivered with passion and eloquence, and not feel compelled toward action.

My second window-on-history choice would be President John F. Kennedy's impassioned plea to have the United States commit to sending a man to the Moon, delivered to the U.S. Congress on May 25, 1961. Here is a small portion of the president's remarks:

> Now it is time to take longer strides—time for a great new American enterprise—time for this nation to take a clearly leading role in space achievement, which in many ways may hold the key to our future on Earth.
>
> I believe that this nation should commit itself to achieving the goal, before this decade is out, of landing a man on the Moon and returning him safely to the Earth.

With these words President Kennedy inspired a generation of citizens and won their commitment to a seemingly impossible task. You may not have to shoulder the responsibility of inspiring millions, but you do have a duty as a leader to help yourself and your employees find meaning in their work and be compelled toward great things.

What Is a Vision Statement?

A vision statement provides a word picture of what the organization intends ultimately to become—which may be 5, 10, or 15 years in the future. Notice the vivid canvas Dr. King paints with his words. He transports the listener to a new and exciting future. While mission statements are often abstract, the vision should contain as concrete a picture of the desired state as possible and provide the basis for formulating strategies and objectives. President Kennedy certainly observed this criterion with his very specific dictum of landing a man on the Moon and returning him safely to Earth. He uses simple language, leaving little room for doubt. With his vision secure, goals and objectives could easily follow.

The vision you create may not change human relations or put a person in space, but it can forever alter the way your organization does business. A powerful vision provides everyone in the organization with a shared mental framework that helps give form to the often-abstract future that lies before us. The vision can inspire every employee and stakeholder to test their boundaries, always stretching to achieve more in pursuit of your overall mission. As organizational learning expert Peter Senge has observed, *"Vision translates mission into truly meaningful intended results—and guides the allocation of time, energy, and resources. In my experience, it is only through a compelling vision that a deep sense of purpose comes alive.* "[23] Let's look at the elements of a vision statement that will serve to enliven the passions of all your stakeholders.

Elements of Effective Vision Statements

Everything discussed in this chapter is critical to your organization and your Balanced Scorecard project, but perhaps the most critical component is the vision. Why? Because it acts as a conduit between your reason for being, as reflected in the mission, the values representative of your culture, and the strategy you'll put into execution to reach your desired future state. Without a clear and compelling vision to guide the actions of all employees, you could wind up with a workforce lacking direction and thus unable to profit from any strategy you put in place, no matter how well conceived. Let's look at some characteristics of effective vision statements:

- *Is Concise.* The very best vision statements are those that grab your attention and immediately draw you in without boring you from pages of mundane rhetoric. President Kennedy didn't mince his words; he simply stated his vision of landing a man on the Moon by the end of the decade. If everyone in your organization is expected to act and make decisions based on the vision, the least you can do is create something that is simple and memorable. Consider it your organizational campaign slogan for the future.

- *Balances external and internal elements.*[24] The external elements of the vision focus on how your public or nonprofit agency will change or improve the world (or your piece of it) should you fulfill your purpose. Rather than saying, "We will have double the current capacity," the external elements of your vision force you to articulate how the world will be a better place as a result of your efforts. For example, "All children will have access to quality health care." Conversely, the internal elements of your vision describe how you will appear as an organization when all the elements you need to meet your external vision are present. Use of staff, service and product mix, partnerships, and technology could be included in the internal portion of your vision. For example, "We will have a 100,000-square-foot gallery that has all the great neon artworks of the twentieth century on display" (Museum of Neon Art).

- *Appeals to all stakeholders.* A vision statement that focuses on one group, to the detriment of others, will not win lasting support in the hearts and minds of all constituencies. The vision must appeal to everyone who has a stake in the success of the enterprise: employees, funders, elected officials, customers, and communities, to name but a few.

- *Is consistent with mission and values.* Your vision is a further translation of your mission (why you exist) and the values of underlying importance to your organization. If your mission suggests solving community problems, and one of your core values is constant innovation in service delivery, then there should be a reference to service delivery innovation in your vision statement. Remember, in the vision, you're painting a word picture of the desired future state that will lead to the achievement of your mission, so ensure that the two are aligned.

- *Is verifiable.* Using the latest business jargon and buzzwords can make your vision statement very nebulous to even the most trained eye. Who within your organization will be able to determine exactly when you become "world class, leading edge, or top quality?" Write your vision statement so that you'll know when you've achieved it. While mission and values won't change, expect the vision to change, as it is written for a finite period of time.

- *Is feasible.* The vision shouldn't be the collective dreams of senior leadership; rather, it must be grounded solidly in reality. To ensure this, you must possess a clear understanding of your environment, its key players, and emerging trends.

- *Is inspirational.* Again, your vision represents a word picture of the desired future state of the organization, so don't miss the opportunity to inspire your team to make the emotional commitment necessary to reach this destination. The vision statement should not only guide, but also arouse the collective passion of all employees. To be inspirational, the vision must first be understandable to every conceivable audience member, from the boardroom to the front lines. Throw away the thesaurus for this exercise and focus instead on your deep knowledge of the business to compose a meaningful statement for all involved. Notice again the simple yet powerful language employed by both President Kennedy and Dr. King.

Developing Your Vision Statement

A rich body of literature exists on the subject of creating a powerful vision. As you might expect given this abundant supply of material, there are many possible ways to craft this important document. In this section I provide you with a number of alternatives. Consider using one of the following or combining those elements that appeal to you.

Ten Key Questions

This exercise challenges a small group of people to formulate answers to 10 important questions. The questions each relate to a specific area of vision creation. Reviewing, combining, and synthesizing your responses will help you document your vision.[25] Here are the 10 questions:

1. How would the world be improved or changed if we were successful in achieving our purpose?
2. What are the most important services that we should continue to provide, change, or begin to offer in the next three years?
3. What staffing and benefits changes do we need to implement to better achieve our purpose?
4. How will our elected officials or board of directors assist us in achieving our purpose?
5. What resource development (funding) changes do we need to influence to better achieve our purpose?
6. What facilities and technology changes do we need to implement to better achieve our purpose?
7. What infrastructure, systems, or communication changes do we need to implement to better achieve our purpose?
8. How could we more effectively or efficiently provide our services? If you could only make three changes that would significantly impact our ability to provide quality services to our clients/customers, what would these changes be?
9. What makes us unique?
10. What do our clients/customers consider most important in our provision of services? What do our clients/customers need from us?

Interview Method

As you might have guessed, senior management interviews are the key component of this technique for developing your vision. Each of the senior leaders of your organization is interviewed separately to gather his or her feedback on the future direction of the organization. I suggest using an outside consultant or facilitator to run the interviews, because a seasoned consultant will have been through many interviews of this nature and will have the ability to put the executive at ease, ensuring that the necessary information flows freely in an environment of trust and objectivity. The interview should last about an hour and include both general and specific questions, as well as a mix of past-, present-, and future-oriented queries. Typical questions may include:

• Where and why have we been successful in the past?
• Where have we failed in the past?
• Why should we be proud of our organization?
• What trends, innovations, and dynamics are currently changing our environment?

- What do our clients and customers expect from us? Our funders and legislators? Our employees?
- What are our greatest attributes and competencies as an organization?
- Where do you see our organization in three years? Five years? Ten years?
- How will our organization have changed during that time period?
- How do we sustain our success?

The results of the interviews are summarized by the interviewer and presented to the senior leader. At this point, the leader will have the opportunity to draft the vision based on the collective knowledge gathered from the senior team. Once the draft is completed, the entire team convenes and debates the leader's vision, to ensure it captures the essential elements they discussed during their interviews. You would not expect the first draft to be accepted by everyone, and that's the idea—to involve the whole team in the creation process. However, by mandating the leader with the initial responsibility for declaring the vision, you ensure his or her commitment to the vision and have a working draft from which to begin the refinement process. Once the team has hammered out the vision statement, it should be reviewed and accepted by people from as many levels in the organization as logistically possible—and with today's technology, that should include just about everyone!

Back to the Future Visioning

I enjoy working with clients on this technique. The exercise can be administered either individually or with a group. I like using it with groups for the initial attempt to develop a draft vision statement, but it also works well in individual settings. In describing the method, I'll assume a group session.

To begin the session, ask the group to imagine they awake the next morning 5, 10, or 15 years in the future (your choice of time increment); and to record their impressions of the future, they've each been given a disposable camera to capture important images and changes they hoped might take place within their organization. At the end of each day's adventure, they must create a caption for the pictures they've taken during the day. Distribute several 3-by-5 index cards to each of the participants for this purpose; then give the participants about 15 minutes to imagine their trip to the future. Encourage them to capture as much detail as possible in their mind's eye. As prompts, ask them: "What has happened with your organization: Are you successful?" "Which customers or clients are you serving?" "What is making you unique?" "What goals have you achieved?" By the end of the trip, they should have cataloged the future in detail.

Once the 15 minutes are up, tell them: "Unfortunately, on the trip back to the present, the reentry was a little rough and the pictures were destroyed; but fortunately for you, the captions remain." (More animated and comedic facilitators can have a field day with this section.) Record the captions from the index cards on a flip chart or laptop computer and use them as the raw materials for the initial draft of a vision statement. I enjoy this approach to vision statement development because it challenges the participants to engage all of their senses in the process, not simply their cognitive abilities. Not only that, it can be fun!

Borrowed Heroes[26]

I opened this section with a short review of two passionate addresses from Dr. Martin Luther King Jr., and former President John F. Kennedy. Of course, these two erudite and articulate men aren't the only ones known to stir a crown with their oratorical genius and powerful visions. Each of you may have your own heroes from the worlds of politics, science, sports, spirituality, or entertainment. In this next exercise you'll create a dialog on your vision by drawing on the words of those who have inspired you.

Here's how it works: First have the group listen to, or read, a stirring and inspirational speech from your own borrowed hero. It could be Martin Luther King Jr.'s "I Have a Dream" speech, President Kennedy's "landing a man on the Moon" address or any other you choose. Next discuss the fact that you've just heard this leader at a specific point in time. Notice that he or she did not address the current state of affairs, but instead tapped the aspiration of all by painting a vivid word picture of future events. What was so inspiring, and why?

Use the discussion to develop a vision for your organization. Imagine that a publication such as *Governing Magazine* or *The Nonprofit Times* is writing a story about your organization 5, 10, or 15 years from now. You've achieved your vision, and the reporter asks how you accomplished the impressive feat. Discuss and record what you've accomplished, how the world is better off because of all you've achived, who you've served, and how you did it. This open and creative discussion should lead you to the elements of a powerful vision for your organization.

The Power of Vision

The preceding are just some of the methods I've found very useful in developing a vision statement. Fortunately for all of us, abundant literature and practice exists on this subject, so you have many resources at your disposal.

Once you've developed your vision you'll be amazed at the power it provides. Here's how Michael Kaiser, president of the Kennedy Center for the Performing Arts in Washington, DC, describes the power of vision for this renowned performing arts center: *"I think what leaders have to do is to provide a vision for the future. And what has been remarkable to me...is the power of a vision. If you can present [that vision] to people, either to people inside the organization who have been damaged, or people outside the organization who have lost faith in what the organization can do, the power is remarkable."*[27] There is little doubt that a powerful vision will confer many benefits to your organization. A summary of potential benefits is outlined in Exhibit 5.4.

Vision Statements and the Balanced Scorecard

Vision statements often describe the desired scope of activities, how the agency will be viewed by its stakeholders (customers/clients, employees, funders, regulators, etc.), areas of leadership or distinctive competence, and strongly held values. When writing a vision for the organization, you're attempting to move away from a paradigm of either/or thinking to embracing the power of "and." It's no longer a matter of satisfying one group using certain competencies at the expense of another. The vision has to balance the interests of all groups and portray a future that will lead to wins for everyone involved. The Balanced Scorecard is the mechanism you use to track your achievement of this lofty goal. The principle tenet of the Scorecard is balance—more accurately, using measurement to capture the correct balance of skills, processes, and customer requirements that lead to your desired future as reflected in the vision.

Exhibit 5.4   Benefits of a Vision Statement

Provides guidance. A clear and succinct vision statement provides all stakeholders the opportunity to see how they fit into the organization's "big picture." The vision supplies clear and compelling guidance of what the future looks like and what is necessary for success.

Creates positive tension. While realistic and feasible, the vision must stimulate people to reach new heights of collective performance. This creates a constructive tension between "what is" and "what could be" if we work to achieve the vision.

Complements leadership. A clear and inspirational vision can empower people to make decisions in accordance with the best intentions of the organization in mind. While leaders cannot, in a practical sense, meet and discuss organizational goals with every stakeholder, the vision can portray the organization's ultimate aims and guide actions accordingly.

Forces the discussion of trade-offs. Even the clearest vision will be open to some interpretation depending on how and where you fit into the overall organizational structure. Visions should be focused enough to guide high-level decision making but flexible enough to encourage active dialog and individual initiative. Achieving the vision should facilitate cooperation and collaboration, not promote isolated win-lose scenarios.

Appeals to a variety of senses. A well-crafted vision taps into the entire human experience. You can literally see, feel, and hear the future as it is elegantly laid out before you. This is why the language of visions is so important. How effective would Dr. King's "I Have a Dream" speech have been if he began by saying, "I have a business strategy"? The best visions resonate within us and appeal to all that is human.

The Balanced Scorecard will provide a new, laserlike focus on your organization's results, and as such the potential problems represented by a misguided vision are significant. We've all heard phrases like, "what gets measured gets done," "measure what matters," and many others. The Scorecard is essentially a device that translates vision into reality through the articulation of vision (and strategy). A well-developed Balanced Scorecard can be expected to stimulate behavioral changes within your organization. The question is, are they the sort of changes you want? Be certain the vision you create for your organization is one that truly epitomizes your mission and values, because the Scorecard will give you the means for traveling first-class to that envisioned future!

SUMMARY

In *The Dilbert Principle*, oft-quoted, and always cynical business sage Scott Adams makes a poignant statement about mission and vision: *"The first step in developing a vision statement is to lock the managers in a room and have them debate what is meant by a vision statement and how exactly it differs from a mission statement. These are important questions, because one wrong move and the employees will start doing 'vision' things when they should be doing 'mission' things, and before long it will be impossible to sort it all out."*[28] It's hard to imagine two more important words that are subject to so much confusion. My goal in this chapter was to clear up some of the clutter surrounding these terms, and to add a third for your consideration: values.

At the essence of every human being, and within every organization, is the desire to make a meaningful contribution. The mission defines this core purpose and articulates why the organization exists. The mission captures the contribution and benefit an organization wishes to deliver to humankind, and provides a star to steer by in our turbulent world. An effective mission should inspire change, be easily understood and communicated, and be long term in nature. The Balanced Scorecard allows an organization to translate its mission into concrete objectives, which align all employees. The measures on a Balanced Scorecard must reflect the aspirations denoted in the mission statement to provide effective direction.

Values represent the deeply held beliefs within the organization and the timeless principles it uses to guide decision making. Values are often reflective of the personal beliefs emanating from a strong leader. While all organizations claim to hold certain values, it's very important to ensure those you espouse truly represent the fiber of your organization. Leaders that "talk the talk" but don't "walk the walk" on values will quickly be seen as hypocrites within the organization. Changing an organization's value systems represents a great challenge but may be accomplished by first openly and honestly identifying current values and providing the mechanisms that facilitate a transition to more appropriate values. The Balanced Scorecard provides organizations with a means of evaluating the alignment of values throughout the organization. The Scorecard may also be used to track the extent to which an organization is living its stated values.

Throughout time, we have been moved by the dynamic visions of impassioned people. Never abstract, the visions they proclaim portray a vivid word picture of what the organization ultimately intends to become. Effective visions balance internal and external elements; appeal to all stakeholders; align with mission and values; and are concise, verifiable, feasible, and inspirational. Vision statements may be created through interviewing of senior executives or by leading any number of group "visioning" exercises designed to enlist the full involvement of your team. The vision statement balances the interest of multiple stakeholders in describing how the organization will create future value. The role of the Scorecard is to capture the correct mix of competencies, processes, and customer value propositions that lead to our desired future.

NOTES

1. Michael Allison and Jude Kaye, *Strategic Planning for Nonprofit Organizations* (New York: John Wiley & Sons, Inc., 1997), p. 56.
2. E.B. Knauft, Renee Berger, and Sandra Gray, *Profiles of Excellence* (San Francisco: Jossey-Bass, 1991).
3. David Osborne and Ted Gaebler, *Reinventing Government* (Reading, MA: Addison-Wesley, 1992).
4. James C. Collins and Jerry I. Porras, "Building Your Company's Vision," *Harvard Business Review,* September–October 1996.
5. Tom Krattenmaker, "Write a Mission Statement that Your Company is Willing to Live," *Harvard Management Update,* March 2002.
6. Peter F. Drucker, *Managing the Non-Profit Organization* (New York: HarperBusiness, 1990), p. 5.
7. Michael Allison and Jude Kaye, *Strategic Planning for Nonprofit Organizations* (New York: John Wiley & Sons, Inc., 1997), p. 57.
8. Julia Kirby and Diane L. Coutu, "The Beauty of Buzzwords," *Harvard Business Review,* May 2001.
9. Rudolph W. Giuliani, *Leadership* (New York: Hyperion, 2002).
10. James C. Collins and Jerry I. Porras, "Building Your Company's Vision," *Harvard Business Review,* September–October 1996.
11. John M. Bryson, *Strategic Planning for Public and Nonprofit Organizations* (San Francisco: Jossey-Bass, 1995), pp. 76–78.
12. Tom Krattenmaker, "Write a Mission Statement That Your Company Is Willing to Live," *Harvard Management Update,* March 2002.
13. Thomas Wolf, *Managing a Nonprofit Organization in the Twenty-First Century* (New York: Fireside, 1999), p. 347.
14. Diane L. Coutu, "How Resilience Works," *Harvard Business Review,* May 2002.
15. Patrick M. Lencioni, "Make Your Values Mean Something," *Harvard Business Review,* July 2002, pp. 113–117.

16. Amy C. Edmondson, "When Company Values Backfire," *Harvard Business Review*, November 2002, pp. 18–19.
17. Patrick M. Lencioni, "Make Your Values Mean Something," *Harvard Business Review*, July 2002, pp. 113–117.
18. James C. Collins and Jerry I. Porras, *Built to Last* (New York: HarperBusiness, 1997).
19. Henri-Frederic Amiel, *Amiel's Journal: The Journal Intime of Henri-Frederick Amiel* (1852), Mrs. Humphry Ward (trans.) (Macmillan & Co, Ltd., 1889).
20. Richard Barrett, *Liberating the Corporate Soul* (Boston: Butterworth Heinmann1998).
21. Jim Collins, *Leader to Leader* (San Francisco: Jossey-Bass, 1999).
22. Tom Morris, *If Aristotle Ran General Motors: The New Soul of Business* (New York: Henry Holt and Company, 1997).
23. Peter Senge, "The Practice of Innovation," *Leader to Leader*, 9 (Summer 1998): 16–22.
24. Michael Allison and Jude Kaye, *Strategic Planning for Nonprofit Organizations* (New York: John Wiley & Sons, Inc., 1997), p. 69.
25. Ibid., p. 73.
26. This method is adapted from material developed by Robert Knowling, in "Why Vision Matters," *Leader to Leader*, 18, Fall 2000, pp. 38–43.
27. Interview on National Public Radio's Morning Edition, March 26, 2001.
28. Scott Adams, *The Dilbert Principle* (New York: HarperBusiness, 1996).

CHAPTER 6

Strategy: The Core of Every Balanced Scorecard

Roadmap for Chapter Six In writing this book my hope is that readers will find it relevant for years to come—just how many years is anyone's guess. Of course, I can only dream about having the staying power of Sun Tzu, the Chinese general who authored a collection of essays on military strategy. The essays, best known to Western audiences by the title *The Art of War,* have been adapted to suit the needs of businesspeople, athletes, and politicians alike. The book, written more than 2,300 years ago, has been a best-seller for years, and Sun Tzu is undoubtedly the most quoted Chinese personality in history. Such is the power of strategy. Whether you wrote something valuable yesterday or 2,000 years ago, you're sure to find a ready audience.

As the title of this chapter implies, strategy is truly at the core of every Balanced Scorecard. Essentially, the Scorecard is a tool for translating a strategy into action through the development of performance objectives and measures. My purpose in this chapter is to crack the quizzical code of strategy, demystify the concept, and provide you with tools to review your current strategy or enable you to craft a new and exciting future through the development of a freshly minted strategy.

To do that, we'll explore the brief yet prodigious history of the subject and examine what strategy is and, equally important, what it is not. Then, in case you're still not convinced of the value of a strategy, we'll examine some of the benefits a strategy can confer. We'll then look at some of the many schools of strategic thought, and I'll share with you one straight-forward method of strategy development. The chapter concludes with a discussion of why the subject of strategy is central to the Balanced Scorecard.

STRATEGY IS EVERYWHERE

As I was writing my first book on the subject of strategy (*Balanced Scorecard Step-byStep: Maximizing Performance and Maintaining Results*) and how it pertains to the Balanced Scorecard, my wife and I were in the middle of a move to a new house. So, while writing my book, I was simultaneously attempting to catalog the business archives of a lifetime in order to facilitate packing and unpacking—no easy chore for a self-described packrat! I observed, via a not-so-scientific calculation, that approximately 90 percent of the documents I had in my possession made at least some passing reference to the subject of strategy. Now comfortably situated in our new home, my accumulation of business materials continues unabated. According to my "strategy meter," I can tell you that the topic continues to be at least casually addressed in virtually 9 out of 10 documents that come my way.

Strategy truly is everywhere. Interestingly, though, the formal field we label "strategic planning" has a relatively short history. The topic as we know it began to emerge in the 1950s and gained momentum throughout the 1960s and 1970s. As we moved into the 1980s, global competition became an increasing threat, especially to the very vulnerable United States.[1] To regain the advantage they once enjoyed, American businesses moved away from formal planning per se and focused instead on making processes more efficient, eliminating "nonvalue-added" activities, and simply recognizing the new competitive landscape. Many operational improvements ensued, but leaders recognized that simply developing more efficient operations did not represent the path to long-term success. They began to realize the path not taken, one that would lead to sustainable competitive advantage, was paved by a differentiating and defensible strategy.

WHAT IS STRATEGY?

Producing a universally acceptable definition of strategy is truly a Herculean task, so as a mental warm-up, let's start with something a little less controversial: what strategy *is not*. Speaking on the current state of strategy development at many nonprofits, author and consultant Bill Ryan says, "*Some nonprofits develop a big pile of well-intentioned programs, ideas, and directions that try to respond to every need and opportunity that comes along and might vaguely fit under their mission. There is always a reason to do something that no one else is willing to do if it relates to your mission. The harder thing, as is often pointed out in strategy discussions, is to have enough of a strategy to know when to say no, when to drop things, pass up opportunities. Understand that, yes, a need might be real, but you might not be the best response to it.*"[2] So strategy is not about being all things to all people. Deciding when to say no, and determining what you should *not* do constitutes a critical component of strategy.

Public-sector firms are not exempt from the temptation to serve everyone. Scorecard co-developer Robert Kaplan suggests, "*Strategy can be a foreign concept to a public sector organization. These agencies have little incentive to take a longer-term view of their role. They may attempt to do everything for everyone, and can end up doing not much at all.*"[3]

If strategy is not about being the same as everyone else, what is it about? Commonly quoted strategy expert Henry Mintzberg provides this excellent synopsis of the subject: *"My research and that of many others demonstrates that strategy making is an immensely complex process, which involves the most sophisticated, subtle, and, at times, subconscious elements of human thinking."*[4] Maybe so, but that doesn't help us much in crafting a definition! The difficulty with defining strategy is that it holds different meanings to different people and organizations. Some feel strategy is represented by the high-level plans management devises to lead the organization into the future. Others would argue strategy rests on the specific and detailed actions you'll take to achieve your desired state. To others still, strategy is tantamount to best practices. Before I finally jump off the fence and offer a definition of strategy, let's look at some of the key principles of this subject:

- *Different activities.* As explained in the discussion above, strategy is about choosing a different set of activities, the pursuit of which leads to a unique and valuable position in the environment.[5] If everyone were to pursue the same activities, then differentiation would be based purely on operational effectiveness and cost.

- *Trade-offs.* Effective strategies demand trade-offs in competition. Strategy is more about the choice of what *not* to do than what to do. Organizations cannot compete effectively by attempting to be everything to everybody. The entire organization must be aligned around what you choose to do, and create value from that strategic position.[6]

- *Fit.* The activities chosen must fit one another for sustainable success. Many years ago Peter Drucker articulated the "Theory of the Business." He suggested that assumptions about the business must fit one another to produce a valid theory. Activities are the same, they must produce an integrated whole.[7]

- *Continuity.* Generally, strategies should not be constantly reinvented. The strategy crystallizes your thinking on basic issues, such as how you will offer customer value and to which customers. This direction has to be clear to both internal (employees) and external (customers, funders, other stakeholders) constituents.[8] Changes may bring about new opportunities that can be assimilated into the current strategy—new technologies for example.

- *Various thought processes.* Strategy involves conceptual as well as analytical exercises.[9] As the Mintzberg quote at the outset of this section reminds us, strategy involves not only the detailed analysis of complex data, but also broad conceptual knowledge of the organization, environment, and so on.

Using the preceding discussion as a backdrop, I offer the following, admittedly succinct, definition of strategy: Strategy represents the broad priorities adopted by an organization in recognition of its operating environment and in pursuit of its mission. Though short on words, this definition is long on implications.

"Broad priorities" means just that: the overall directional areas the organization will pursue to achieve its mission. For many, there is a tremendous appeal of turning their strategy document into an endless wish list of programs or initiatives. Robert Kaplan has seen this in action: *"Most nonprofits don't have a clear succinct strategy. Their 'strategy' documents often run upwards of 50 pages, and the so-called strategy consists of lists of programs and initiatives, not the outcomes the organization is attempting to achieve."*[10] Consider a small, local AIDS organization. Its strategy could detail every initiative it plans to undertake for the upcoming year. A better approach is to inform its stakeholders and employees as to the overall approach it will take in serving the community. Perhaps it will choose to focus on education, or prevention, or building community support. These are strategies. They set direction and provide a context for the development of objectives and measures, which will follow with the Balanced Scorecard.

A criticism I have of many public and nonprofit strategy documents is the order in which they present their plans. Frequently, they will outline their mission, then a number of specific initiatives, and finally key goals and objectives. In my opinion, this is backwards. Mission always begins the process, on that we agree. However, next comes values and vision, then strategy, which represents the broad, overall priorities of the organization. Translating that strategy is accomplished through the development of objectives, measures, and targets on a Balanced Scorecard. Finally, specific initiatives are put in place to help the organization achieve its Balanced Scorecard targets. Chapter Seven provides a closer examination of the Scorecard's role in the overall Performance Management process of the organization.

DO WE NEED A STRATEGY?

I recently had a very telling conversation with a consultant to nonprofit organizations. He continually encounters organizations whose boards of directors haven't accepted that they need to develop a strategy. This is quite ironic to him since in the nonprofit model it is the board that is charged with setting the direction of the organization. The irony is extended when you consider the fact that most leaders are expressing a desire to spend more time on strategic issues and less on operational demands.

The uplifting words contained in mission, value, and vision statements represent nothing but wishful thinking unless accompanied by a strategy. The strategy gives life to the lofty aims declared in these documents. While mission, values, and vision dwell in the realm of "why" and "who," the strategy gets deep into the trenches of "how." A well-conceived and skillfully executed strategy provides the specific priorities on which you'll allocate resources and direct your energies.

Here are but a few of the many benefits that arise when you develop and commit to executing a strategy[11]:

- *Strategic thought and action are promoted.* Rather than focusing on the rote details of the moment, a strategy directs the energies of all employees toward what is truly important within your organization.

- *Decision-making can be improved.* The important decisions in your organization can be considered through the prism of strategy, not the glare of urgent activities.

- *Performance is enhanced.* A strategic focus ensures your entire organization is focused on achieving overall goals. Add to this potent mix aligned processes for decision-making, resource allocation, and performance management, and performance is almost certain to improve.

Of course, strategy is central to the Balanced Scorecard. To grab hold of the maximum benefit the Scorecard has to offer, you should use it as a mechanism for translating your strategy into action. The final section of this chapter details the vital link between strategy and the Balanced Scorecard.

MANY APPROACHES TO STRATEGY FORMULATION EXIST

Strategy setting is definitely messy business, and that may be putting it euphemistically. One corporate executive told researchers that *"strategy setting is like some primitive tribal ritual. There is a lot of dancing, waving of feathers, and beating drums. No one is exactly sure why we do it, but there is an almost mystical hope that something good will come out of it."*[12] That's a frightening attitude when you consider the crucial importance of a sound strategy to any organization's chances for success.

Part of the confusion surrounding strategy stems from the fact that the field is as crowded as a Tokyo subway, but with approaches and methodologies instead of people. Military applications notwithstanding, never has a field with such a relatively short history spawned such a multitude of techniques. Just a partial listing of strategic modes would include: strengths and weakness analysis, portfolio approaches, shareholder value, economic value-added, core competencies, strategic intents, profit zones, and disruptive technologies. And new entrants are constantly joining the fray. One of the latest techniques is known as "value innovation." Developed by Professors Chan Kim and Renee Mauborgne, this approach seeks to, *"push for a quantum leap in buyer value while simultaneously lowering the industry's cost structure."*[13] Is your head spinning yet? Well, to really get it going, I'll reintroduce a book I first mentioned in Chapter One. *Strategy Safari* extensively documents a whopping 10 different schools of strategic thought, for those intrepid enough to make such a journey. The 10 schools are presented in Exhibit 6.1.

Exhibit 6.1   Ten Schools of Strategic Thought

Design School: Proposes a model of strategy making that seeks to attain a fit between internal capabilities and external possibilities. Probably the most influential school of thought, and home of the SWOT (strengths, weaknesses, opportunities, and threats) technique.

Planning School: Formal procedure, formal training, formal analysis, and lots of numbers are the hallmark of this approach. The simple informal steps of the design school become an elaborate sequence of steps. Produce each component part as specified, assemble them according to the blueprint, and strategy will result.

Positioning School: Suggests that only a few key strategies (positions in the economic marketplace) are desirable. Much of Michael Porter's work can be mapped to this school.

Entrepreneurial School: Strategy formation results from the insights of a single leader, and stresses intuition, judgment, wisdom, experience, and insight. The "vision" of the leader supplies the guiding principles of the strategy.

Cognitive School: Strategy formation is a cognitive process that takes place in the mind of the strategist. Strategies emerge as the strategist filters the maps, concepts, and schemas shaping his or her thinking.

Learning School: Strategies emerge as people (acting individually or collectively) come to learn about a situation as well as their organization's capability of dealing with it.

Power School: This school stresses strategy formation as an overt process of influence, emphasizing the use of power and politics to negotiate strategies favorable to particular interests.

Cultural School: Social interaction, based on the beliefs and understandings shared by the members of an organization, leads to the development of strategy.

Environmental School: Presenting itself to the organization as a set of general forces, the environment is the central actor in the strategy–making process. The organization must respond to the factors or be "selected out."

Configuration School: Strategies arise from periods when an organization adopts a structure to match to a particular context, which gives rise to certain behaviors.

Adapted from *Strategy Safari*, by Henry Mintzberg, Bruce Ahlstrand, and Joseph Lampel (New York: The Free Press, 1998).

Unfortunately, no single "right" method exists. What works for one organization at a distinct point in time may not work for another organization at a different juncture. Conversely, I could also say "fortunately" there is no single right approach, because the importance of the field has stimulated never-ending research, and despite some confusion and head-scratching around the lexicon produced by the field of strategy, we're all the better for the efforts. In the next section I present the most common elements of a strategic planning effort.

STRAIGHTFORWARD APPROACH TO STRATEGY DEVELOPMENT

Entire books, seminars, and MBA courses have been dedicated to this topic, and though formal and detailed strategic planning techniques are beyond the scope of this book, strategy and the Balanced Scorecard are so inextricably linked that it would be a disservice not to share at least the basics of strategic planning for those of you with limited experience in this area. Therefore, consider what follows a primer on the subject. It will serve you well in assessing your current process against common practice, as it provides the essentials of developing a unique strategy for your organization.

The strategic planning method that is given here represents a composite of many different techniques advocated by a wide range of practitioners, consultants, and academics. The five steps are: getting started; conducting a stakeholder analysis; analysis of strengths, weaknesses, opportunities, and threats (SWOT); identifying strategic issues; and developing strategies. When developing a strategy, most pundits suggest you first develop your mission, values, and vision, which set the foundation for your strategy work. We covered mission, values, and vision in Chapter Five, so for the purposes of this discussion, I'm assuming they are present when you begin your strategy efforts.

Step 1: Getting Started

As with your overall Balanced Scorecard implementation, you must ensure your organization is ready to embark on a strategic planning process. As a first step you should review the effectiveness of your current planning process. Exhibit 6.2 provides a number of questions to consider regarding your current processes. Items with lower scores are ideal candidates for improvements that can be addressed in the current strategy development process.

Strategic planning requires the commitment of time and attention from your top leaders, as well as a willingness to provide ample resources for the effort. If your leaders are mired in current crises or anticipating a key legislative change, then perhaps this isn't the best time to embark on the task of developing a new strategy. To make the decision, you'll have to weigh the importance of the undertaking against the probability of success resulting from limited leadership involvement.

Once you're ready to plan, it's then time to consider your *objectives* for drafting a new strategy. Any gap you've uncovered as a result of answering the questions in Exhibit 6.2 will provide an impetus for developing a new strategy. You could be facing any number of issues that necessitate the development of a new strategy. However, it's important to distinguish between issues of truly strategic significance and those of operational dilemmas. Any crisis situations, or issues with a time window of less than a year, probably fall into the latter category. Fundamental issues of a longer-term nature that relate to your core service are more likely to be strategic.

Exhibit 6.2   Evaluating Your Current Strategy Process

1. Our strategy efforts result in a clear picture of organizational priorities for the future.
2. Our strategy works as a unifying force for the entire organization.
3. Senior leaders within the organization view our strategy process as valuable and relevant.
4. As a result of our strategy, all employees know our key priorities and how we intend to serve customers/clients.
5. Our strategy has been the basis for the development of new initiatives to take advantage of opportunities or safeguard current operations.
6. If we execute our current strategy, our operational efficiency will increase.
7. Accountabilities are clear, whether individual or shared, for each aspect of our strategic plan.
8. We have developed performance measures to track our progress in executing our strategic plan.

Assign a score to each of the questions using the following scale:
1 – No value on this goal
2 – Some help on this goal
3 – Quite helpful on this goal
4 – Extremely valuable on this goal

Once you've answered the questions, total your ratings. A value under 16 suggests there is much room for improvement in your strategy process. A score between 18 and 24 would indicate value in your current process, but also room for improvement. If your total was over 24, you are most likely enjoying the benefits of a well-coordinated strategy management process.

Adapted from Bob Frost, *Crafting Strategy* (Dallas, TX, Measurement International, 2000).

At the risk of sounding overly simplistic, do you know your formal and informal *mandates?* The formal mandates of your organization spell out in detail what it is you are specifically required to do, and not to do. Laws, ordinances, articles of incorporation, and charters are likely sources of information on this topic. No less important are the informal mandates or expectations key stakeholders require from you. Recall the definition of strategy as the broad priorities adopted by an organization in recognition of its operating environment and in pursuit of its mission; with that in mind, be sure any strategy you develop is consistent with the mandates you're required to observe.

The final step in getting started actually requires you to take a step back. To develop context for your effort, it's often illuminating to view your organization from an *historical perspective.* Chronicle the history of your public or nonprofit agency from its earliest developments to the present-day realities you face. Along the way you can document programs and services you've offered, milestones reached, any shifting priorities, and external events such as demographic or legislative changes. We all know experience is the best teacher, and you can use the history of your own organization to learn from both past missteps and successes alike.

Participants engaging in an exercise such as this frequently have a tendency to magnify past transgressions and to focus primarily on faults of the organization. If you find this is the case at your agency, consider using the Appreciative Inquiry approach to balance the deck. Developed in the early 1990s by David Cooperrider at Case Western Reserve University, Cleveland, Ohio, this approach focuses on an organization's achievements rather than its problems.[14] Participants are encouraged to share personal accounts of the organization operating at "peak performance." The stories describe the organization at its most alive and effective state. Participants then seek to understand the conditions that made peak performance possible (values, relationships, enabling technologies, and so on). From this input, a strategy is developed that draws on the very best the organization has to offer its customers, clients, employees, and all other stakeholders.

Step 2: Conducting a Stakeholder Analysis

You could develop the most insightful strategy ever conceived, but unless it is responsive to the needs of your stakeholders, it won't be worth the three-ring binder it's bound to end up in. All organizations, whether private, public, or nonprofit, exist primarily to serve and satisfy the needs of key stakeholders. Only by meeting their needs, and in some way improving their lives, will an organization be able to work toward the fulfillment of its mission.

The first step in any stakeholder analysis is to identify specifically who your key stakeholders are. This can prove to be a complicated endeavor for any organization, but given the web of relationships that exist for most public and nonprofit agencies, it can be a real challenge. Exhibit 6.3 outlines some of the many stakeholder groups that might apply to your organization. When compiling your list of stakeholders, it's best to cast the net as widely as possible. Don't limit yourself to the obvious choices; instead, attempt to identify all those who are touched by your organization.

With stakeholder groups identified, you can move on to a determination of their requirements. Interviews and surveys are proven methods for gathering this intelligence. Of course, experiences gleaned from working directly with these groups should also provide you with some excellent insights for capture. Be sure to challenge your assumptions, however, because what you think your stakeholders require and what they actually desire from you could be two very different things. A good example comes from the U.S. Forest Service. You might think the average visitor to a national forest would be looking for easy-to-read maps and lots of recreational opportunities, right? That could be part of it, but what years of complaint data has yielded is the enlightening finding that visitors really just want toilets that don't stink! In response to this most critical of stakeholder needs, the U.S. Forest Service dubbed 1990 the "Year of the Sweet-Smelling Toilet," as it adopted the latest research and science to construct state-of-the-art "facilities," which expunged the air of any malodorous offenses.[15]

Exhibit 6.3   Partial List of Public and Nonprofit Stakeholders

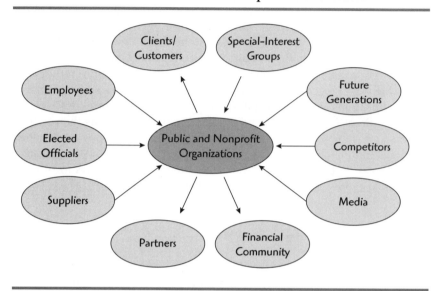

Adapted from *Strategic Planning for Public and Nonprofit Organizations,* by John M. Bryson (San Francisco: Jossey-Bass, 1995).

Chapters Eight and Nine will include a discussion of objectives and measures for the Customer perspective of the Balanced Scorecard. As part of the dialog, I will advocate that you attempt to strike a balance between what your customers or clients need from you and what you need from them. Nonprofit and public-sector employees are justifiably proud of their altruistic heritage; however, clients (and all stakeholders for that matter) must be engaged in a manner that produces results for them while simultaneously allowing the organizations to sustain themselves. By focusing now on the proper stewardship of human and financial resources, you'll ensure your organization is around to satisfy the needs of future generations of stakeholders.

Step 3: The SWOT Analysis

Strategies emerge out of a deep understanding of your organization's place in its current and anticipated operating environment. An excellent tool to make this assessment is the *strengths, weaknesses, opportunities, and threats* (SWOT) analysis. This widely recognized methodology is simple to administer and facilitate and can yield swift and profound results. The SWOT analysis consists of finding answers to four fundamental questions:

- What are our organization's strengths?
- What are our organization's weaknesses?
- What opportunities are present for our organization, the pursuit of which will lead us toward our mission?
- What threats do we face that may endanger the pursuit of our mission?

When discussing *strengths,* you should ask what it is you really do well, or what advantages you have that others cannot easily duplicate. *Weaknesses* represent areas in which improvements are necessary if you are to work toward fulfilling your mission. Changes in your environment, be they demographic, legislative, or pertaining to public opinion may represent *opportunities* to the organization. Finally, *threats* represent the converse of opportunities, and can be viewed as changes that may potentially hinder your ability to serve stakeholders.

Typically, strengths and weaknesses pertain to issues residing within the organization. Among the subjects frequently encountered in a discussion of strengths and weaknesses are: employee competencies, organizational structure, customer and client service, reputation of the agency, governance, facilities and equipment, fiscal position, technology, communication, culture, and values. Opportunities and threats are normally considered to be external issues that affect the organization. Discussions on these topics will often yield comments relating to: changing client needs, demographic shifts, economic stability (or instability), competition, legislative changes, and technology.

While SWOT is well known and universally utilized, many organizations forget the suffix "analysis" that forms such a crucial part of this process. Perhaps the crying out of strengths, weaknesses, opportunities, and threats serves enough of a cathartic purpose that no energy is reserved for the important task of actually analyzing these findings. However, insights will often bloom out of a critical examination of the interplay among the elements. Two intersections are of particular interest: strengths and opportunities and weaknesses and threats. When crafting strategy, it makes great sense to exploit the matching of particular strengths with outstanding opportunities. That's how breakthroughs in performance are made. Consider the example of one prenatal health clinic. Among the many strengths it cataloged during a SWOT exercise was "highly knowledgeable workforce." It was also fortunate enough to list a number of opportunities, one of which was, "New prenatal care techniques that can greatly help our clients." Until this point in its evolution, the clinic had focused almost entirely on service delivery. But when analyzing the results of the SWOT the clinic's leaders saw the potential for a new strategic direction to emerge: Why not combine the core strength of knowledgeable workers with the opportunity presented by new prenatal techniques and focus on providing education services? They recognized they were in the unique and enviable position of employing some of the brightest professionals in the field who could quickly assimilate the latest research and effectively articulate it to their clients. They hypothesized that by providing education services and increasing awareness of the latest techniques available, clients would be armed with the knowledge required to make better health choices. Ultimately, the clinic's leaders believed this would lead to a reduction in prenatal care issues later in a pregnancy. A new strategy was born.

SWOT analyses are by necessity "point-in-time" exercises. Given the many insights you can garner from this process, consider making it part of your ongoing Performance Management process. While you wouldn't want to engage in a SWOT analysis every month, it's not unreasonable to suggest, given the unprecedented pace of change in today's world, a review at least annually, if not semiannually.

Step 4: Identifying Strategic Issues

Thus far in the process you've considered your objectives for developing a strategy, reviewed the organization's mission and mandates, identified key stakeholders, and considered strengths, weaknesses, opportunities, and threats. Some may consider these steps almost academic in nature, hence not "real," since they do not reflect a bias toward action. All that will change in step 4 as you carefully analyze the material you've captured to date and frame the key strategic issues facing your organization.

Strategic issues can be defined as, "*fundamental policy questions or critical challenges that affect an organization's mandates, mission, and values; product or service level and mix; clients, users, or payers; or cost, financing, organization, or management.*"[16] Thus a strategic issue could be anything from "a shortage of long-term office space requirements" to "potential funding shortfalls" to "changing demographics of key clients." When documenting issues, it's important to phrase them as a challenge facing the organization, then outline the specific ramifications that await you should you choose to ignore this issue. Given the input you have at your disposal to help you generate issues—mission, mandates, SWOT, stakeholder needs—it should not come as a surprise to learn that many organizations can quickly compile dozens. Distinguishing between the truly strategic issues and merely operational ones will assist you in keeping the list at a manageable level. Strategic items are those that:

- Appear on the agenda of your board or elected officials and leaders.
- Are longer term in nature.

- Affect the entire organization.
- Have significant financial ramifications.
- May require new programs or services to address.
- Are "hot buttons" for key stakeholders.
- May involve additional staff.

Identifying the key issues facing your organization may be accomplished in a number of ways. Brainstorming as a group is one option. Using this technique, a facilitator will instruct the strategic planning team to generate as many possible issues as they can within a limited time frame. All issues are captured on flip charts or on a computer, with the contents projected onto a screen in the room. Once all issues have been identified, the group begins the sometimes arduous task of clarifying and classifying the issues, ensuring there is a common understanding among the team of exactly what the issue is, why it is an issue in the first place, and what the consequences are of not directly addressing it.

Another possible method of capturing issues is a derivative of the Appreciative Inquiry approach presented earlier in the discussion of chronicling the organization's history. Recall that this approach focuses on an organization's achievements rather than its problems. This exercise may be applied to the discussion of issues. Participants are encouraged to envision the organization operating at peak performance, and then consider any obstacles standing in the way of their achievement. The obstacles will represent strategic issues that must be mitigated in order for the organization to reach its desired state.

Step 5: Developing Strategies

With the issues facing the organization clearly enumerated, it's now time to develop strategies that directly address the issues and allow you to work toward fulfilling your mission. One effective method of producing strategies centers on providing responses to five key questions relating to each of your strategic issues.[17] The questions are:

1. What are the practical alternatives we could pursue to address this issue?
2. What potential barriers exist in the realization of the alternatives?
3. What action steps might we take to achieve the alternatives or overcome the barriers to their realization?

4. What major actions must be taken within the next year (or two) to implement the action steps?

5. What actions must be taken in the next six months, and who is responsible?

Have you ever heard the term *green-field brainstorming?* It suggests an activity in which people engage in the purest form of the brainstorming art, assuming nothing and simply listing any and all aspects of a particular situation or issue. Generating strategies using this technique may yield many options; but as you know, it's the implementation of strategy that produces real benefits. Therefore, your goal should be to elicit strategies that have a reasonable chance of successful execution. Using the five questions presented will stack that deck in your favor. The first question is straightforward and is reminiscent of the brainstorming technique just discussed. However, beginning with the second question, the level of pragmatism is quickly escalated. Discussing barriers at this point will lead to open and frank discussions about the real probability of successfully implementing the proposed strategy. Not that barriers should be considered insurmountable brick walls; in fact, question 3 promotes the use of creative thinking in overcoming the barriers to success. The final two questions prompt the team to consider specific steps necessary in implementing the strategy, and equally important, assigning ownership for results.

In the discussion of the SWOT technique I emphasized the use of the word "analysis," suggesting you look at the interplay among the elements. So it is with strategy. While some strategies will stand on their own, you may find some will tend to form clusters that emerge into themes. Public and nonprofit organizations will often find their strategies contain overarching strategic themes that are further decomposed into specific strategies. Typically, the themes will form around broad service areas within the organization. A good example comes from Prince William County, Virginia. To help make the community's future vision a reality, the board of supervisors approved their first strategic planning effort in 1991. Since that time, Prince William County has been consistently lauded as a leader in public-sector performance management. Its current strategic plan contains five focus areas or themes: economic development, education, human services, public safety, and transportation. Within each of these broad areas are specific strategies. For example, the theme of human services contains seven specific strategies, including: preventing abuse, neglect, and exploitation of county residents of all ages; and assisting elderly residents, low-income residents, and persons with disabilities to remain in the community as independent and productive as possible. The City of Charlotte, North Carolina, also used strategic themes to craft its Balanced Scorecard. Chapter Thirteen reviews the process it followed.

In a similar fashion, the Southeastern Pennsylvania chapter of the American Red Cross has identified four strategic "priorities." These priorities emerged after conducting both an internal and external assessment of strategic challenges and opportunities. The four priorities are:

- Become a more customer-focused organization and heighten visibility in every way.
- Grow financial resources available for programs.
- Continuously improve systems to achieve operational excellence.
- Maximize people resources.

Each of the strategic priorities contains a number of additional, and more specific, strategies that must be successfully executed should the chapter hope to fulfill its mission of *"...Providing relief to victims of disasters and helping people prevent, prepare for, and respond to emergencies."*[18]

Did you notice anything about the Red Cross's strategic priorities? All are extremely noble and admirable themes, indeed. But what jumps out at me is how nicely they map to a Balanced Scorecard framework. And, in fact, that is exactly what this chapter of the Red Cross did: It made each of these priorities the cornerstones of the four Scorecard perspectives, as shown in Exhibit 6.4.

While the situation presented in Exhibit 6.4 is convenient, don't feel you have to "force-fit" your strategies to the Scorecard perspectives. That said, it certainly doesn't hurt to keep in mind that success is a product of strategic execution, and the vehicle of that execution is the Balanced Scorecard. I'll conclude the chapter with a look at precisely why strategy is so important to the development of the Balanced Scorecard.

Exhibit 6.4   Sample BSC Priorities

Customer Perspective	Financial Perspective
Become a more customer-focused organization and heighten visibility in every way.	Grow financial resources available for programs.
Internal Process Perspective	**Employee Learning and Growth Perspective**
Continuously improve systems to achieve operational excellence.	Maximize people resources.

STRATEGY AND THE BALANCED SCORECARD: A CRITICAL LINK

While writing this book, 2002 passed into 2003. During the past holiday season I had the chance to read a newspaper article chronicling some of the many New Year's resolutions one reporter heard when speaking to patrons at a particular nightclub. (Appropriate choice of venues for such an assignment, don't you think?) I can just hear the resolutions becoming more grandiose with each passing hour (and drink). The list was replete with the usual suspects: quit smoking, lose weight, get my financial house in order, and so on. But one gentleman's declaration stood out from the crowd. He resolved to get in shape, and to that end had decided to buy books on fitness, join a health club, and cook more balanced meals. I was impressed by the specific accounting he made of what he was going to do, and thought it lent an air of authenticity and legitimacy to his resolve. But then I realized that deciding is not doing. He could buy a thousand books on fitness and watch the Food Network from dusk 'til dawn and still not get in any better shape. Execution is the key. So it goes with organizations. While the formation of a strategy may initially impress your stakeholders, it's the results borne of strategic execution that really get their attention. The Balanced Scorecard helps you turn the good ideas and potential of strategy into actual results.

The Scorecard provides the framework for an organization to move from *deciding* to live its strategy to *doing* it. A well-constructed Balanced Scorecard will describe the strategy, breaking it down into its component parts through the objectives and measures chosen in each of the four perspectives. Far from an academic exercise, this process will force you as an organization to specifically articulate what you mean by typical strategy terms such as: "excellent customer service," "continuous improvement," or "enhanced staff competencies." Using the Scorecard as a lens through which to view these terms, you may determine that "excellent customer service" equates to meeting client requests within 24 hours. Now you have created a focus for the entire organization. While "excellent customer service" could be debated endlessly, depending on your personal point of view, meeting requests within 24 hours is objective, measurable, and can act as a focal point for channeling the energy of employees across the agency.

Can you develop a Balanced Scorecard without a strategy? Sure, and some organizations will do just that. But consider for a moment what such a Scorecard would consist of. You would still have a mix of financial and nonfinancial indicators straddling the four perspectives. What you would not possess, however, is a common linkage or theme running through the Scorecard. Your strategy is the common thread that weaves through the Scorecard tying the disparate elements of customers, processes, employees, and financial stakeholders into one coherent whole. Without the unifying theme represented by your strategy you're left with a collection of good ideas that lack a coherent story or direction. The Balanced Scorecard and strategy truly go hand in hand. Kaplan and Norton sum up this subject very well. *"The formulation of strategy is an art. The description of strategy, however, should not be an art. If we can describe strategy in a more disciplined way, we increase the likelihood of successful implementation. With a Balanced Scorecard that tells the story of the strategy, we now have a reliable foundation."*[19]

SUMMARY

Although the formal study of strategy in the business world has existed for only approximately four decades, the field has produced thousands of works and hundreds of theories. While many organizations struggle with the subject of strategy, public and nonprofits may find it particularly vexing. Given the mission-driven nature of their operations, these organizations will often approach their stakeholders with an "all things to all people" strategy, which is really tantamount to no strategy at all.

Strategy may be defined as the broad priorities adopted by an organization in recognition of its operating environment and in pursuit of its mission. "Broad priorities" means just that: the overall directional areas the organization will pursue to achieve its mission.

Some organizations will question the need to have a strategy. Given the pace of change in their environments, they wonder if the time required developing a strategy would be better spent responding to current conditions. This is not the case, especially for mission-driven nonprofit and public-sector agencies. Without a clear strategic direction, the lofty goals of the mission and vision remain hollow and empty. Organizations can glean several benefits from the development and execution of strategy: the promotion of strategic thought and action, improved decision-making, and enhanced performance.

A plethora of strategic planning approaches are used in practice. This chapter reviewed one straightforward method, which represents a composite of many effective techniques. The five-step model is composed of:

1. *Getting started.* Assessing your readiness to plan, developing objectives for the planning process, reviewing organizational mandates, and viewing the organization from an historical perspective.

2. *Conducting a stakeholder analysis.* Identifying all key stakeholders and their requirements from your agency. It's also important to consider what you need from your stakeholders in order to achieve success.

3. *Performing an analysis of strengths, weaknesses, opportunities, and threats (SWOT).* Strengths and weaknesses tend to be internal to the organization, while opportunities and threats represent external phenomenon. It's very important to view the interplay between SWOT elements in order to generate strategic insights.

4. *Identifying strategic issues.* The fundamental policy questions or critical challenges that affect an organization's mandates, mission, and values; product or service level and mix; clients, users, or payers; or cost, financing, organization, or management.

5. *Developing strategies.* The broad overall priorities the organization will pursue.

Strategy helps bring life to mission, values, and vision, but on its own will not transform an organization. Only through the execution of the strategy will breakthrough results be accomplished. The Balanced Scorecard provides the framework for translating the strategy into action and results through the development of performance objectives and measures in each of the four perspectives.

NOTES

1. Bob Frost, *Crafting Strategy* (Dallas, TX: Measurement International, 2000), p. 7.
2. From interview with Bill Ryan, September 17, 2002.
3. Robert S. Kaplan, *BSC Report*, vol. 2, no. 6, pp. 1–4.
4. Henry Mintzberg, "The Fall and Rise of Strategic Planning," *Harvard Business Review*, January–February 1994, pp. 107–114.
5. Michael E. Porter, "What Is Strategy?" *Harvard Business Review*, November–December 1996, pp. 61–78.
6. Ibid.
7. Ibid.
8. Keith H. Hammonds, "Michael Porter's Big Ideas," *Fast Company*, March 2001, pp. 150–154.
9. E.E. Chaffee, "Three Models of Strategy," *Academy of Management Review*, October 1985.
10. Robert S. Kaplan, "The Balanced Scorecard and Nonprofit Organizations," *Balanced Scorecard Report*, November–December 2002, pp. 1–4.
11. John M. Bryson, *Strategic Planning for Public and Nonprofit Organizations* (San Francisco: Jossey-Bass, 1995), p. 7.
12. Eric D. Beinhocker and Sarah Kaplan, "Tired of Strategic Planning?" *McKinsey Quarterly*, 2002, No. 2.
13. From a presentation by Francis J. Gouillart at the Balanced Scorecard Summit, San Francisco, CA, 2002.
14. Based on a paper delivered by Gervase R. Bushe at the 18th Annual World Congress of Organizational Development, Dublin, Ireland, July 1998.
15. John M. Bryson, *Strategic Planning for Public and Nonprofit Organizations* (San Francisco: Jossey-Bass, 1995), p. 74.
16. Ibid., p. 30.
17. Ibid., p. 139.
18. From the strategic plan of the Southeastern Pennsylvania Chapter of the American Red Cross.
19. Robert S. Kaplan and David P. Norton, *The Strategy-Focused Organization* (Boston: Harvard Business School Press, 2001).

CHAPTER 7

A Balanced Scorecard within Your Performance Management Framework

Roadmap for Chapter Seven The Balanced Scorecard has emerged as a proven tool for organizations around the globe in their quest to execute their strategies. However, it is not the first tool that has risen to the aid of challenged organizations, nor will it be the last. Although the monikers vary widely, all organizations employ some process of Performance Management. In this chapter we'll seek to determine precisely where the Scorecard should fit in your performance framework.

As just stated, Performance Management comes in many guises and goes by a multitude of names, and each and every term may connote different meanings to different people. For that reason, the chapter begins with a discussion of the power of words, those seemingly harmless things that Jean-Paul Sartre once termed "loaded pistols." We'll explore the potential danger of not reaching consensus on the definitions of your Performance Management terms and discuss an exercise designed to help you avoid this pitfall.

Once you've defined your terms, we'll consider how they weave together to form a Performance Management process. Using a mapping approach, you'll determine how the Balanced Scorecard ties into your overall performance framework.

A WORD OR TWO ABOUT WORDS

In his 1833 book *On War,* Karl von Clausewitz declared, "The first task of any theory is to clarify terms and concepts that are confused....Only after agreement has been reached regarding terms and concepts can we hope to consider the issues easily and clearly, and expect others to share the same viewpoint...." I'm generally not a big fan of military metaphors in the business world since, unlike the results of war, I believe organizations should strive for an outcome in which everybody wins. However, I am particularly struck by the power of this German general's words. Reaching "agreement

145

on terms and concepts" is not as easy as it sounds, especially when you consider there are more than 14,000 meanings for the 500 most common words in the English language. It's amazing we're able to communicate at all!

Language can have a profound impact on an organization. Listen to what Organizational Learning expert Peter Senge has said on the topic: *"Words do matter. Language is messy by nature, which is why we must be careful in how we use it. As leaders, after all, we have little else to work with. We typically don't use hammers and saws, heavy equipment, or even computers to do our real work. The essence of leadership (what we do with 98 percent of our time) is communication. To master any management practice, we must start by bringing discipline to the domain in which we spend most of our time, the domain of words."*[1] This is especially relevant in a world dominated by knowledge workers, one in which success is derived primarily from the transformation of intangible assets. Never has communication been so vital to the prospects of organizations; and, of course, words are at the core of communication. If you think this is an academic exercise, think again. As Wes Schaffer, a Senior Principal Consultant from the Touchstone Consulting Group told me, *"Shared understanding of terminology can be one of the first challenges to overcome in the early stages of implementing a Balanced Scorecard."*[2]

Consequences of Not Agreeing on Definitions

Confusing our words can lead to the transmission of confusing signals to employees and result in less than desirable outcomes for the organization. The two terms on the organizational landscape most prone to obfuscation are *mission* and *vision*. Recently, when working with a new public-sector client, I engaged the Balanced Scorecard team in a discussion of mission and vision. I provided my definitions for these terms—those that I shared with you in Chapter Five—and they appeared to resonate with everyone—everyone, that is, but one person. To her, the vision was the core purpose of the organization and the mission was the desired future. We went back and forth on the issue several times, both of us articulating our best prose on the subject, but neither budging.

This is far more than a philosophical difference. Consider the ramifications when my client begins to communicate these terms to a broader audience. The vast majority will understand mission to be the core purpose of the organization, but one small pocket, those reached by the person holding a contrary opinion, will understand core purpose to mean vision. Undoubtedly, these employees will speak with one another, and of course we want people talking about these terms. But in this case they'll be using different words to convey the meanings of two fundamental principles. I can hear the conversations now:

Wanda: "Hey Mike, I hear we have a new mission statement."

Mike (with a light chuckle): "No, no Wanda, that's a vision, or at least that's what my manager calls it."

Wanda: "Well, I'm sure whatever it is they'll spend about a year figuring it out, so I guess it doesn't matter to us."

As the dialog demonstrates, confusion will surely reign. Equally discouraging, the leaders of the Scorecard initiative will undoubtedly lose credibility in the eyes of the employee base, the very group they must win over if they hope to achieve success on the initiative.

You won't be surprised to read that I recommend you use the definitions and connotations given in this book. However, in the end it really doesn't matter what you call the concepts (remember Shakespeare's admonition: "What's in a name? That which we call a rose by any other name would smell as sweet.") just as long as you use them with unwavering consistency throughout the organization. If you've deliberated with your team on the concepts of vision and mission, and as a group feel your *raison d'etre* is best described as a vision, then so be it. Just ensure there is true consensus on the point and that the term is communicated clearly to all stakeholders.

A Terminology Exercise

In the spirit of General von Clausewitz, I would like to introduce a terminology exercise. The task is designed to help you foster agreement on the key terms of your Performance Management Process so that, as von Clausewitz aptly advises, we can hope to consider the issues easily and clearly, and expect others to share the same viewpoint.

The activity will be completed in two phases over the course of a week or two, depending on the current demands and pressures you face. Phase one is an individual exercise, while phase two draws the entire team together. Begin by circulating to your Balanced Scorecard team a simple template that contains the Performance Management terms you use, or plan to use, in your organization. Advise the group members that they each have one week (or whatever time frame you designate) to complete the template and return it to the Scorecard champion (Exhibit 7.1 contains a sample template). Once all templates have been returned, the Scorecard champion will prepare a document compiling all definitions supplied for each term.

In addition to the terms displayed in Exhibit 7.1, I would suggest you consider including the following: Performance Management, Balanced Scorecard, budget, stakeholder, public input, strategic planning, Performance Measurement, programs, and business plan. Of course, you should add any other terms that are germane to your situation. For example, a local government organization would most likely include the term general plan. But, and this is a big but, don't overload the request with dozens of terms. It can prove to be a taxing exercise for those completing the templates, after which it may take hours, if not days, to come to consensus on definitions in the group setting that follows. Focus on the key terms you will be using, and attempt to keep the list under 15.

Exhibit 7.1   Performance Management Definition Template

Balanced Scorecard
Terminology Template

Before we develop a Balanced Scorecard and communicate it to our employees, it's important to ensure we're all in agreement on the many Performance Management terms we will soon be sharing with the entire organization.

Please take a moment to provide a working definition for each of the terms contained in this package. The definition should convey your current understanding of the term, not a dictionary reference. Please support your definition with an example or a sentence using the term in order to provide context.

We will discuss the terms at our next Balanced Scorecard meeting. Thank You.

Mission: _____
_____
_____
_____
_____
_____

Vision: _____
_____
_____
_____
_____
_____

Values: _____
_____
_____
_____
_____
_____

Strategy: _____
_____
_____
_____
_____
_____

To facilitate the discussion of terms at the Scorecard meeting that follows, I suggest you use a combination of high-tech and low-tech devices. For example, capture the definitions for each term in either an MS Word or

PowerPoint document, then display the document on a screen from a computer so that everyone can easily view what has been shared. Also distribute paper copies of the definitions, and have a flip chart and markers at your disposal.

The facilitator will begin the meeting by thanking everyone for their submissions, and reiterating the importance of reaching consensus on Performance Management terms. He or she will then display the first term on the screen, read a portion of the definitions and examples provided, and, finally, invite comments. You can record any changes to your terms "live" using your computer or the flip charts you've stationed in the room. The range of discussion you can expect will depend almost entirely on the level of consensus reflected in the definitions you receive from the participants. If everyone agrees in principle, it will simply be a matter of "wordsmithing" to concoct a formal definition with which all can concur. I can imagine your eyes rolling as you read that last sentence. Yes, wordsmithing can prove to be an onerous chore. To alleviate the pain of the effort, try instituting a time limit for each term. If you cannot develop an adequate definition that meets everyone's requirements within 10 minutes, assign an individual or smaller group to work on it "offline," and move on to the next term.

As a consultant I've had the opportunity to facilitate a number of these terminology sessions, and I'm always pleasantly surprised at the amount of dialog and learning that results. The learning comes in a variety of forms. First and foremost, the team will have reached agreement on specifically what they mean by the terms that form their Performance Management lexicon. They've also constructed a solid foundation from which to launch both their Scorecard building efforts and educational initiatives throughout the organization. Finally, and perhaps most importantly, this exercise gives team members an insight to the unique perspectives held by their colleagues. Exploring the perceptions of others, freely exchanging ideas, and being open to new points of view will all lead to a stronger team.

FINDING A PLACE FOR THE BALANCED SCORECARD IN YOUR PERFORMANCE MANAGEMENT FRAMEWORK

The previous two chapters of the book have explored a number of elements you'd typically find as part of a Performance Management system: mission, values, vision, and strategy. But Performance Management is a broad subject and in the preceding section I encouraged you to define the many terms you may turn to when building your overall system. The question is, where does the Balanced Scorecard fit into this mix?

Rather than acting as yet another individual component of the Performance Management process, the Balanced Scorecard can act as a unifying force, tightening the links between the various dimensions of the system and making the whole significantly stronger than the sum of the parts. To serve this role, the Scorecard must find a place in the overall system, a place that allows it to maximize the considerable value it has proven to deliver. Mapping your current framework will help you uncover the perfect place for your Balanced Scorecard.

Mapping the Performance Management Framework

Mapping your framework entails identifying all Performance Management elements and sorting them in systematic and chronological order. This is easily accomplished when considered an "add-on" to the terminology exercise just described. Here's how the mapping exercise unfolds:

1. Once you've finalized the definitions for each of your Performance Management terms, convene a new meeting to map those same terms.
2. Conduct the meeting in a room that has at least one long wall on which you can affix paper.
3. Distribute the terms to all participants. Each person should have a packet containing all terms, with each term on a single 8½ by 11 sheet of paper.
4. Begin by asking the group which term would most likely represent the starting point for your Performance Management process. For most organizations, *mission* will be the chosen starting point.
5. Take a page with the word "mission" (or whichever term is considered your entry point) and tape it to the wall. Now poll the group for the term that should follow *mission. Vision* will frequently be identified as that term. Tape the piece of paper with the term you selected to the right of *mission*—remember you're moving both chronologically and systematically.
6. Continue until you've mapped all the terms selected as pertaining to your Performance Management process.
7. Review the completed map as a group to determine whether it accurately reflects your ideal Performance Management process.
8. Solicit a volunteer to record your map in the software program of your choice, and distribute to the team for final approval.
9. When all edits have been completed and the document is considered final, distribute to all team members and other key stakeholders.

Assuming *Balanced Scorecard* was one of the terms you chose for inclusion in this task, you should now have dedicated a place on your map for this new system of performance measurement (a sample Performance Management map is outlined in Exhibit 7.2). Note in this map that the tasks associated with the Balanced Scorecard have been elaborated and shown in the order in which they will occur.

Exhibit 7.2   Performance Management Map

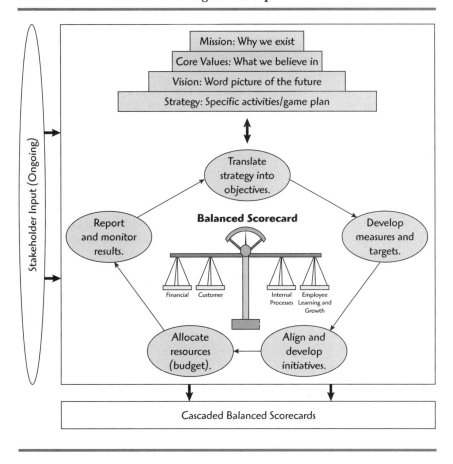

A word of caution: When conducting this exercise, don't feel you must obey convention and map a tired process that has been in place at your organization longer than anyone cares to remember. Some processes have a nasty habit of remaining intact far beyond their useful life. Challenge all assumptions and, if necessary, forge a bold new approach that will allow you to best serve the needs of your customers and clients.

The City of Chula Vista, California, has recently embarked on an initiative to introduce the Balanced Scorecard, and as a first step, it has mapped its ideal Performance Management framework. Director of Development and Strategic Planning, Roderick Reinhart, describes an immediate benefit of the process: *"The Framework, or outline, we developed neatly categorizes and formalizes mission/vision/values development, strategic planning, general planning, public input, and performance measurement into a holistic and logical process."*[3] Chula Vista City Manager Dave Rowlands recognizes the importance of including the Balanced Scorecard as part of the overall Performance Management framework. He explains: *"I like to think of our strategy as the direction we want to go in, and our staff and budget as the vehicle for taking us there. In this analogy, the Balanced Scorecard serves as our compass by giving us the information we need to focus our resources and efforts on what's important: achieving results for our citizens."*[4]

SUMMARY

The French writer Emile de Girardin once remarked, *"The power of words is immense. A well-chosen word has often sufficed to stop a flying army, to change defeat into victory, and to save an empire."* The corollary to this is, of course, that a poorly chosen word will snatch defeat from the jaws of victory and may lead to the demise of an empire! We often confuse the word for the thing it is describing, a phenomenon sometimes described with the phrase, "the map is not the territory." Of course, meanings reside within our heads and not within words. Thus, ensuring we understand the meanings attached to key terms is critical to any endeavor, including the Balanced Scorecard. Failing to reach consensus on definitions, and broadcasting this confusion to an often-skeptical employee base can rapidly diminish the credibility of any Balanced Scorecard effort. Working together as a group to define the key terms comprising your Performance Management is an effective way to short-circuit any potential misunderstandings.

Mapping your Performance Management framework entails identifying all Performance Management elements and sorting them in systematic and chronological order. This exercise allows you to critically examine your current process and determine specifically how the Scorecard fits into the system. Affixed in the right location, the Scorecard can fuse together the many disparate elements of the system, making the whole significantly stronger than the sum of the parts.

NOTES

1. Peter M. Senge. "The Practice of Innovation," *Leader to Leader,* 9, Summer 1998, pp. 16–22.
2. From interview with Wes Schaffer, September 27, 2002.
3. From interview with Roderick Reinhart, January 10, 2003.
4. From interview with David C. Rowlands, Jr., January 10, 2003.

PART THREE

Developing Your Balanced Scorecard

CHAPTER 8

Developing Performance Objectives on a Strategy Map

Roadmap for Chapter Eight This is a good point in the book to pause and reflect both on where we've been, and where we're going. The early chapters provided background on the Balanced Scorecard, and how you can adapt the model to fit your government or nonprofit agency. We then explored the elements necessary to construct a solid foundation for your Scorecard effort; determining your "burning platform," building your team, gaining executive support, and training, to mention just a few. Then we turned to the building blocks of any Balanced Scorecard: mission, values, vision, and strategy. Exhibit 8.1 displays the Scorecard expedition beginning at that point. Chapter Seven discussed the important role of terminology, and challenged you to find the appropriate place for the Scorecard in your wider performance management process. I now turn your attention to the actual construction of your Balanced Scorecard. This chapter and Chapter Nine focus on the steps necessary to develop a strategy map of objectives, translate those into measures, and develop corresponding targets and initiatives. As the arrows in Exhibit 8.1 indicate, performance results from your Scorecard will allow you to learn about your strategy, and ultimately move you toward your mission. Now, on to strategy maps!

Describing his North African adventures, Mark Jenkins had this to say about maps in his book *To Timbuktu: "Maps encourage boldness. They make anything seem possible."*[1] And you thought a map was just something to get you from point A to point B. For many organizations, executing strategy can feel like an impossible task, one in which boldness, while often in short supply, is in great demand.

In this chapter we'll discuss the use of *strategy maps*. We'll explore how these devices provide a powerful method of graphically describing your strategy, bringing your performance objectives to life and boldly proclaiming your intent to implement your strategy. But before you can build a strategy map that tells your strategic story, you must determine which Balanced Scorecard perspectives are right for you. That is our starting point in this chapter. From there we'll delve into the world of strategy mapping, examining what is necessary to begin the effort, how to develop maps, and, finally, how to maximize the effectiveness of your strategy map.

Exhibit 8.1   Where We Are, Where We Are Going

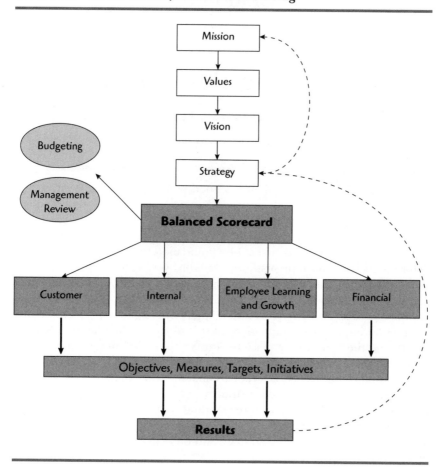

BEFORE YOU BUILD YOUR MAP

Selecting Perspectives and Perspective Names That Are Right for You

A fundamental question to ask prior to building your agency's Balanced Scorecard is, "Which perspectives will we use to tell the story of our strategy?" As you know, Scorecard architects Kaplan and Norton originally conceived of four perspectives in the Balanced Scorecard: Financial, Customer, Internal Processes, and Employee Learning and Growth. However, they did so with the private sector in mind. As use of the Scorecard has evolved and expanded over many years, the founding fathers realized their original perspectives may not be appropriate for all organizations. They have since suggested the four perspectives *"should be considered a template, not a strait jacket."*[2] Let's look at how many creative public and nonprofit agencies have modified the architecture and nomenclature of the Balanced Scorecard to better reflect their needs.

Mission May Appear at the Top of the Balanced Scorecard as a Fifth Perspective

Unlike your colleagues in the private sector, public and nonprofit organizations don't exist to produce wealth for shareholders. Financial measures still have a place in your Scorecard but they don't represent the final destination toward which you are striving. You exist to serve a higher purpose, for example, to: "improve the prospects of youth living in low-income communities," or "reduce discrimination." Therefore, you might consider placing a mission objective at the top of your Balanced Scorecard to signify the socially important goals you are working toward.

Some public and nonprofit agencies may hesitate to include such lofty objectives on their Balanced Scorecard claiming, "We don't have total control over our mission," or "We can't influence the outcomes." Both points have merit, but should not preclude you from attempting to measure the impact you are having on your key constituencies. It's only through the act of measurement that you can gauge real difference in the lives or circumstances of those you aim to serve. However, as I pointed out in Chapter Two, you won't achieve your mission overnight, and in fact may see only periodic movement. This is precisely why the other perspectives of the Balanced Scorecard are so vital. Monitoring performance, and learning from the results in the Customer, Internal Process, Employee Learning and Growth, and Financial perspectives will provide you with the short- to medium-term information you require to guide you ever closer to achievement of the mission.[3]

Customer Perspective May Be Split

Public and nonprofit organizations frequently encounter a dilemma when selecting objectives and measures for the Customer perspective. The process is complicated by the fact that different groups pay for the service, perform the service, and ultimately receive the service. Any one or all of the groups involved in the broad customer experience could, and should, be considered candidates for inclusion on a Balanced Scorecard. Fortunately, the Balanced Scorecard model does not require you to choose one set of customers at the exclusion of others. Any individual or group who fits the criterion of a "customer" may be included in that perspective of your Scorecard.

The Customer perspective is typically populated by examining the "stakeholders" of your organization—any person or group who has a stake in the success of your agency. While all stakeholders may be included in the perspective, some organizations opt to develop an entirely new perspective based on salient characteristics defining the groups. The Naval Undersea Warfare Center (NUWC), Division Newport, is one such organization. When developing its Balanced Scorecard, organizers originally combined all stakeholders within the Customer perspective. They soon discovered, however, that while some groups could wear the dual hats of stakeholders and customers, there was clearly a distinction that warranted the inclusion of a new perspective. Customers, for example, could include the fleet, the sailor, Congress, and the U.S. taxpayers. While these groups could be considered customers, NUWC determined a better definition of customer would include only those organizations and program managers that actually pay directly for the products and services they offer. Program executive officers and the Naval Sea Systems Command fit this description and were thus labeled as customers. Other groups then formed the basis of the new stakeholder perspective.[4] NUWC Division Newport's modified Scorecard framework is shown in Exhibit 8.2.

Exhibit 8. 2   Naval Undersea Warfare Center Division Newport's Balanced Scorecard Framework

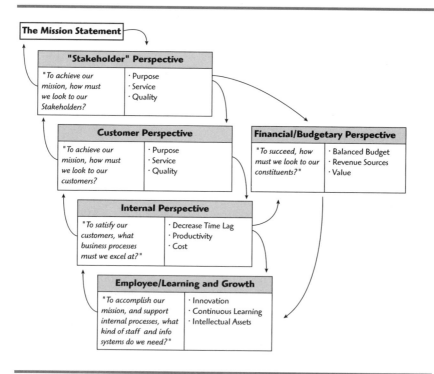

Balanced Scorecard model tailored for NUWC Division Newport. Reprinted with permission from *Perform* magazine.

Interestingly, one study of public sector Balanced Scorecard usage discovered that approximately two-thirds of respondents used the same four perspectives typically found in corporate Scorecards.[5] However, as noted, many organizations find it necessary to make modifications to the Scorecard perspectives in order to fit their culture or unique circumstances. Frequently, the changes are in name only, with new monikers more readily accepted within the organization. For example, the Financial perspective is frequently renamed the "budget perspective," or "resources perspective." Internal Processes are sometimes labeled "operations," or "enabling processes." Finally, the Employee Learning and Growth perspective may be repositioned as "people enablers," "building for our future," or "internal infrastructure."

The Dallas Family Access Network recognized the importance of labeling the perspectives in a way that represented its purpose. This Dallas-based nonprofit began its life in 1989 as a pediatric health care project. Since then, the organization has grown into an integrated network service delivery organization, providing unique and unduplicated services to individuals and families impacted by the HIV epidemic. Organizers wanted a Scorecard that closely reflected the important work they carry out. To that end, they not only renamed the four perspectives and added a fifth, but they also changed the name of the Scorecard itself, calling it the "Balanced Workplan." Their five perspectives are outlined in Exhibit 8.3.

Exhibit 8.3   The Five Perspectives of the Dallas Family Access Network

FIVE BALANCED PERSPECTIVES "THE GOALS"	
HEALTH CARE PERSPECTIVE	Maintaining health and wellness for HIV-infected clients.
SOCIAL SERVICES PERSPECTIVE	Provide supportive and social services for women, children, youth, and families.
OPERATIONAL PERSPECTIVE	Determine the effectiveness of the network in providing care for HIV-impacted populations.
CONSUMER PERSPECTIVE	Expand the consumer role in planning, implementing, and evaluating the network.
FINANCIAL PERSPECTIVE	Secure adequate funding to operate Dallas FAN.

Choosing Your Perspectives

Ultimately, the choice of perspectives should be based on what is necessary to tell your strategic story. When you examine your strategy and attempt to translate it, who or what are the key constituents necessary to describe it? The original four perspectives are broad enough to capture most constituents; however, as discussed, you may choose to include an overarching mission perspective and a stakeholder perspective. Partners, suppliers, and elected officials all represent other groups that could, depending on their importance to your success, be given distinct Scorecard perspectives.

As important as the articulation of stakeholders is, don't make the mistake of creating a "stakeholder Balanced Scorecard." This model outlines everyone even remotely connected to your organization and ignores the other Scorecard perspectives. The danger in doing this lies in missing the "how" of success. You may list noble objectives related to every group, but remember that a well-constructed Balanced Scorecard dictates how you'll achieve success through the interplay of processes in the Internal Processes perspective, resources in the Financial perspective, and enabling infrastructure in the Employee Learning and Growth perspective. When combined, these objectives and measures will drive the success you desire for identified stakeholders. The true test is whether you can easily intertwine your perspectives to tell a coherent story. Stand-alone perspectives that describe a constituent group but fail to link together with the other perspectives don't belong on a Balanced Scorecard.

REVIEWING BACKGROUND INFORMATION ON BALANCED SCORECARD RAW MATERIALS

Gathering and Reviewing Background Information

Very soon you and your Scorecard team will gather enthusiastically around a conference room table, and someone will say, "Okay, so what are our key objectives?" The first few will come with great ease—after all, you're experts on the operations of your organization and undoubtedly have years of experience. However, after the initial euphoria that results from identifying the "no-brainer" objectives, the room will quiet. Identifying the true drivers of your success is more difficult than it first appears. For that reason, it's important to provide the team with as much background on the organization as you can reasonably muster given your time and staff resource constraints. Each of the sources outlined here will provide input that may be used when developing the Balanced Scorecard:

Mission statement. Chapter Five outlined the importance of mission to the Balanced Scorecard. Your objectives and measures should act as faithful translations of the sentiments reflected in the mission.

Values. Has your organization established its guiding principles?

Vision. The vision represents a word picture of what the organization ultimately intends to become. Use this picture of the future to help populate your Scorecard.

Strategic plan. Chapter Six was dedicated to the discussion of strategy and strategic planning. Use the broad priorities articulated in your strategy to guide the development of your Balanced Scorecard.

Annual plans. Many nonprofits, and an increasing number of public agencies, will issue annual plans or reports to key constituents. The document will outline key stakeholders, financial resources, and current metrics used to gauge success. All can be considered raw materials for the Balanced Scorecard.

Consulting studies. Consultants have been known to generate their fair share of paper. Fortunately, most of it contains valuable information that may provide relevant background material for your review process.

Mandates/bylaws. What are the parameters that guide the operations of your organization? Your Scorecard should be firmly rooted in reality, as reflected by the mandates within which you've been chartered to operate.

Organizational histories. Chapter Six discussed the importance of developing context for the strategic planning effort by looking back at your organization's history. The story often reveals programs and services you've offered, milestones reached, any shifting priorities, and external events such as demographic or legislative changes.

Customer surveys. Taking the pulse of your key customers is a popular and proven technique in the private, public, and nonprofit sectors. Information gleaned from these surveys may lead directly to Balanced Scorecard objectives and measures.

Published studies. Both the nonprofit and public sectors are closely scrutinized by ravenous watchdog groups waiting to pounce on your tiniest of missteps. Despite the often-critical nature of the material these groups produce, it will undoubtedly prove helpful in the development of a robust Balanced Scorecard.

Benchmarking reports. One of the best attributes of the public and nonprofit sectors is their willingness to openly share and learn from colleagues. This is a refreshing change from the secretive and hypercompetitive world occupied by most for-profit enterprises. Benchmarking studies are available on a wide variety of sectors and functional specialties. While these documents provide good background, and may stimulate discussion of potential measures, I caution against a reliance on them. Your Balanced Scorecard should tell the story of *your* strategy. The measures you choose to represent that strategy may in some cases mirror those of other organizations, but it's the determination of the *key drivers for your particular organization* that will ultimately differentiate you from other agencies.

Not every document will produce objectives and measures that can be used word for word in your Balanced Scorecard. However, this prospecting exercise is bound to yield a number of potential Scorecard elements. Catalog all of your findings using the four perspectives of the Balanced Scorecard as categories, and return to the list when you begin the work of building your Scorecard.

Conducting Interviews to Gather Executive Input

The sources outlined in the previous section will help you unearth many possible objectives and measures for your Balanced Scorecard. But there is one additional source potentially more potent than any other: the knowledge, experience, creativity, and desire that resides within the minds of your senior leadership team.

Interviewing your top leaders provides a number of benefits: First, as noted previously, you'll receive your leaders' input on the key drivers of your success. Second, this is a tremendous opportunity to directly engage your leadership in the process. To earn their support for the Balanced Scorecard, they must first learn what this tool is all about, how it can produce results, and what specifically it can do for your organization. This is your chance to answer all these questions, and more—whether they're asked or not! Finally, interviews are a great way to detect potential trouble spots that may lie ahead. You'll be able to tell after a short period of time whether a leader is truly committed to the idea of performance measurement and the Balanced Scorecard or is merely paying it lip service. A quorum of lip servers will necessitate action on your part to demonstrate the value of the Balanced Scorecard.

To get the most out of these interviews, it is absolutely critical that your leaders feel comfortable and be willing to share. For that reason, it's often preferable to have the interviews conducted by an outside facilitator or consultant. While the questions are certainly not controversial, the answers provided could shed light on some sensitive topics and lead the executive to take a position of reticence should they not feel psychologically safe in divulging such information to a Scorecard team member. Using a consultant is not a steadfast requirement, however. Many fruitful executive interviews have been conducted by members of Scorecard teams. Again, the key to success lies in ensuring that the executive feels psychologically safe in sharing information with the individual. A Balanced Scorecard team member who is well respected throughout the organization, and has ample experience liaising with senior leaders will normally be welcomed openly.

I suggest this outline for your interviews, delineated in the following subsections.[6]

Review Purpose

In most implementations, your executive team will be among the first in the organization to receive Balanced Scorecard training. Therefore, you don't want to expose the time-constrained executive to 20 slides of Scorecard theory. However, it is important to at least display the Scorecard framework you'll be adopting, and solicit questions. Perhaps this executive was unsure about the meaning of an objective, or didn't quite grasp what was meant by a strategy map. This is the time to win his or her support by providing clear and concise answers to any and all outstanding questions. Also take the opportunity to share the objectives for the interview (receiving the executive's input); briefly outline what will be covered and define the expected duration.

Mission, Values, Vision, and Strategy

These are the building blocks of the Balanced Scorecard so it's important to determine how executives feel about each. Unless directly asked, don't share what you've uncovered in your research. You're attempting to determine how your leaders view these items and whether alignment exists among your senior team. Ask the following questions:

- Has the mission for the organization been defined? If so, what is that mission?
- What core values are essential in pursuit of the mission?
- Has the organization developed a vision statement? If so, what is the vision?
- Which key strategies will lead us to the achievement of our vision?

You may need to define specifically what you mean by these terms in order to receive any feedback. *Mission, vision,* and *strategy* are often confused even at the highest echelons of the organizational hierarchy. If confusion seems to be reigning, consider directly asking these questions:

- Why do you feel we exist as an organization (mission)?
- What core values do we hold?
- Where do you see us in 5, 10, or 15 years (vision)?
- What must we do to reach that desired future (strategy)?

The goal of this component of the interview is to determine the level of consensus that exists across the organization in relation to mission, values, vision, and strategy. Should you find that every executive is saying something different, that will make it exceedingly difficult to craft a Balanced Scorecard that suits all of their individual preferences and perceptions. In this case, reverting back to a discussion of mission, values, vision, and strategy at the senior level may be necessary before the implementation can continue.

Balanced Scorecard Perspectives

By this point in your implementation you should have determined the perspectives that will comprise your Balanced Scorecard. Ask the executive for his or her input on each of the four (assuming you're using four) perspectives. Use this component of the interview to accumulate the executive's thoughts on which objectives and measures are critical to the organization's success.

- *Customer.* Who are our customers (or clients), and what must we do well to satisfy them?
- *Internal processes.* At which processes must we excel if we are to meet customer and client needs?
- *Financial.* Financially, what is most critical to us?
- *Employee Learning and Growth.* What skills or competencies do we require to succeed?
- *Employee Learning and Growth.* Do we have the proper organizational climate (culture, alignment, etc.) necessary for success?
- *Employee Learning and Growth.* Do our employees have the tools they need to meet customer requirements?
- Which measures do we currently use to gauge our success?

The last question does not relate to an individual perspective of the Scorecard but seeks to determine how this executive currently tracks success. Objectives or measures repeated consistently here should form part of your Scorecard.

Implementation and Use

In this phase of the interview you're attempting to move away from the Scorecard as an academic exercise to probe what it will actually mean for your organization. A constant communication theme for Scorecard-implementing organizations has to be separating the idea of the Balanced Scorecard as a theoretical construct from that of the Scorecard as a practical management solution. Ask these questions:

- How would you like to see the Balanced Scorecard used here?
- What are some of the barriers we may face in implementing the Balanced Scorecard, and how do we overcome them?

Chances are, unless they campaigned for the Scorecard, this is the first time your executives will be pressed to consider how they would like to use the tool and the roadblocks you might face. This is valuable input for a couple of reasons. One, the answer to "How would you like to see the Scorecard used?" will provide some parameters for the actual Scorecard the team designs. If, for example, five out of five executives say they want a complex management reporting tool, then your Scorecard development team will most likely construct a Scorecard consisting of many objectives and measures. Conversely, if "communication tool" is the answer most commonly cited, a Scorecard with fewer measures will most likely satisfy executives. Asking executives which barriers you face not only challenges them to enumerate issues, but puts psychological pressure upon them to be part of any solution.

Interviews should be scheduled for one hour, and questions limited to about 10. (I've included a total of 13 in the interview sections outlined here, which in all honesty may be difficult to plough through in an hour.) Choose those questions that are most vital for your implementation. You don't want to lose the rapport you're establishing with an executive by stopping them midsentence with, "Okay, I'm sorry but we have to move on now." Of course, you have to ensure the interview remains focused as well, which can sometimes prove to be a delicate balancing act. For example, I like to start my interviews on a casual note, engaging the executive on a comfortable topic like the weather, general business news, or sports. This method can be a great icebreaker, but there have been occasions in which 15 minutes have passed and I'm still hearing about the executive's last round of golf! Be on guard for "hot button" issues as well. One executive I interviewed felt passionate about a casual dress policy. Suffice it to say that at the end of our time together I knew far too much about the organization's dress code and far too little about its key objectives!

Once all of the interviews have been completed, have your consultant or Scorecard champion sort, summarize, and compile all responses. Names, of course, will be removed, as will any quotes that could easily identify a specific individual. Then distribute the condensed notes to the Scorecard team for reference purposes during your development sessions.

BUILDING THE STRATEGY MAP

Importance of Cause and Effect

Which would you find easier to remember, a passage from the novel you're currently reading or a paragraph from this book? I'm pretty sure I can guess how most of you would answer that question—and don't worry, you didn't hurt my feelings. Fortunately for my ego, I believe I know why the novel is easier to remember, and I'm sure you do as well: it's a story. There is nothing like a good story, whether it's the latest best-selling novel or blockbuster movie to draw us in and capture our full attention. Now a second question for you: Can an organizational model accomplish the same results? I believe the answer is yes. A good organizational model is really just a story that explains how the organization works. The best-told stories help every employee see what the organization is trying to accomplish and how they fit into that context.[7] But how do you tell your strategic story? Through the objectives and measures on the Balanced Scorecard.

A powerful story is composed of a number of elements: an intriguing plot, interesting characters, and stimulating dialog, to name but a few. If any of these elements is missing from the story, the whole suffers as a result. Now think for a moment about your organization, and how you measure success. You could, for example, measure customer satisfaction, adherence to budget, and quality, but what is missing? What ultimately drives success in any enterprise? Employees. If you don't include measures to capture employee issues, a hole develops in your story. And it isn't just employees. You could measure skills, training, and dozens of other employee-related attributes, but if you then choose to ignore how these effect outcomes for your customer, you've again failed to tell a coherent story. All of your organization's constituents must be present in your measurement system if you hope to create a captivating story that draws in all of your stakeholders.

A well-constructed Scorecard should describe how your organization works, and what is critical to your success, through a series of interconnected objectives and measures running through the four perspectives. Rather than focusing exclusively on any one element of success, you're painting a full canvas of what is necessary to succeed. Your story should include outcomes for customers, the processes at which you must excel to drive customer outcomes, the enabling infrastructure required, and the financial resources necessary to sustain your service delivery. Each element represents a vital link in the powerful chain of cause-and-effect relationships that run through the Balanced Scorecard.

For many Scorecard-adopting organizations, the greatest benefit has not been a ready supply of answers to all that ails their agencies; rather, the provocative questions generated from an analysis of Balanced Scorecard results have proven to be the greatest boon. Questions lead to discussions,

discussions may lead to debate, debate contributes to insight, and insight often leads to breakthroughs. The questions arise as you analyze the results of Balanced Scorecard measures and begin to contemplate the hypothesis you originally put in place when constructing your cause-and-effect relationships. It is only by linking your measures together in a coherent whole that you can begin to truly analyze and learn about your strategy.

Rick Pagsibigan from the Red Cross of Southeastern Pennsylvania described the importance of cause and effect to me this way: *"The first thing we have to do is take care of internal customers—our staff. How do we make this a worthwhile environment? Then, if we have the right skill sets and the right talent in place, it will impact our ability to perform our critical business processes. That in turn impacts our ability to fund-raise and to sell, because we do have products and services we sell, which add to our revenue. Finally, the more we can raise money, the greater impact we have both in quality and quantity for our customers."*[8]

What Are Performance Objectives?

Before you begin the development of your strategy map, I want to clarify the meaning of the term *objective*. Consider objectives a bridge that spans your strategy of broad overall priorities and your measures, which are the quantitative means by which you will gauge success. Performance objectives describe what you must do well in order to effectively implement your strategy. They are more specific than what is contained in your strategy, but less precise than performance measures. Objectives typically begin with an action verb.

Objectives translate strategic priorities, which are often vague and nebulous, into directional and action-oriented statements of what must be done to execute the strategy. The objectives are then further translated into more granular performance measures. It would prove quite difficult to develop meaningful performance measures without the context established by objectives. For example, it is not uncommon for an organization to adopt a strategy of "maximizing people resources." Given that approximately 75 percent of value in today's organization is driven by intangible assets, developing the people in an organization makes great sense. Consider the dilemma facing Scorecard developers at an institution should they be required to leap directly from a strategy as broad as this to specific performance measures. Their choices are practically unlimited, and those measures ultimately selected may not represent the true essence of the strategy. In contrast, a focused discussion of what must be done well to capture the essence of the strategy—in other words, the objectives—will lead to more focused and refined performance measures. Upon reflection, this organization might determine that maximizing people means "increasing skill sets," "improving communication," and "building organizational alignment." These objectives now set the stage for precise measurements.

Exhibit 8.4 graphically displays the bridging function of objectives and provides a sample of action verbs.

What Is a Strategy Map?

To help answer the question just posed, let's break it down into two parts. First, we'll examine the word "map," and then we'll take another look at "strategy."

A map provides a graphical representation of the whole or part of an area. As we all know, a good map is essential to help us navigate unfamiliar terrain. Speaking of unfamiliar terrain, although I make my home in California, I'm originally from the province of Nova Scotia, in Canada. Perhaps some of you have visited my beautiful home. For those of you who have not, consider this an invitation. Let's say for a moment you decide to

Exhibit 8.4 Performance Objectives

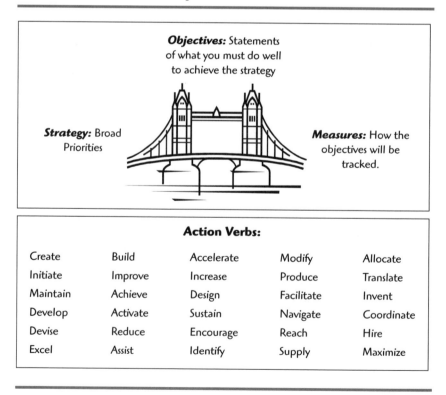

Objectives: Statements of what you must do well to achieve the strategy

Strategy: Broad Priorities

Measures: How the objectives will be tracked.

Action Verbs:

Create	Build	Accelerate	Modify	Allocate
Initiate	Improve	Increase	Produce	Translate
Maintain	Achieve	Design	Facilitate	Invent
Develop	Activate	Sustain	Navigate	Coordinate
Devise	Reduce	Encourage	Reach	Hire
Excel	Assist	Identify	Supply	Maximize

take me up on my offer and plan to visit Nova Scotia during your next vacation. I suggest that if you fly to Nova Scotia, you drive from Halifax, the provincial capital, to my hometown of Sydney, on Cape Breton Island. I'm certain you'll find the scenery breathtaking. Now look at the two maps I've provided of the province in Exhibit 8.5. With the map on the left, do you think could you find your way from Halifax to Sydney? Without some advance knowledge of the province, the answer is probably no. The picture becomes much clearer with the map on the right, because now, in addition to a map of the province, you have landmarks to guide you from place to place, simplifying your navigational challenges significantly. Following the landmarks will lead you to your chosen destination.

Let's now return to the word "strategy." Like your fictional visit to Nova Scotia, strategy is a new destination for most organizations, one to which they have never traveled. As much as it is discussed and debated, it is frequently not implemented with any degree of success. In many ways, strategy is reminiscent of the map on the left side of Exhibit 8.5. It's a guide of where we would like to go, but the landmarks to guide us on our journey are missing. This is where performance objectives come in. The objectives on a strategy map serve as the landmarks on the road to strategy execution. Scorecard architects Kaplan and Norton explain: *"Strategy implies the movement of an organization from its present position to a desirable but uncertain future position. Because the organization has never been to this future place, the pathway to it consists of a series of linked hypotheses. A strategy map specifies these cause-and-effect relationships, which makes them explicit and testable."*[9] The "linked hypotheses" Kaplan and Norton reference are represented by the performance objectives you choose as translations of your strategy. With a strategy map in place, you possess a clear and concise one-page document outlining what you believe is most critical in the effort to execute your strategy.

Exhibit 8.5   Landmarks Are Critical to Any Map

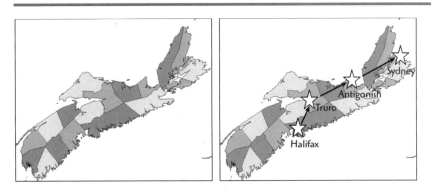

One final point on strategy maps: Some of you may be wondering if a strategy map is a Balanced Scorecard. Can the terms be used interchangeably? (Warning: Typical consultant answer approaching.) The answer is, it depends. Going back to the discussion of terminology in Chapter Seven, how you use the words "Balanced Scorecard" and "strategy map" depend on your definitions. Typically, a strategy map is a one-page document that graphically displays your performance objectives. A Balanced Scorecard complements the strategy map by once again outlining the objectives; but it also provides the measures, targets, and initiatives used to gauge success on the objectives. The strategy map is frequently used as a communication tool, while the Balanced Scorecard serves as a reporting tool.

Another Reminder: The Balanced Scorecard Translates Mission, Values, Vision, and Strategy

As a consultant, I fly frequently, and could probably recite the preflight announcements of every major airline verbatim. Nevertheless, I always heed the plea of the flight attendant when he or she announces, "We know many of you fly frequently, but for your safety we ask that you give us your full attention for the following safety reminders." Consider what follows to be your preflight announcements, as I ask that you allow me to reiterate the core purpose of the Balanced Scorecard: translation.

Take a look at Exhibit 8.6. This graphic is a representation of the development of your Balanced Scorecard. Chapter Five discussed mission, values, and vision. Strategy was addressed in Chapter Six. This chapter explores how the Balanced Scorecard brings these concepts to life through the selection of objectives and measures. The arrows in the diagram indicate the Scorecard is both a top-down and bottom-up process. Normally, you will construct the Balanced Scorecard by starting at the top and translating mission, values, vision, and strategy. Equally important, however, is the bottom-up strategic learning, which results from using the Balanced Scorecard. The objectives and measures you choose will tell the story of your strategy, and over time the analysis of results will provide you with a gauge of the effectiveness of your implementation. As you develop objectives and, later, measures, continually evaluate them in light of the mission, values, vision, and strategy you've selected. Only then will you build a Balanced Scorecard that is capable of transporting you to your desired future.

DEVELOPING YOUR STRATEGY MAP OF PERFORMANCE OBJECTIVES

This section provides the full agenda for a one-day strategy mapping session. We'll work through the entire event, including: what to do before the meeting, how to structure the session, facilitation tips, and next steps.

Exhibit 8.6   Translating with the Balanced Scorecard

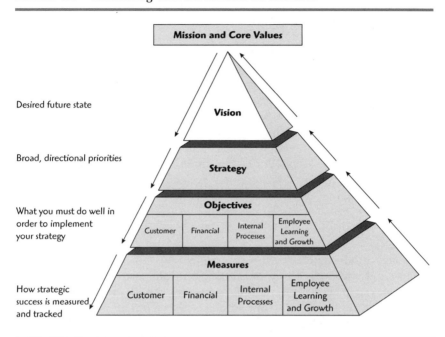

Adapted from material presented in *Balanced Scorecard Step-by-Step: Maximizing Performance and Maintaining Results,* by Paul R. Niven (John Wiley & Sons, Inc., 2002).

Before the Session

Whom to Invite to Your Strategy Mapping Session

The strategy map should be developed by the members of your Balanced Scorecard team. Additionally, you should request the attendance of your executive sponsor. His or her input will prove invaluable as you debate and discuss potential performance objectives. The executive sponsor will supply both organizational knowledge and wisdom regarding what is politically possible and strategically sound.

I suggest using an outside consultant or facilitator to conduct the meeting. Certainly, the Scorecard champion could fill the facilitator role, but it would demand his or her complete attention, leaving little in the way of contribution to the topic at hand. A skilled consultant or facilitator will apply proven techniques and spark the group creativity necessary to build a dynamic strategy map. This is far from simply self-serving advice. I've had many calls from clients and potential clients who tell me, "We tried to do this ourselves, but...." Save yourself important time by bringing in an outside consultant to help you with this important step.

Logistics

As noted in the opening of this section, you should reserve a full day for the strategy mapping session. Holding the event off-site is always advisable. A fresh new location can do wonders for the energy and creativity of a group. Rooms with windows that open to allow fresh breezes to glide through, and offer pleasing views are an excellent touch.

Hotel conference rooms seem to be the default choice when booking an event such as this, but don't neglect to consider other venues in your area. I've held workshops in quaint country inns, elegant former estate homes, and serene nature centers. Wherever you decide to hold your session, you'll need a room supplied with the usual accoutrements of any workshop: flip charts, markers, Post-it notes, paper, and a screen and projector for a notebook computer.

Assign Homework

It's a classic understatement to say everyone is busy these days. With shrinking funding and burgeoning workloads, it's difficult to fit in yet another seemingly critical task. However, preparation is vital to the effort to draft a strategy map that truly tells your strategic story. To that end, ensure your Scorecard team is well equipped with the latest copies of your mission, values, vision, and strategy. Notes from the executive interviews and other materials gathered during your research phase should also accompany them. Advise each team member to carefully review the materials prior to the event and arrive prepared, ready, and willing to share possible Scorecard objectives. As the Roman Statesman Seneca long ago advised, "Luck is what happens when preparation meets opportunity."

Facilitating the Strategy Mapping Session

Balanced Scorecard SWOT Analysis

Anyone who has ever exercised—or, more accurately, anyone who has ever injured themselves exercising—knows the value of warming up first. The same advice readily applies to a strategy mapping workshop. The mental muscles required for this event should be limbered up prior to turning loose your talented team. The Balanced Scorecard SWOT analysis is a great way to tune up the team.

The topic of strengths, weaknesses, opportunities, and threats was introduced during the strategy discussion in Chapter Six. Here, we're going to modify this old standard to allow for an examination of SWOT as it relates to the four perspectives of the Balanced Scorecard. The Balanced Scorecard SWOT technique was introduced to me by Patricia Bush of the Balanced Scorecard Collaborative. She and two colleagues developed the process a number of years ago, and I have since used it with many organizations spanning the private, public, and nonprofit sectors.

The purpose of the exercise is twofold. First, it will highlight many possible issues and opportunities that may be likely candidates for translation into Balanced Scorecard objectives. Second, it provides real-time learning on what is typically captured in each of the four perspectives. What someone advances, for example, as a Customer opportunity, may in fact belong in the Internal Process perspective. Clarifying the nature of exactly what you hope to populate each perspective with is immensely valuable before you actually begin the work of developing the strategy map. Disagreements about what belongs where are better hashed out now, before the real work begins.

Use the grid displayed in Exhibit 8.7 to help you facilitate the discussion. You'll notice I've added a fifth column entitled "Wild Card." You can be certain that at various points in your discussion someone will raise an excellent issue but is unable to find a proper home for it. The Wild Card column is the repository for such insights. Begin your analysis with the Customer perspective and advise participants to contemplate your strengths, weaknesses, opportunities, and threats from the customer's perspective. Allow 15 to 20 minutes for everyone to collect their thoughts on the matter. When time has expired, solicit input from around the room on what should be captured in each column. Writing the findings on flip charts is always popular, but in addition, make sure someone is assigned to simultaneously capture the material on a computer. Continue the exercise until you've completed all four perspectives. The material supplied by this analysis will prove to be extremely valuable during the development of strategy map objectives. For that reason, the notes should be immediately printed and distributed to the team as they begin their deliberation on objectives.

Exhibit 8.7 BSC SWOT Analysis

- What are our financial strengths, weaknesses, opportunities and threats?
- From the customer's perspective, what are our strengths, weaknesses, opportunities and threats?
- Internally, what are our process strengths, weaknesses, opportunities and threats?
- From an employee-enabling perspective regarding culture, leadership, technical infrastructure and competencies/ skills, what are our strengths, weaknesses, opportunities and threats?

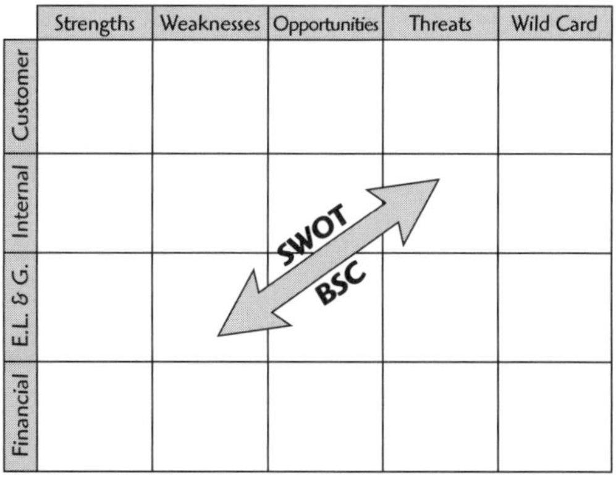

Not only does the Balanced Scorecard SWOT technique give you instant results in the form of potential objectives, but it will also highlight potential areas for Balanced Scorecard initiatives. We'll return to the story of initiatives in Chapter Nine.

Developing Objectives for Each of the Four Perspectives

An effective method for generating strategy map objectives is to examine each Scorecard perspective in the form of a question or questions. Objectives may be based on the responses your team provides to the questions outlined here.

Customer perspective. There are a number of thought-provoking questions related to the Customer perspective. Consider framing your discussion with any or all of these:

- *Who are our targeted customers?* Not always an easy answer in the public and nonprofit sectors. Critically examining this question may lead to the development of an entirely new perspective as you distinguish between "customers" and "stakeholders."

- *How do we "add value" for our customer?* Value proposition is a term frequently bandied about in the for-profit world. In that sector, many organizations have embraced the work of Michael Treacy and Fred Wiersema, as articulated in their 1995 book *The Discipline of Market Leaders.* Exhibit 8.8 outlines the three value disciplines they have

Exhibit 8.8   Customer Value Propositions

Product Leadership	Customer Intimacy	Operational Excellence
Product leaders push the envelope of their firm's products. Constantly innovating, they strive to offer simply the best product in the market.	Doing whatever it takes to provide solutions to unique customers' needs help define the customer-intimate organization. They don't look for one-time transactions, but instead focus on long-term relationship building.	Organizations pursuing an operational excellence discipline focus on price, convenience, and, often, "no frills."
Sony Mercedes Johnson & Johnson Intel	Home Depot Nordstrom	Costco McDonalds Dell Computer Wal-Mart
Most Innovative Product	**Best Solution**	**Best Total Cost**

Adapted from material developed from *The Discipline of Market Leaders,* by Michael Treacy and Fred Wiersema (Perseus Books, 1995).

seen used in practice. Many organizations, public and nonprofit included, have used these disciplines as a guide in evaluating the perceptions customers hold of them. How do your customers see you? Are you operationally excellent, a product leader, or customer intimate? What do you aspire to be? Answering these questions may lead you to consider entirely new customer objectives.

- *Which services or products do our customers require and expect from us?* Don't overlook the obvious in trying to fashion the perfect strategy map. The best objectives may be right under your nose.

Internal Processes perspective. The Internal Processes perspective sheds light on the critical processes at which you must excel as an organization in order to continue adding value for your customers or clients. Despite the fact that you may already have dozens of processes, if not more, the strategy mapping exercise may lead to the development of entirely new processes. Creating a strategy map will often lead to the development of never-before considered objectives. Chances are, if the item under consideration wasn't being measured, there may not be an accompanying process. New objectives may require new processes, new employee skills, and even additional resource requirements. Here are a couple of questions to consider when developing internal process objectives:

- To continue adding value for our customers and clients, at which processes must we excel?

- After analyzing current trends, which processes might we be expected to develop and excel at in the foreseeable future?

Employee Learning and Growth perspective. In his foreword to the book *The HR Scorecard,* Balanced Scorecard co-developer David Norton had this to say about understanding of human capital issues in most organizations: *"The worst grades are reserved for...understanding of strategies for developing human capital.... The asset that is most important is the least understood, least prone to measurement, and, hence, least susceptible to management."*[10] The Employee Learning and Growth perspective is often overlooked during the development of strategy maps and the Balanced Scorecard. It's not uncommon for a team to diligently unearth every rock of information pertaining to Customer, Internal Processes, and Financial objectives, and then say something to the effect that, "HR will take care of the employee objectives." Organizations that make such a decision do so at their own peril. The objectives in this perspective are the enablers of everything that takes place within the Scorecard. You can't possibly hope to succeed in today's knowledge economy without skilled motivated employees, operating with the right tools in an environment that provides the conditions of success. Here are some questions to consider when developing objectives for the Employee Learning and Growth perspective:

- Which organizational infrastructure elements are necessary if we are to achieve our process and customer objectives?
- Which skills and competencies do our employees require now?
- Which skills and competencies will be required in the years ahead?
- Do our employees have access to the information they need to help us achieve our customer outcomes?
- Is our organizational climate conducive to success? Do we have a strong culture and alignment of goals throughout?

Financial perspective. Operating efficiently and safeguarding resources is critical to all organizations, whether they are private, public, or nonprofit. In an era of diminishing budgets and cries for accountability, financial objectives take on a prominent role. Consider framing your discussion of this perspective with any or all of these:

- *Is our service delivered at a good price?* You may think so, but comparing with other organizations or jurisdictions may be enlightening.
- How can we maintain current service levels while remaining within our budget?
- What opportunities do we have for enhancing revenue?

Facilitation Tips

The questions just outlined have the potential to generate hours of stimulating discussions. Nevertheless, even the most energetic and committed groups will occasionally suffer lapses in productivity and output. Therefore, in this subsection, I provide some tips for your facilitation toolkit.

If your group suddenly becomes reticent, and you see a lot of them are staring down at the table, consider breaking the silence with some carefully selected *keywords* gathered during your executive interviews and research phase. I normally have a list of five or six words for each of the four perspectives, gleaned during interviews and in my review of organizational documents. For example, the facilitator might say, "I heard the word 'productivity' mentioned frequently during the executive interviews: How can we incorporate a productivity theme into our map?"

Nothing can slow the momentum of your map-building exercise quite like *wordsmithing the objectives.* Remember, the goal is not to get this thing 100 percent right the first time. You're charged with developing a draft map that can be refined and clarified during subsequent sessions. Though you definitely want your objectives to be unique, and to adequately represent you as an organization, that shouldn't require twenty words! Abbi Stone and Katy Rees of California State University San Marcos originally fell victim to the allure of wordsmithing, but made an enlightening discovery along the strategy mapping path. *"The tendency is to focus on wordsmithing when developing objectives—you simply need to capture the essence of the objective at this point. A single word isn't going to make or break this thing. You can wordsmith it later."*[11] It's important to remember that a next step in the mapping process will be the development of objective statements. These two- or three-line narratives clarify and expand on the objectives appearing in the map. Therefore, you don't have to break the word bank just yet.

Another valuable facilitation tip was passed on to me by John Ramont of the County of San Diego, California. When working with the county's Animal Control department, he began the discussion by challenging the group with this question: *"Who is the very best Animal Control unit in the country?" "What makes them the best?" "What is keeping us from being the best?"*[12] Out of these simple questions the group began to think of their own business and develop strategic objectives that focused on what they needed to do to become the best. These questions could be used in a discussion of any of the four Scorecard perspectives. A warning, however: You can't simply duplicate a competitor—your objectives must reflect *your* strategy and mission.

Of course, maybe I'm all wrong; perhaps your group will get together and within no time at all will have drafted the first absolutely perfect strategy map known to man. You might enjoy complete and unwavering agreement on each and every objective worthy of appearing on your map. Sounds good, doesn't it? Well, actually, it's not so good. When developing objectives you should encourage some *creative tension* among the group. If everyone immediately agrees on an objective, it could mean one of two things: either it is in fact the perfect objective—which is a good thing—or the group has not given it the deliberation it deserves. Peter Drucker supports this notion of creative tension. *"All the first-rate decision makers I've observed, beginning with Franklin D. Roosevelt, had a very simple rule: If you have consensus on an important matter, don't make the decision. Adjourn it so that everybody has a little time to think. Important decisions are risky. They should be controversial. Acclamation means that nobody has done the homework."*[13]

How Many Objectives on a Strategy Map?

I really enjoyed the movie *Finding Forrester.* I saw it just as I had begun to write my last book, *Balanced Scorecard Step-by-Step: Maximizing Performance and Maintaining Results* (John Wiley & Sons, Inc., 2002). At one point in the movie, author William Forrester, played beautifully by Sean Connery, advises his young protégé to always write a first draft "from the heart." I remember very well how that advice, albeit from a fictional character, resonated with me. As I continued my writing, I did just as Forrester/Connery suggested and wrote my first draft from the heart. Fortunately, for you, you didn't have to wade through those first drafts. The problem with writing from your heart is that virtually everything seems critical to the topic, and it's very difficult to leave anything out when that topic is so very important (and close) to you. Like all authors, I benefited greatly from a skilled editor who helped me hone my lengthy drafts into a more concise final version that was bound between the covers of the book.

So, other than providing a movie review, what does the preceding paragraph have to do with your strategy map? Well, you and your Scorecard team are the authors of your strategy map. And, as such, that map will undoubtedly convey the strongest feelings of all involved on what is absolutely important to the organization. Like the writer who feels compelled to empty his or her soul in a work, you won't want to leave anything on the table. As a result, it's not uncommon to see first-draft strategy maps that contain 35 to 40 objectives.

A number of factors conspire to see the number of first-draft strategy map objectives balloon to an unmanageable number. The atmosphere in the meeting room is generally very positive; after all, you've convened a team that was chosen for both their knowledge and enthusiasm. You're all talking about what you do every day, about your organization; and, truthfully, how often do you have the opportunity to spend an entire day analyzing your operations? It's exciting, liberating, and fun! I've even seen chief executives get caught up in the frenzy. Prior to one strategy mapping session with a client, the CEO stressed to me the importance of keeping the total number of objectives capped at around 10. I agreed that a low number was better for this small company, and together we vowed to curb any attempts at raising the objective total. But when we got into the session, his tune changed, and changed dramatically. He was the one I couldn't rein in! Suddenly everything seemed critical to the company's success, and before we knew it there were 31 objectives on the map.

There is no hard-and-fast rule for the "right" number of objectives, but a good guideline is "less is generally more." Keep in mind that every objective on the strategy map may spawn two performance measures to accurately capture the intent of the objective. So, for example, 20 objectives would take you up to 40 measures for one Scorecard. Multiply that by several cascaded Scorecards throughout your organization and you've quickly ascended to hundreds of measures, and a challenging process to manage. To harness the power of the Balanced Scorecard as both a measurement and communication system, you have to keep the number of objectives to a manageable level. Only you can make the determination of what is manageable, however. That said, I will offer you some advice: Cap your objectives between 10 and 20. Katy Rees and Abbi Stone of Cal State San Marcos offer some excellent input on this point: *"We wanted to start out with a small number of objectives, and then maybe grow. We were trying very consciously not to overwhelm ourselves, our managers, and our staff with work. You have to be cognizant of the environment you're in; people are busy. We don't want to turn people off with this.* "[14] Careful reflection and consideration of measurement and management issues will often aid you in your rationalization effort.

Reviewing and Refining the Strategy Map

Immediately upon completion of the draft map, it makes sense to test its efficacy in telling your story. A fun and creative method to do so is the "*USA Today* interview." Suggest to your group that you're now three years in the future. A reporter from *USA Today* would like to do a story on your organization because of the great success you've achieved. How would the headline for the story read? Do the objectives on your map lead you to that headline?

If envisioning the future isn't your thing, try evaluating the map with these probing questions:

- Is the cause-and-effect logic in the map complete? Are all the necessary elements to tell our story accounted for?[15]
- Is the logic reflected in the map theoretically sound? Do all the elements fit together logically?[16]
- Will the objectives outlined on the map lead to the effective execution of our strategy?
- Does the map represent balance in our efforts to achieve our vision?

Creating the strategy map is intense and fatiguing work. As much as we all know and care about the organizations in which we work, plumbing the depths of our knowledge on the subject for an entire day can prove to be draining for even the best of us. Therefore, give your Scorecard team some time to reflect individually on the map before reconvening as a team. Between sessions, each team member can quietly review the map, critically examine the logic it portrays with a fresh eye, and conjure up any possible modifications.

It's always a good idea to circulate the draft strategy map among key stakeholders for review and feedback. Employees, senior management, funders, customers, and partners, to name but a few, should have the opportunity to test the logic of the document. Executive input is especially critical. As we all know, for the Scorecard to gain a foothold in the organization, it must be embraced, and viewed as a legitimately valuable tool, by the senior management.

An effective strategy map should tell the story of your strategy, with the objectives chosen helping to make your story leap from the page. If, upon review, your stakeholders don't understand or agree on the priorities you're asserting, you should revisit the map. The Balanced Scorecard can serve as a powerful communication tool, signaling to everyone the key drivers of your success. If your map is overly complex, poorly designed, or difficult to understand, your communication efforts may be severely compromised.

Once your team has had the opportunity to reflect individually on the map, and you've gathered feedback from all key stakeholders, reconvene the team for a final discussion of the map. Make any recommended changes and, if necessary, conduct a vote to determine the final objectives for the map.

Clarifying Objectives with Objective Statements

Exhibit 8.9 displays the strategy map developed by the Finance and Administrative Services division of Cal State San Marcos University. It's a terrific example of a well-constructed strategy map. The limited number of objectives is testimony to their commitment of measuring only the critical few drivers of success. The map also portrays clear cause-and-effect linkages among the objectives, making the division's strategic story easy to read, understand, and share with others. And, in keeping with an earlier admonition, the group's objectives are very concise.

Brevity is certainly an important attribute of performance objectives. However, in order to continue your translation efforts from objectives to measures, you must ensure there is clear understanding of exactly what is meant by each objective. Consider for example an objective of "increase workplace productivity." That's a very broad and nebulous statement. Any number of performance measures could serve as able translations. Objective statements serve the purpose of providing clarification and elaboration on the objectives as displayed on the strategy map. These two- or three-sentence narratives clearly articulate what is meant by the objective, while providing guidance as to what type of performance measures may be appropriate. Well-written objective statements will share the following traits:

- Provide precise clarification of the meaning suggested by the objective.
- Outline why this objective is important to customers, employees, or other stakeholders.
- Briefly discuss how the objective will be accomplished.
- Describe how the objective links in the chain of cause and effect evident in the strategy map.

Exhibit 8.9 Cal State San Marcos Finance and Administrative Services Strategy Map

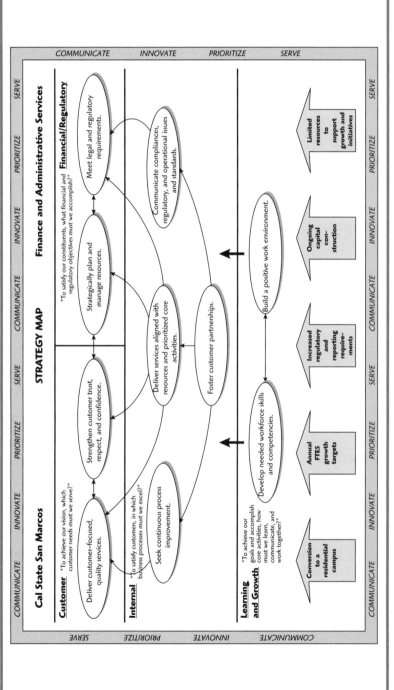

181

Here is an example of a sharply written and cogent objective statement:

> Attract, Develop, and Retain Talent
> Knowledgeable and experienced employees are the key to our success. Our objective is to reduce staff turnover and recruitment challenges by creating an appealing work environment built upon role clarity, personal motivation, satisfaction and accountability. We will provide all employees with an opportunity to directly impact officewide performance and achieve goals that meet customers' needs. [17]

As important as the objective statements are, getting people to take the time to write them can, admittedly, be like pulling teeth—not a fast and painless process. Some organizations will impose a two-week deadline for the submission of all statements. Though the looming deadline poses some urgency, most people will wait until the fourteenth day to craft something, and it will often reflect a lack of time and attention. One of my clients came up with an innovative solution to keep objective statements at the forefront of everyone's attention. This organization holds a morning management meeting each day, and decided that, until the objective statements were completed, updates would be shared at the meeting. Each day, one person was assigned to present at least one objective statement for review with the group. This is a great idea for a couple of reasons: First, and practically speaking, it ensures that objective statements are crafted in a timely fashion; second, and equally important, by following this method, the entire management team can hear and see what is being developed, and discuss it as a team. The feedback offered helps the writer tighten the statements, while others in attendance learn the "best practices" of objective statement writing and can apply it to their endeavors.

SUMMARY

Among the first decisions any Scorecard-adopting organization must make is, which Balanced Scorecard perspectives will we use? Kaplan and Norton originally designed the Scorecard with profit-seeking enterprises in mind, and developed four broad perspectives to satisfy that group: Financial, Customer, Internal Processes, and Employee Learning and Growth. Research has indicated that a majority of public-sector organizations use these same four perspectives. However, adaptability is possibly the Balanced Scorecard's greatest attribute, the point being that you should choose perspectives that are right for your organization. Many nonprofit and government agencies will choose to place an overarching mission perspective at the top of their Scorecard. Others will choose to split the Customer perspective in two, including both customers and stakeholders. Perspective names are often changed to reflect the work done in the public and nonprofit sectors.

Before developing a strategy map of performance objectives, the Balanced Scorecard team should endeavor to gather and review as much organizational background as possible. There are a number of potentially illuminating sources of information, including: mission statements, values, vision, strategic plans, consulting studies, bylaws, mandates, annual plans, organizational histories, customer studies, and benchmarking studies.

Interviewing senior executives prior to developing a strategy map also offers many benefits. You'll gain insight into their thinking on key performance objectives, have an excellent opportunity to win their support for the process, and discover any doubts or issues they may harbor. The key components of the interview are: review of purpose; discussion of mission, values, vision, and strategy; exploration of the Balanced Scorecard perspectives; and review of implementation and use.

Performance objectives describe what must be done well in each Scorecard perspective if the organization hopes to achieve the strategy. Objectives are more precise than strategies, but less granular than performance measures. Beginning each objective with an action verb helps associate them with a "bias toward action."

Strategy maps are one-page documents that clearly articulate, and graphically represent, the key objectives spanning the four perspectives of the Balanced Scorecard. The objectives on a strategy map serve as landmarks on the organization's journey toward strategy execution.

Building the strategy map can be accomplished during one-day off-site sessions attended by the Balanced Scorecard team, executive champion, and an outside facilitator or consultant. The Balanced Scorecard SWOT analysis is a great way to warm up the team prior to jumping into the waters of map building. The exercise analyzes your strengths, weaknesses, opportunities, and threats in the context of Balanced Scorecard perspectives.

Performance objectives are frequently developed through the analysis of questions relating to each of the four perspectives:

- *Customer.* Who are our customers, and how do we add value for them?

- *Internal Processes.* Which processes must we excel at in order to continue adding value for customers?

- *Employee Learning and Growth.* Which organizational infrastructure elements are necessary if we hope to execute our strategy?

- *Financial.* How do we maintain service levels while adhering to budgetary constraints?

There is no single "right" number of objectives for a strategy map. However, many Scorecard adopters have found that adhering to the adage of "less is more" will pay dividends. A large number of objectives may lead to an unmanageable amount of measures, and obscure the Balanced Scorecard's communication abilities.

Your first strategy map should be considered a draft and be circulated to all key stakeholders for review and input. Incorporating recommendations will help build support for the map. When reviewing the map, ask yourself if all essential elements are present if you hope to execute your strategy, and if they fit together in a logical fashion.

Objective statements are two- to three-sentence narratives that clarify and expand on what appears in the strategy map. An objective statement outlines why the objective is important to stakeholders, briefly discusses how it will be accomplished, and describes how it links in the chain of cause and effect weaving through the Balanced Scorecard.

NOTES

1. Mark Jenkins, *To Timbuktu* (New York: William Morrow & Company, 1997).
2. Robert S. Kaplan and David P. Norton, *The Balanced Scorecard* (Boston: Harvard Business School Press, 1996).
3. Robert S. Kaplan, "The Balanced Scorecard and Nonprofit Organizations," *Balanced Scorecard Report,* November–December, 2002, pp. 1–4.
4. Georgia M. Harrigan and Ruth E. Miller, "Managing Change through an Aligned and Cascaded Balanced Scorecard: A Case Study," *Perform,* Vol. 2, No. 2, pp. 20–26.
5. Jake Barkdoll, "Balanced Scorecards in the Federal Government," *Public Manager,* Fall 2000, pp. 43–45.
6. Paul R. Niven, *Balanced Scorecard Step-by-Step: Maximizing Performance and Maintaining Results* (New York: John Wiley & Sons, Inc., 2002), p. 103.
7. Joan Magretta, "Why Business Models Matter," *Harvard Business Review,* May 2002, pp. 86–92.
8. From interview with Rick Pagsibigan, September 19, 2002.
9. Robert S. Kaplan and David P. Norton, "Having Trouble with Your Strategy? Then Map It," *Harvard Business Review,* September–October 2000, pp. 167–176.
10. As quoted in Brian E. Becker, Mark A. Huselid, and Dave Ulrich, *The HR Scorecard* (Boston: Harvard Business School Press, 2001).
11. From interview with Abbi Stone and Katy Rees, September 18, 2002.
12. From interview with John Ramont, December 6, 2002.
13. Peter F. Drucker, *Managing the Non-Profit Organization* (New York: HarperBusiness, 1990), p. 124.
14. From interview with Abbi Stone and Katy Rees, September 18, 2002.
15. John A. McLaughlin and Gretchen B. Jordan, "Logic Models: A Tool for Telling Your Program's Performance Story," *Evaluation and Program Planning,* 1999, pp. 65–72.
16. Ibid.
17. Adapted from the objective statements of Horizon Fitness, DeForest, Wisconsin.

CHAPTER 9

Performance Measures, Targets, and Initiatives

Roadmap for Chapter Nine When Kaplan and Norton originally conceived the idea for a Balanced Scorecard, they were attempting to solve a measurement problem: How do organizations balance the historical accuracy and integrity of financial numbers with the drivers of future success? Since that time, over a dozen years ago, the Balanced Scorecard has evolved from a measurement system to a strategic management system and a powerful communication tool. Creative Scorecard adopters are finding ever new ways to harness this revolutionary tool. However, at its core, the Scorecard retains a commitment to performance measurement. In this chapter we examine the final elements necessary to develop a Balanced Scorecard measurement system: measures, targets, and initiatives.

We'll begin the chapter by considering the types of measures most used by public and nonprofit organizations. We'll then examine each of the four Scorecard perspectives in detail, providing information and techniques you can use to develop your performance measures. To help you choose the most appropriate measures for your organization, a number of criteria are presented.

The critical role played by targets is the next stop in our Balanced Scorecard journey. Different types of targets will be examined, and sources of target information reviewed. Finally, we'll review organizational initiatives. Initiatives describe the steps, processes, projects, and plans that will bring the targets to life. Using the Balanced Scorecard as a lens, we'll explore a method of determining whether your current initiatives are acting as allies in the campaign to execute your strategy.

WHAT ARE PERFORMANCE MEASURES?

Modern organizational vocabulary is flooded with references to measurement: "You get what you measure." "Measurement matters." "Measurement gets results." You've probably heard these and many more in your working life. The truth is, though sounding cliché, each is absolutely sound. Measurement does matter and it does drive results.

Performance measures may be considered standards used to evaluate and communicate performance against expected results. Granted, that's a rather banal description when you consider the undeniable power of a good performance measure. Not only do measures provide managers and executives with a tool to gauge organizational progress, but, when well crafted, they can inspire and motivate all employees, set direction for the organization, and encourage alignment from top to bottom.

The idea of measuring performance existed well before Kaplan or Norton conceived of something called a Balanced Scorecard. Organizations have long been devoted to the art and science of tracking performance. That said, there is a cavernous gap between the simple act of measurement and measuring the right things. Consider these dubious examples of measurement[1]:

- The single goal for the Department of Defense (DoD) procurement is the percentage of procurement funds requested and appropriated by Congress compared to DoD identified needs. This is a measure of inputs and lobbying success, but says nothing about results achieved with the appropriated funds.
- The Health Resources and Services Administration provides grants to increase the number of primary care providers, encourage better distribution of health professionals, and increase the number of minorities in the health professions. Program performance has been measured, not by the number or distribution of health care professionals, but rather by the number of grants made to academic institutions, hospitals, or students.

Measurement is about more than "counting widgets." Real benefits accrue to those who view the full range of measurement's vast potential, drawing on a range of measurement alternatives. Next we'll explore several types of performance measures you can draw upon when designing your Balanced Scorecard.

Types of Performance Measures

Traditionally, three types of performance measures have been encountered in practice. Each is discussed in turn.

Input Measures

At the lowest end of the performance measurement spectrum is the tracking of program inputs. Typical inputs include staff time and budgetary resources.

Inputs are generally the simplest elements to measure, but provide limited information for decision-making and analysis of actual results.

Output Measures

Results generated from the use of program inputs are the domain of the output measure. These metrics track the number of people served, services provided, or units produced by a program or service. They may sometimes be referred to as activity measures. Depending on the nature of the program or service, output measures may provide information on whether desired results are being achieved. An immunizations program, for example, would gauge its effectiveness based on the number of inoculations delivered. However, for the majority of agencies, these too fail to disclose whether customers or clients are better off.

Outcome Measures

As noted, input and output measures demonstrate effort expended and numbers served, but reveal little about whether these interventions are making a difference—whether the targeted population is any better off as a result. The outcome measure answers this call.

Outcomes track the benefit received by stakeholders as a result of the organization's operations. Whereas inputs and outputs tend to focus internally on the program or service itself, outcomes reflect the concerns of the participants (clients, customers, other stakeholders). Outcome measures shift the focus from activities to results, from how a program operates to the good it accomplishes.[2] Outcome measures offer many advantages:

- Outcomes demonstrate results, and in today's environment that is exactly what everyone, from the general public to the world's most generous philanthropists, are demanding from public and nonprofit organizations.

- Outcomes provide guidance in resource allocation decisions. Funding can be directed in alignment with those actions that produce documented results.

- Focusing on outcomes, rather than inputs or outputs, serves to guide the entire organization toward its true aims.

- Accountability is enhanced when the focus shifts to outcomes. Administrators cannot hide behind data indicating numbers served, but must outline specifically how targeted audiences are better off as a result of their program or service.

Your Balanced Scorecard will likely contain a mix of input, output, and outcome measures weaving through the perspectives chosen. Exhibit 9.1

provides an example for a prenatal health clinic. In this example, the clinic measures new revenue received in the Financial perspective. Funding dollars will be used to support the clinic's ongoing operations, and is thus considered an input. The clinic will dedicate a least a portion of its enhanced funding to support training of staff on the latest prenatal care techniques. Number of staff trained is a metric chosen in the Employee Learning and Growth perspective. Trained staff will use their knowledge in the delivery of services, and hence training may be considered an input. Possessing additional knowledge will allow the staff to deliver new and highly informative presentations to their targeted audience of low-income mothers. Number of presentations delivered is the output measure chosen in the Internal Processes perspective. The clinic is hypothesizing—remember, a Balanced Scorecard is designed to capture your business hypothesis—that informative presentations will help clients make better decisions, which will ultimately result in better choices and clients feeling better about themselves. This will be reflected in an outcome measure of

Exhibit 9.1   Mix of Input, Output, and Outcomes in a Balanced Scorecard

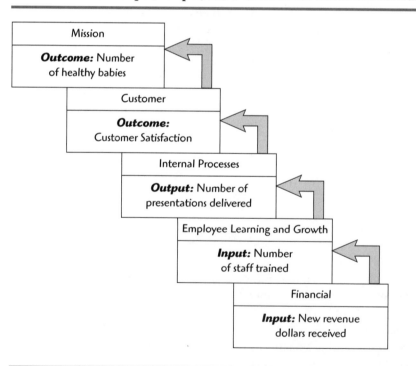

customer satisfaction. Finally, those patients who feel satisfied are more-
likely to maintain the healthy habits necessary for a safe delivery, which will
lead to a greater number of healthy babies. The number of healthy babies
is chosen as an outcome under the mission perspective of the Scorecard.

Other Types of Performance Measures: Lag and Lead Indicators

Later in the chapter when discussing the Employee Learning and Growth
perspective, we'll explore employee satisfaction. You'll learn that taking the
pulse of your employees' attitudes, opinions, and beliefs is immensely
popular. While employee satisfaction is an important metric worthy of any
Balanced Scorecard, it is essentially a *lag* indicator of performance.
Satisfaction will typically be gauged once, maybe twice, a year, with findings
being incorporated into plans for the following year. By the time you survey
your employees, the actions they're reflecting upon and assessing in the
survey have already occurred. Thus, you need to balance this historical
view with a predictive, driving metric that leads to improved employee
satisfaction—in other words a *leading* indicator of performance. Perhaps
you hypothesize that absenteeism is a leading indicator of satisfaction, thus
you monitor employees' time away from work in the belief that higher
absenteeism is an early warning sign that overall satisfaction is falling.
This gives you information you can take action upon now, not a year from
now when you complete your next employee satisfaction survey. Should
absenteeism increase, you must mount a campaign to determine why this
is taking place, and enact programs to mitigate it.

Deborah Kerr of the Texas State Auditor's Office describes lag and lead
measures this way. *"Lag measures tell you basically whether or not you have
met your target. Lead measures tell you how you are doing along the way and allow
you to adjust performance so that you can be more successful in achieving your goal.
Lead measures can be identified by mapping your processes and noting critical milestones, which can be used as lead measures to flap possible performance problems."*[3]
An interesting example comes from the Department of Corrections in
New York City.[4] Using its performance measurement system, this department tracks commissary sales in its jails. Prison officials have determined
that if sales of cigarettes and candy suddenly increase, a riot may be in
the planning stages. Inmates realize that they'll be confined to their cells
immediately after any kind of uprising, and therefore stock up on supplies.
A spike in candy and cigarette sales in this case is a leading indicator of
the number of prison riots. Knowing this relationship exists allows prison
officials to take action and attempt to avert a potentially dangerous
confrontation.

The Balanced Scorecard should contain a mix of lag and lead indicators of performance. If you have nothing but lag indicators, historical representations of performance, you know little about the "how" of your operation. Conversely, a preoccupation with leading indicators will not reveal whether improvements are leading to improved process and customer results.

I warn you, some people on your Scorecard team may suggest that every measure is in effect "lagging" because it is historical in nature. It's very easy to get off track and engage in a discussion of this nature, but in the end it boils down to a simple principle: When selecting measures ask yourself, "What drives this measure?" Whenever you choose one measure, and can hypothesize a relationship with a related metric you feel drives the performance of the first measure, you've determined a lag and lead relationship. Exhibit 9.2 outlines some of the key differences between lag and lead indicators.

Exhibit 9.2   Lag and Lead Performance Measures

	Lag	Lead
Definition	Measures focusing on results at the end of a time period. Normally characterizing historical performance.	Measures that "drive," or lead, to the performance of lag measures. Normally measures intermediate processes and activities.
Examples	· Revenue · Employee Satisfaction	· Grants written · Absenteeism
Advantages	Normally easy to identify and capture.	Predictive in nature, and allow the organization to make adjustments based on results.
Issues	Historical in nature and do not reflect current activities. Lack predictive power.	May prove difficult to identify and capture. Often, new measures with no history at the organization.
The Balanced Scorecard should contain a mix of lag and lead measures of performance.		

Adapted from material presented in *Balanced Scorecard Step-by-Step: Maximizing Performance and Maintaining Results*, Paul R. Niven (John Wiley & Sons, Inc., 2002).

DEVELOPING MEASURES FOR THE FOUR PERSPECTIVES

In the following sections we'll explore each of the Scorecard's four perspectives in turn, and discuss how you can develop performance measures for each. Sometimes, the hardest part of any task, developing performance measures included, is getting started.

To kick-start your measurement efforts, try this technique, which the Department of Energy (DoE) calls "binning." That interesting term means taking the metrics that your organization already has to collect and putting them in the four Balanced Scorecard perspectives, or "bins." This is an easy and nonthreatening way to begin thinking about what to measure on the Balanced Scorecard. Once you've filled your bins, you can then take a more critical view of the metrics and determine whether they deliver a truly well-rounded view of your performance.

MEASURES FOR THE CUSTOMER PERSPECTIVE

Frances Hesselbein served as the national executive director of the Girl Scouts of the United States of America from 1976 until 1990. Her tenure at that venerable institution was marked with both progress and innovation. Speaking on the topic of customers, she once commented, *"Rarely does a nonprofit organization have 'a' customer. If we market to only one of our customers, I think we fail."*[5] The same can be said for a government organization at any level.

Customers come by many names and represent many groups. Legal service and human service agencies serve "clients," health care organizations serve "patients," arts organizations serve "patrons," advocacy groups serve "constituents."[6] The key is not the nomenclature, but the recognition that these different groups exist, and that while they may all fall under the broad umbrella of the "customer," they all possess different needs, which must be addressed if the organization is to succeed. The Balanced Scorecard may act as a repository for all of your varied, and seemingly disparate, customer groups.

A simple, but very effective, question to ask when generating customer measures is: "What do our customers demand or expect from us?" Empathy is critical to the success of this exercise; you must literally attempt to walk a mile in your customer's shoes to find a sincere response. While each customer group may produce different answers to the question, requiring different measurements, they will often fall under one of the following categories:

- *Access.* Metrics relating to the ease with which customers can avail themselves of your products or services.

- *Timeliness.* Time expended, or saved, by clients as a result of your offerings.

- *Selection.* Depending on the nature of your organization, you may be in a position to offer more than one product or service. Are your offerings meeting the expectations of your customers?

- *Efficiency.* Customers of public sector organizations especially value a transaction that can be completed easily and accurately in one stop.

In a twist on former President Kennedy's famous dictum of "Ask not what your country can do for you, but what you can do for your country," I would suggest you not only ask what you can do for your customers, but also what you need from them. You're attempting to produce a service and deliver it efficiently and in a timely fashion, but what do you require in return? This isn't a selfish question, just a pragmatic one. For example, you may require greater visibility in the community, or greater support from donors. Now we have a balance reflected in the Customer perspective that ensures everybody is better off, and you're not jeopardizing your ability to provide future services because you cannot afford to continue operating.

Customer Satisfaction Surveys

Customer satisfaction surveys have been used successfully in both the public and nonprofit sectors for many years. Prince William County in Virginia, a recognized leader in performance management, has been doing annual telephone surveys of hundreds of community households since 1993. The auditor's office of the City of Portland has been even more aggressive, undertaking an annual mail survey of approximately 10,000 households since 1991.[7] At the federal level, customer satisfaction is monitored annually by the American Customer Satisfaction Index. (In case you're interested, overall customer satisfaction with the federal government declined by 1.5 percent in 2002 to 70.2.[8])

While many organizations devote significant resources of both money and time to query about satisfaction, not all surveys are created equal. Designing an effective evaluation tool requires moving beyond simple questions such as, "Overall, how would you rate your satisfaction with our services?" to an examination of variables that exist on several levels. Based on interviews with more than a billion—that's right, a billion—customers, the Gallup organization has identified these four expectations inherent in the study of customer satisfaction:[9]

- *Accuracy.* Whatever your product or service, customers expect it to be delivered accurately every time.

- *Availability.* Services should be available in locations, and at times, that meet customers' needs.

- *Partnership.* Customers and clients want to feel that you understand them and are "on their side."
- *Advice.* This is the real barometer of nonprofit and public-sector success. How can you help your customers in some way, thereby improving their situation in a demonstrable fashion?

Customer satisfaction surveys should attempt to probe customers' feelings about your offerings in each of the four categories.

Customer Value Propositions

The concept of value propositions was introduced during the discussion of customer objectives in Chapter Eight. The idea, introduced by Michael Treacy and Fred Wiersema in 1995, suggested that any business should face the market using one of three value propositions:

- *Product leadership.* These organizations constantly push the envelope of product and service design. While you might expect to pay a little more for their offerings, you expect a superior product or experience. Sony is an example of a product leader.
- *Operational excellence.* Wal-Mart is the classic operationally excellent company. You probably don't shop there for outstanding customer service or cutting-edge products; rather, what you expect is a huge selection and great prices. It can offer you this value because of flawless execution of hundreds of operational processes affecting your store experience.
- *Customer intimacy.* Organizations pursuing a customer intimacy strategy strive to provide total solutions to customer needs. Rather than focusing on a transaction as a one-time event, they strive to build long-lasting relationships with customers. Home Depot prides itself on providing helpful solutions to customers' needs.

When the idea of value propositions hit the mainstream in the mid- to late-1990s, it was quickly applied by those organizations developing Balanced Scorecards. The challenge of identifying a value proposition and determining appropriate metrics seemed very well suited to the demands of the Customer perspective. However, organizations quickly realized they could not focus exclusively on one value proposition, to the exclusion of the other two. Rather, they concluded, at least a baseline of acceptable performance must be achieved in two propositions, with a focus of efforts devoted to the third. Thus, many Scorecard adopters now use the value proposition model when populating the Customer—and, as you'll soon see—the Internal Processes perspectives.

The question is, do the value propositions apply to nonprofit and public sector organizations? Actual practice is limited at this point, but anecdotal evidence suggests the answer is yes. All organizations, regardless of structure, must attempt to forge meaningful bonds with their customers. This is the case even if your service is currently a monopoly. Hence, customer intimacy readily applies to governments and nonprofits. Operational excellence, too, is a natural fit. Given shrinking funding and increasing demands, efficient internal operations are a must if you hope to survive. Finally, even product leadership is possible in public and nonprofit sectors. Approaching your customers in a new way, providing new services to meet demands, and creatively applying technology to simplify the customer experience are all examples of product leadership propositions.

The Michigan Department of Transportation used the notion of value propositions when developing its Balanced Scorecard. Staff described the benefit this way: *"Using the value proposition concept was one of the most insightful pieces for us. We learned a lot about things we could do more of, and it drove home more quickly the importance of building relationships, communicating value, and focusing on innovation. It's not only applicable, but was one of the real benefits of doing this."*[10]

MEASURES FOR THE INTERNAL PROCESSES PERSPECTIVE

If you hope to drive continuous value for customers and clients, and ultimately work toward your mission, process excellence is a must. Every organization is different, and will derive value from a different combination of processes. However, there are several core processes you should consider when developing measures for the Internal Processes perspective, each discussed in turn in the following subsections.

Quality

Total Quality Management, or TQM, became a household (or at least organizational) word in the 1980s. This unrelenting focus was long overdue, as many organizations saw eroding results due to substandard quality. As with many concepts, however, the quality movement bore an unintended consequence for some devotees. Their maniacal attention to this one variable of performance led to less attention on customer satisfaction, innovation, and, in many private-sector examples, financial results. Many quality standouts of the 1980s paid the ultimate price for their lack of balance and ended up in bankruptcy.

Using a Balanced Scorecard approach allows you to mitigate this substantial risk. You can do so by balancing the admirable goals of quality improvement with measures that demonstrate whether the improvement is leading to increased value for customers or clients.

Innovation

Your customers are changing, the environment in which you operate is changing, your own staff is undoubtedly changing; the question is, are you responding? Innovation must be built into every organization, from the smallest local nonprofit to the largest federal government department. Embracing the status quo is no longer an option for organizations that wish to be relevant today, tomorrow, and years into the future. Here are some characteristics practiced by organizations excelling at the art of innovation[11]:

- *Innovation is treated as a process.* A structured process is put in place for the systematic practice of innovation. This imposes a discipline and allows for measurement, and, ultimately, improvement.
- *Cross-functional teams are used.* Leading innovators recognize that creative insights are often struck from the eclectic exchanges among participants representing every discipline.
- *Customers are at the center.* Organizations committed to innovation learn primarily from their current customers and clients, analyzing their needs, wants, and "must-haves."
- *Passion and creativity are supported.* Some pundits describe the role of leadership as that of establishing the conditions for success to flourish, then getting out of the way. Innovating organizations recognize this tenet of leadership and put in place structures and environments conducive to creativity.

Consider the case of the Youth Voice Collaborative (YVC).[12] An innovative after-school program of media literacy and leadership training, YVC provides young people between the ages of 13 and 18 with the information they need to become critical consumers of media, and the skills they need to create and distribute messages that reflect their realities. This innovative idea was the brainchild of the Boston YWCA, and resulted from its commitment to getting at-risk kids off the streets after school hours. Upon hearing one young woman explain that her life was changed by "walking into a boys and girls club and picking up a camcorder," YWCA President Marti Wilson-Taylor sprang to action. She spoke to other kids, organized a collaborative effort with other youth service agencies and set about to develop a program dedicated to the natural attraction of kids and media. The YWCA had never done anything quite like this in the past, but was committed to improving society and used innovation to help it achieve its goals.

Partnering

Partnering has become emblematic of modern private sector organizations. The technology sector in particular has grown in large part due to powerful and synergistic unions between organizations. Partnering offers many opportunities for public and nonprofit organizations as well. One area of emerging interest for nonprofits is the potential link to corporate philanthropy efforts. Private-sector organizations are beginning to realize they can use their charitable efforts to improve their "competitive context"—the quality of the business environment in the location where they operate.[13] They are beginning to seek out nonprofit (and government) partners in order to improve their business prospects. Consider, for example, the State Museum of Auschwitz-Birkenau in Poland. It has partnered with Grand Circle Travel, a leading direct marketer of international travel for older Americans. Grand Circle provides donations to the museum, which allow it to maintain the aging facilities, and offer innovative exhibitions. Grand Circle patrons benefit from the relationship by receiving special visiting and learning opportunities at the museum.

Marketing

Getting the word out about your organization has never been more important. However, it seems every organization is clamoring for attention these days, leaving precious little room for individual voices to be heard above the din. Marketing is a long-standing method of telling your story, your way. Here are the "four Ps" of marketing, each of which could lead to important performance measures[14]:

- *Product.* The product of service offered. In order to stand out, it must at least live up to, if not exceed, what customers and clients demand.
- *Promotion.* Going from the best-kept secret in town to a household name is the goal of promotion. Products, services, and image are all potential targets of promotional campaigns.
- *Price.* Price in this context refers to perceived value. Ironically, in the nonprofit world, bewildered consumers often associate greater value with higher price.
- *Place.* Where the product or service is delivered. Public and nonprofits must ensure they develop an effective distribution system for their products and services. In other words, if clients can't come to them, organizations should go to the clients.

Fundraising

It would be difficult, if not impossible, to raise your profile, provide quality products and services, attract potential partners, and constantly innovate without a steady stream of revenue. Many sources of performance measures exist throughout the fundraising process, from finding potential donors to developing proposals to building budgets.

Other Sources of Internal Processes Measures

Measures in the Internal Process perspective should flow directly from your choices in the Customer perspective. After all, you're attempting to tell the story of your strategy through the measures you choose, and to do so they must link together in a cause-and-effect chain throughout the four perspectives. Once you've developed your customer objectives and measures, ask yourself, "At which processes must we excel in order to meet these customer goals?"

If you subscribe to the customer value propositions we've discussed, they will provide a convenient technique for creating Internal Processes metrics. Should you choose a focus of product or service leadership in the Customer perspective, you would most likely develop measures around the processes of innovation, research and development, and partnering. Customer-intimate organizations will place a spotlight on customer relationship processes and their ability to learn more about their targeted clients. Finally, operational excellence will demand a concentration on processes affecting cost, quality, and timeliness of current product and service offerings.

MEASURES FOR THE EMPLOYEE LEARNING AND GROWTH PERSPECTIVE

In his foreword to the *HR Scorecard*, David Norton wrote, *"The worst grades are reserved for [executives'] understanding of strategies for developing human capital. There is little consensus, little creativity, and no real framework for thinking about the subject.... The asset that is the most important is the least understood, least prone to measurement, and, hence, least susceptible to management."*[15] Research has indicated that upwards of 75 percent of value in today's organization is derived from intangible assets, principally human capital. However, as Norton aptly asserts, the failure to recognize and respond to this undeniable fact has reached epidemic proportions.

My experience as a consultant echoes Norton's findings. In conducting Scorecard sessions with a wide variety of clients, I have often detected a worrisome pattern. Enthusiasm abounds as we discuss customer objectives and measures. Internal processes and financial measures can be tough going, but the groups consistently remain strong and generate active discussion on the points. Inevitably, employee learning and growth issues will be the last area of dialog. Perhaps I'm mistaking fatigue for disinterest, but in a disturbingly high number of cases, when I introduce this perspective I'll be greeted with, "Oh, HR will take care of those measures." The majority of organizations, while paying constant lip service to the importance of employees, have yet to make the realization that the value of human capital truly is the distinguishing feature among today's organizations. Public and nonprofit leaders must pay particular heed to this warning since the yield from human capital in your organizations is particularly high.

In this section we'll look at three areas that comprise the measurement challenge of the Employee Learning and Growth perspective: *human capital*, *information capital*, and the *climate for positive action*.

Measuring Human Capital

I frequently encounter strategy maps that include objectives in the Employee Learning and Growth perspective related to competencies. No one would argue the importance of tracking key competencies in today's knowledge-worker-dominated environment. However, confusion exists over specifically what a competency entails. Is it skill, habit, or talent?[16] The ability to distinguish between the three seems to rest on what comes naturally and what is teachable.

- *Skills* are attributes or behaviors that, with some practice and determination, most people can demonstrate with at least some degree of proficiency. The ability to effectively use software systems, for example, is a skill.

- *Habits* represent our natural proclivities. You may be intensely competitive, or exhibit sincere compassion; both are habits cultivated over a lifetime. With some fierce determination and a good dose of self-awareness, most people can change their habits over time.

- *Talents* are recurring patterns of thought, feeling, or behavior that distinguish a person.[17] They are innate and, therefore, very difficult to teach. Demonstrating "calm under fire" is a talent some people are fortunate enough to possess. Those of us who can't claim this talent could sign up for training classes on the attributes of grace under pressure, but unless you're born with such a talent it is difficult to cultivate through practice.

When measuring human capital, skills are the easiest to identify, measure, monitor, and improve. Your task is to identify the skills you require now and in the future, catalog your current inventory of skills, determine the gap, and then put in place a plan to close the gap.

Talents pose a more significant measurement challenge. If someone simply does not have a talent that you intend to measure, all the training and motivation in the world will not change that situation. All you can do is attempt to match talented people with the right roles: Look at the roles within your organization and determine which talents, not skills, differentiate the job. Upon reading that, you might think I'm referring only to management positions, but that's not the case. No job is too simple or too complex to require talent. Early in my career I worked with a large bank where one person in our lending group was responsible for ensuring all the loan documentation was completed accurately and on time, to ensure smooth processing. Talk about a paper pusher! Her desk was constantly being piled with a seemingly endless flow of paper. But just as quickly as it arrived, it was gone. Not only did she have the skills necessary to complete the documents, but she was in possession of a talent for processing paperwork. For many people, the job would have been overwhelming and stressful, trying to meet all the demands and keep the process flowing in a smooth and orderly fashion. I recall her proclaiming proudly to me, "The world needs paper pushers too, Paul." The point is, give all your roles a second look through the lens of talent. You'll be surprised at what you discover.

Employee Training

As just discussed, talents are difficult to teach, thus are not good candidates for training. Skills, however, are ideal. Responding to the moniker Employee Learning and Growth, most organizations will have at least one performance measure related to training. And why not, since the person trained gains valuable new skills, and will be in a better position to contribute to overall organizational success.

The great temptation with training metrics is to simply count the amount of training hours per week, month, or year. Using the vernacular developed earlier in this chapter, this would probably represent an input measure. But remember, inputs reveal little about real success. Training is certainly an important component of employee success, but what really drives that success are the *results* of training, not the simple act of attendance. Therefore, measures of employee training must balance participation with results. What specific skills or behaviors do you expect to see demonstrated as a result of the training? Measure and monitor those as well, to see the whole picture of training.

Retaining Employees

The federal government in the United States is at its lowest staffing level since 1950. At approximately 1.8 million people, the ranks have been diminished by almost 325,000 since 1993.[18] Proponents of smaller government will applaud, but those of you charged with managing programs realize the tremendous challenges you face. You're not alone. Inspectors general at nine major federal agencies have listed workforce problems among the top 10 most serious management challenges facing their agencies. Only 7.5 percent of the federal workforce is under age 30, while 38 percent is over age 50. If you've never considered retention and succession an issue, this is your wake-up call.

While the statistics are alarming, they are just that, statistics. You may prefer the approach utilized by the Australian Department of Defense, which also faces the challenge of an aging workforce. Its Balanced Scorecard champion recognized this fact and felt it must be addressed in the department's Scorecard. Rather than quoting dry statistics to reflect the crisis, she showed the senior leadership team a group picture of themselves. Then she asked what they saw. A picture truly does tell a thousand words—or, in this case, one word: gray! Faced with the stark reality of their aging ranks, the department rallied to support her cry for succession metrics.

Within the nonprofit world, the problem of succession may be dwarfed by issues of retention. Many people are drawn to nonprofits in the hope of advancing beliefs they hold dear, but are eventually repelled by the often stressful nature of the work. Measurement sometimes unintentionally exacerbates this issue. Strapped for financial resources, many agencies will monitor the cost per hire, doing everything in their power to keep it as low as possible. However, this admirable goal of austerity may result in hiring employees who are ill-suited to advance the cause of the organization. Poor hires leave, or are involuntarily removed, which results in higher overall costs in relation to lost time, training investments, and benefits.

Measuring Information Capital

In the preceding section I mentioned that the federal government had significantly reduced its workforce over the past several years. Fewer people means the government must do everything it can do enhance productivity—do more with less as they say. In keeping with that credo, the federal government has become the world's largest consumer of information technology (IT). Estimates suggest the government spent a whopping $45 billion in 2002 alone.[19] The problem, a significant one, is that despite this prodigious infusion of IT, there have been no measurable gains in productivity. At least part of the blame can be pinned on the tail of measurement. Agencies tend to assess the performance of their IT applications according to how well they serve the agency's requirements, not how well they meet customer needs. Reversing this situation represents a simple, yet profoundly fundamental shift in perspective. IT serves your organization in order for you to better serve your customers. It's that simple. Performance measures must balance the extent to which IT investments improve your ability to serve and the corresponding influence on customer results.

The Bureau of the Census offers a glimpse into how technology may improve performance. The agency uses an electronic hiring system that provides managers with online access to applicant resumes. Within 24 hours of receipt, managers can be reviewing the latest candidate resumes. Using the new system, the Census Bureau has reduced the time required to fill some positions from six months to as little as three days. The next challenge for the bureau is to develop performance measures that track customer service or other customer-related metrics in an attempt to ensure that its new-found internal capabilities are boosting results for its customers.

Information is more than just the ability to log on to the latest IT applications. Access to information is every bit as critical. Employees must be able to access information about key customers, donors, and other stakeholders in order to make informed decisions. However, investments of this nature are considered "overhead" by many nonprofits, and as a result are shunned in deference to an allocation of the same funds to direct service provision. This may prove to be a shortsighted decision. Though in the short-term funds will be directed toward clients and customers, in the long run, as conditions inevitably change, if employees don't have critical information on trends and environmental shifts, future service delivery will be placed in severe jeopardy.

Creating a Climate for Positive Action

Earlier in the chapter I described a model in which leaders provide the conditions necessary for success in their organizations, and leave it to their clever and dedicated employees to achieve success. What constitutes these conditions? Let's look at three factors that many organizations will focus on when attempting to create a positive climate.

Employee Satisfaction

Possibly the single most popular metric appearing in the Employee Learning and Growth perspective is employee satisfaction. If you're attempting to create a climate of positive action, one that will improve your performance and ultimately benefit customers, it's virtually impossible without committed staff. As a result, workplace surveys abound in organizations large and small, public, private, and nonprofit alike. Putting your ear to the ground and finding out what your people think is critical, but traditional methods for gathering that data often leave much to be desired. Survey experts suggest most organizations are applying survey design principles formulated 40 or 50 years ago.[20] To bring your surveying techniques out of the dark ages, here are a number of recommendations[21]:

- *Ask questions related to observable behavior, not thoughts or motives.* This allows respondents to draw on first-hand experience, not inference.
- *Measure only those behaviors that are linked to your organization's performance.* Awareness of your new cafeteria hours may be interesting, but is it relevant to your results?
- *Structure approximately one-third of the questions to lead to a negative response.* This avoids the natural tendency to agree to things.

- *Avoid questions that require rankings.* People tend to remember the first and last things in a list, which may bias their answer to the question.
- *Make sure the survey can be completed within 20 minutes.* Recognize that everyone is busy, and taking an hour to complete a 100-question survey may elicit a negative response that shows up in the respondent's answers.

Of course, surveying is one thing, taking action on the findings is another. To generate commitment from employees, you must demonstrate a willingness to act on the concerns raised in the surveys. Anything less and your survey efforts will be dismissed as hollow, dust-collecting make-work projects.

Communication

In a recent study, fewer than one-third of respondents believed their company communicates effectively with them.[22] Shakespeare said, *"If music be the food of love, play on."* Modern organizations would be well advised to say, "Communication is the food of success; communicate on." Employees are frequently drawn to careers in the public and nonprofit arenas by the allure to make a difference. The fire behind that bright-eyed idealism can be quickly extinguished without constant communication to employees of the organization's goals, how they fit in, and what is expected of them going forward. In Chapter Thirteen you'll read the story of Charlotte, North Carolina's, journey with the Balanced Scorecard. Among organizers' words of wisdom to Scorecard-adopting organizations is communicate, communicate, communicate. They recognize the value of providing constant information to all employees, and have seen the results it can bring. Their advice could be easily expanded into communication regarding all realms of the organization.

Alignment

In my ongoing effort to stay in some sort of shape, I recently bought a treadmill. It was with great anticipation that I plugged it in for the first time and climbed aboard. When I pressed the start button, I was greeted by a horrendous and violent shrieking noise. A quick examination determined the track had been jolted out of alignment during shipping. Things just don't work when they're not aligned. Now, my treadmill was easily remedied, and will undoubtedly provide me with years of service, but if your employees are not aligned to your overall goals, the results can be devastating. Conflicts of interest, misallocated resources, wasted performance management efforts, and missed opportunities can all result from poor alignment. Without a workforce that understands your mission, vision, and strategy, and is aligned toward their achievement, you will never produce the results you desire.

Alignment is frequently measured anecdotally through employee sur-veys: "Do you understand the goals of your department?" "Do you work col-laboratively with other groups to achieve success?" And so on. While this approach can prove effective, a simple method is to assess the degree of alignment of Balanced Scorecards in your organization. Chapter Ten will discuss cascading the Scorecard—driving it to lower levels of the organiza-tion in an effort to promote goal alignment. Once you've cascaded, you can perform a quick alignment diagnostic by evaluating how well your Scorecards work together to tell your strategic story.

MEASURES FOR THE FINANCIAL PERSPECTIVE

Last year here in the United States, 46 states struggled to close a combined budget gap of $37 billion. Of course, the news is even bleaker this year, with the state of California alone facing a deficit of almost $35 billion. Every day, newspapers and television reporters deliver doomsday predictions of how these shortfalls will inevitably affect public service. For self-preservation alone, public and nonprofit agencies must demonstrate their effective stew-ardship of what meager financial resources they have to a confused and skeptical public and funding bodies.

Measures in the Financial perspective of the Balanced Scorecard help demonstrate how you are providing your services in a manner that balances effectiveness with efficiency and cost consciousness. Here are some factors to consider:

- *Price of product or service delivery.* Determining the real cost of your efforts will go a long way toward inspiring you to continuously improve. Techniques such as Activity-Based Costing (ABC) have been utilized by a number of public agencies in their quest to accurately capture true cost information.

- *Revenue enhancement.* Ask: "What opportunities exist for broadening our sources of revenue?" "Do we currently provide services for which we could charge a fee?" "How diversified are our funding sources?"

- *Financial systems.* Regardless of how you view the accountants in your organization, financial systems are the backbone of most operations. Reliable, relevant, and timely financial information fuels virtually every type of decision you'll make. Financial errors can amount to huge sums of money and waste. For example, the Department of Agriculture esti-mated $976 million in food stamp overpayments, and $360 million in underpayments, for a total of $1.34 billion in erroneous payments in 2000. That's a payment error rate of an astonishing 8.9 percent.[23] Robust and reliable financial systems not only produce accurate data, they can also enhance your credibility.

CRITERIA FOR SELECTING PERFORMANCE MEASURES

Not all performance measures are created equally. Effective metrics provide direction, align employees, improve decision-making, and serve as a basis for resource allocation decisions. Here are several criteria to consider when attempting to narrow down your measures to the critical few that articulate your strategic story.

- *Linked to strategy.* The Balanced Scorecard was designed to facilitate the description of strategy. It does so by translating your strategy into a set of objectives and measures used to evaluate performance. All measures on the Scorecard should link back to your broad priorities as articulated in the strategy.

- *Easy to understand.* You and your employees shouldn't require a graduate degree from M.I.T. to comprehend what is meant by your Scorecard performance measures. The tool will be used simultaneously as a measurement, management, and communication tool. Communication is difficult, if not impossible, if your audience is unable to understand what is portrayed on the Scorecard.

- *Link in a chain of cause and effect.* The measures you select should link together through the four perspectives of the Scorecard. When you have a coherent story emerging from your measurements, communication efforts will be greatly enhanced, as will your opportunities to learn from performance results.

- *Updated frequently.* Your primary motivation in launching a Balanced Scorecard was most likely to improve results. Results can only be enhanced through the provision of timely information upon which you can take action. "Timely" in this context refers to measures that are updated frequently—monthly or quarterly. Semiannual and annual performance measures allow little room for midcourse corrections. By the time you receive your results, the actions that led to the performance are long past.

- *Accessible.* Research suggests that upwards of 30 percent of your performance data may be unavailable when you launch a Balanced Scorecard. Many organizations are disappointed to learn this, until they realize the missing data represent entirely new ways of monitoring performance that had been neglected in the past. Proclaiming a measure as critical enough to appear on the Scorecard, regardless of initial data availability, signals a strong commitment to focusing on what really matters. While 30 percent is palatable, 70, 80, or 90 percent is not. Never let the best be the enemy of the good. Sounds profound (maybe) but simply means a Balanced Scorecard you can use now with 70 percent of data available is better than a Scorecard you have to wait a year for, because of data availability issues.

- *Average-cautious.* Let's say you pick up your local paper tomorrow and see a headline that reads, "County incomes increase by record margin." Sounds like great news, worthy of celebrating and patting the backs of your elected officials. But what if you later discovered that in the past year Bill Gates, Warren Buffett, and Oprah Winfrey all decided to take up residence in the cozy confines of your town. Think about the effect their galactic-sized incomes would have had on your town's average. Typical townsfolk might be no better off, and perhaps suffered through a year in which income had fallen. Such is the danger of averages. Look for performance measures that portray the true picture of the process or event you're attempting to capture.

- *Resistant to "date"-related measures.* It's not uncommon for Scorecard developers to include at least a measure or two to the effect, "Complete X project by September 30." This reflects more of an initiative—an action taken to assure success on the measure—than a measure itself. Should they be fortunate enough to complete the project, does the measure simply vanish from the Scorecard? In this case, the Scorecard creators should ask, "What happens on September 30? How are we better off as an organization? How are prospects improved for our customers or clients?" In other words, "Why are we embarking on this initiative?" Answering these questions may lead to the development of a more appropriate performance measure.

- *Quantitative.* For all the men out there who are fashion-challenged, what would your wife say if you were about to leave for a romantic dinner dressed in a striped shirt and plaid pants? To put it mildly, she might suggest the two just don't go together. And so it is with subjectivity and performance measurement. Evaluation of performance should reflect objectivity as much as possible. Using quantitative indicators ensures any subjective biases are barred from the system. With a little creativity, you can transform even the most challenging measurement issue into a number. I can recall a medical services unit I worked with at a county government. A key performance metric was the distribution of its trauma reports in a timely fashion. The original measure was "reports issued." In other words, a simple yes or no would suffice as the indication of performance. With a little tweaking, we improved the measure by restating it as the "percentage of trauma-report recipients receiving the document on time."

- *Dysfunctional.* Dysfunctional is a word that has gradually crept into the mainstream. We have dysfunctional families, dysfunctional workplaces, dysfunctional teams. Basically, anywhere humans congregate seems to breed the potential for dysfunction. Measures can be dysfunctional too, in that they may drive the wrong behavior in your organization. Consider the example of one restaurant chain. Concerned with a large amount of food being thrown away at the end of the day, managers instructed their staff not to cook any food within one hour of closing until ordered by a customer. Great for waste, bad for customer service. Customers had to wait an inordinately long period of time for their orders, and soon business dried up. Measuring waste in this case drove the wrong behavior. Consider the behavior your measures will drive before including them on your Balanced Scorecard.

To help you make the hard choices among competing measure alternatives, I've developed a worksheet, shown in Exhibit 9.3, for ranking your metrics. List your measures under the appropriate perspective, and award a score in relation to each criterion. Consider rating each out of a possible 10 points.

How Many Measures on a Balanced Scorecard?

This is the $64,000 question: Just how many measures should your Scorecard contain? The standard response suggests you use as many measures as are necessary to adequately describe your strategy. If that means 10 measures, great; if it translates to 30 measures, so be it. When discussing objectives in Chapter Eight, I suggested you cap your number at between 10 and 20. Ten objectives would equal at least 10 performance measures. However, measures and objectives don't always exhibit a one-to-one relationship. Some objectives may require two measures to adequately capture their essence. For those objectives to which you do feel comfortable in assigning only one performance measure, a closer examination may reveal it to be a lagging indicator, which requires the balance of a leading indicator, again translating to more than one measure for the objective. A minimum of one and a half measures per objective is a good rule of thumb to follow. Therefore, 10 objectives would translate into at least 15 performance measures; 20 objectives would mean 30 measures; and so on.

My bias is toward fewer performance measures, under 20 whenever possible. There is a lot of "noise" in modern organizations, and a good Balanced Scorecard should rise above the crowd, providing you with a view of the real drivers of success in your organization. Limiting your measures means making the commitment to monitor strategic measures and place less relevance on operational indicators. This can prove to be a vexing challenge, especially in the public sector, where measures in the hundreds are not uncommon. You're not alone; recent research from a Hackett Benchmarking study found the typical monthly performance report to contain 140 different measures.[24]

Exhibit 9.3   Worksheet to Select Balanced Scorecard Measures

Perspective	Linkage to Strategy	Easily Understood	Cause and Effect Linkage	Frequency of Updating	Accessibility	Reliance on Averages	Date-Driven?	Quantitative	Dysfunctional?	Comments
Balanced Scorecard **Measure Selection Worksheet**										
Customer										
Measure 1										
Measure 2...										
Internal Processes										
Measure 1										
Measure 2...										
Employee Learning and Growth										
Measure 1										
Measure 2...										
Financial										
Measure 1										
Measure 2...										

Adapted from material in *Balanced Scorecard Step-by-Step: Maximizing Performance and Maintaining Results.*

207

Concentrating on the strategic doesn't mean the operational necessarily vanishes. My car monitors speed, fuel, temperature, and a few other critical variables, but that doesn't mean I don't care about what happens under the hood. I just don't need to be monitoring those myriad activities unless something occurs out of a normal range. Your organization is the same; as leaders, you have an obligation to focus on the strategic, the core drivers of performance. Examining performance measures related to activities three levels below you is an inefficient use of your time and the organization's resources. Maximize your time, abilities, and effectiveness by choosing to monitor only those few variables that truly correspond to success.

Gathering Employee Feedback on Your Performance Measures

Creativity tends to flourish in workplaces where employees are informed, inspired, and involved. The Balanced Scorecard can certainly inform all stakeholders of your progress, and positive results will no doubt prove inspiring. The other aspect of this triad is not to be overlooked. Before you can expect employees to embrace and use the Scorecard, you should provide them with the opportunity to provide input on this most critical of organizational documents.

Feedback can be gathered in a number of ways. Here is how the County of San Diego, California, accomplished the task.[25] This county, the sixth most populated in the country, recently instituted a wide-ranging performance management program to better serve its citizens. Leaders began their efforts by developing Balanced Scorecards for the Health and Human Services Agency (HHSA). With a budget of over $1 billion, and 5,000 employees, the HHSA is larger than many corporations. Given the diverse nature of services offered throughout the agency, the HHSA asked each of its program areas to develop Balanced Scorecards that demonstrated how they successfully serve their customers. A Balanced Scorecard project team made up of county personnel and consultants worked with each program to develop Scorecards over a four-month span.

Once preliminary Scorecards were built, the team looked for a way to share what had been developed with all employees and gather their feedback. They decided to hold what they termed "validation sessions." Four sessions were held over a two-day period—two in the morning and two in the afternoon. Upon entering the conference room, participants were greeted by project staff and given a folder to hold the information they would gather during the event. Each session was kicked off with a short presentation from the project team leader. He provided an overview of the project, benefits to be derived from performance management, and the work that lay ahead. Once the presentation concluded, participants were free to roam the large room and visit any one of the several booths staffed by project team members. Each booth featured a number of different Scorecards that the participants could review and discuss with the team. A kiosk was also set up, where employees could test-drive the Scorecard software that would be used to report results. Feedback forms were distributed, and participants were encouraged to provide their input to the team. The event was a great success since employees from across the agency had the chance to participate in the evolution of performance measures and see how other groups within the HHSA were measuring their outcomes.

Another client took an even more direct approach. After much deliberation, the Scorecard project team could not reach a consensus on how to measure the objective of "creating a safe and healthy environment." Rather than debating the topic endlessly, the chief executive used his weekly e-mail message to all employees to seek their input. Here is what he said:

> I would like to update you on our progress with our Balanced Scorecard (BSC) program. Last week, the executive team met with the implementation team to review the latest version of the BSC as we prepare to bring our five-year and line-of-business scorecards to the board of directors. We had very productive discussions and are close to finalizing the objectives, measures, and targets for the Balanced Scorecard.
>
> One objective, which is very important to our organization and generated significant discussion and dialog, was related to creating an organization that is "well"—including the physical, mental, and emotional well-being of all of our employees. Specifically, our objective is to: "Create a safe and healthy environment that supports balance in people's lives." Both the implementation team and executive team have debated a variety of measures—everything from measuring absenteeism to insurance claims to the number of accidents on the job to the amount of wellness programs we offer—and we just can't seem to find the ideal measure for gauging how "well" our organization is. We agreed that, with the wealth of knowledge resident across our organization, we would likely be able to find the answer. So, here's what I propose: Please think about what the best way to measure our organization's wellness might be, and drop me a note via e-mail sometime before next week. We'll gather up the responses and attempt to complete our work with your input on this last objective we're struggling with. I'm really looking forward to your input on this one.

Not surprisingly, many possible measures were advanced by employees across the organization (I'd like to tell you which they selected but as of this writing, their Scorecard is still under development). This is a true win-win situation. Not only does the organization's Scorecard benefit from the input of knowledgeable employees at all levels, but the chief executive reinforced both his commitment to the Balanced Scorecard and his faith in employees to deliver whatever is necessary to succeed.

RECORDING YOUR MEASURES ON A DATA DICTIONARY[26]

Creating a Performance Measure Data Dictionary

Once you've settled on a group of performance measures, you're ready to catalog the specific characteristics of the measures in a data "dictionary."

My dictionary's definition of the word "dictionary" reveals the following: "Book that lists....the topics of a subject." That is precisely what you're crafting in this step of the process: a document that provides all users with a detailed examination of your Balanced Scorecard measures, including a thorough list of measure characteristics.

Creating the measure data dictionary isn't a very glamorous task, but it is an important one. When you present your Balanced Scorecard to senior managers and employees alike, they will undoubtedly quiz you on the background of each and every measure: "Why did you choose this measure?" "Is it strategically significant?" "How do you calculate the measure?" "Who is responsible for results?" These and numerous other queries will greet your attempts to share your Scorecard with colleagues. The data dictionary provides the background you need to quickly defend your measure choices and answer any questions your audience has. Additionally, chronicling your measures in the data dictionary provides your team with one last opportunity to ensure a common understanding of measure details.

Exhibit 9.4 provides a template you can use to create your own measure dictionary. There are four basic sections of the template you must complete. In the first section, shown at the top, you provide essential background material on the measure. The second section lists specific measure characteristics. Calculation and data specifications are outlined in the third component of the dictionary. Finally, in the bottom section, you provide performance information relating to the measure. Let's examine each of these sections in some detail.

Measure Background

At a glance, readers should be able to determine what this measure is all about and why it's important for the organization to track.

- *Perspective.* Displays the perspective under which the measure falls.
- *Measure Number/Name.* All performance measures should be provided a number and name. The number is important should you later choose an automated reporting system. Many will require completely unique names for each measure; and since you may track the same measures at various locations or business units, a specific identifier should be supplied. The measure name should be brief, but descriptive. Again, if you purchase software for your reporting needs, they may limit the number of characters you can use in the name field.

Exhibit 9.4 Balanced Scorecard Data Dictionary

Perspective: Customer	**Measure Number/Name:** C01/Customer Satisfaction	**Owner:** L. Hess

Strategy: Expand program offerings	**Objective:** Increase Satisfaction with Programs

Description: Customer Satisfaction measures the percentage of surveyed customers stating they are satisfied with our current service offerings. Satisfaction is judged using a number of criteria, including: access to services, timeliness, and overall quality. We feel that only by ensuring current customers are satisfied will we be able to expand our offerings.

Lag/Lead: Lag	**Frequency:** Quarterly	**Unit Type:** Percentage	**Polarity:** High values are **good**

Formula: Number of quarterly survey respondents who feel satisfied with current access, timeliness, and quality of our services divided by the total number of surveys received.

Data Source: Data for this measure is provided by our survey company, "SST." Each quarter they perform a random survey of our customers and provide the results electronically to us. Data is contained in the form of MS Excel spreadsheets (CUST SURVEY.xls, lines 14 and 15). Data is available the 10th business day following the end of each quarter.

Data Quality: High – received automatically from third party vendor	**Data Collector:** S. Commons

Target: Q1 2001: 65%   Q2 2001: 68%   Q3 2001: 72%   Q4 2001: 75%

Baseline: Our most recent data received from SST indicates a Customer Satisfaction percentage of 59%

Target Rationale: Achieving customer satisfaction is critical to our strategy of service expansion. The quarterly increases we're targeting are higher than in past years but reflect our increased focus on satisfaction	**Initiatives:**
	1. Tranportation services for targeted customers
	2. Customer management software program implementation
	3. Customer Service Training

211

Adapted from material presented in *Balanced Scorecard Step-by-Step: Maximizing Performance and Maintaining Results.*

- *Owner.* Not only does the Balanced Scorecard transmit to the entire organization what your key strategies for success are, but it also creates a climate of accountability for results. Central to the idea of accountability is the establishment of owners for each and every measure. Simply put, the owner is the individual responsible for results. Should the indicator's performance begin to decline, it's the owner you look to for answers and a plan to bring results back in line with expectations. The example lists a specific individual as the owner of the measure; however, some organizations feel more comfortable assigning ownership to a function, not a person. They rationalize that while people may come and go, functions tend to remain, and assigning the ownership to a function assures the responsibilities inherent in the task are not lost when a new person comes on board. This argument has merits, but I recommend you use actual names rather than functions. Not that people will hide behind their titles, but an employee who sees his or her name associated with the performance of a key organizational measure will tend to promote more action and accountability than will a job function.

- *Strategy.* Displays the specific strategy you believe the measure will positively influence.

- *Objective.* Every measure was created as a translation of a specific objective. Use this space to identify the relevant objective.

- *Description.* After reading the measure name, most people will immediately jump to the measure description, and it is therefore possibly the most important piece of information on the entire template. Your challenge is to draft a description that concisely and accurately captures the essence of the measure so that anyone reading it will be able to quickly grasp why the measure is critical to the organization. In the example, we rapidly learn that customer satisfaction is based on a percentage, what that percentage is derived from (survey questions), and how the measure will help to achieve the strategy of expanding program offerings.

Measure Characteristics

This section captures the "meat and potatoes" aspects of the measure you'll need when you begin reporting results.

- *Lag/Lead.* Outline whether the measure is a core outcome indicator or a performance driver. Remember that your Scorecard represents a hypothesis of your strategy implementation. When you begin analyzing your results over time, you'll want to test the relationships you believe exist between your lag and lead measures.

- *Frequency.* How often do you plan to report performance on this measure? Most organizations have measures that report performance on a daily, weekly, monthly, quarterly, semiannual, or annual basis. However, I have seen unique time frames, such as school year for one government agency. I also recommend that you attempt to limit the number of semi-annual and annual measures you use on your Scorecard. A measure that is updated only once a year is of limited value when you use the Scorecard as a management tool to make adjustments based on performance results.

- *Unit Type.* This characteristic identifies how the measure will be expressed. Commonly used unit types include numbers, dollars, and percentages.

- *Polarity.* When assessing the performance of a measure, you need to know whether high values reflect good or bad performance. In most cases, this is very straightforward. We all know that lower costs and increased employee satisfaction are good, while a high value for complaints reflects performance that requires improvement. However, in some cases, the polarity issue can prove quite challenging. Take the example of a public health organization. If it chooses to measure caseload of social workers, will high values be good or bad? A high number of cases per social worker might suggest great efficiency and effectiveness on the part of the individual workers. Conversely, it could mean the social workers are juggling far too many clients and providing mediocre service in an attempt to inflate their caseload numbers. In cases like this, you may want to institute a "dual polarity." For example, up to 25 cases per social worker may be considered good, but anything over 25 would be a cause for concern, and necessitate action.

Calculation and Data Specifications

Information contained in this section of the dictionary may be the most important, yet most difficult to gather. To begin reporting your measures, precise formulas are necessary, and sources of data must be clearly identified.

- *Formula.* In the formula box, provide the specific elements of the calculation for the performance measure.

- *Data Source.* Every measure must be derived from somewhere—an existing management report, third-party vendor-supplied information, customer databases, the general ledger, and others. In this section you should rigorously attempt to supply as detailed information as possible. If the information is sourced from a current report, what is the report titled, and on which line number does the specific information reside? Also, when can you access the data? This information is important to your Scorecard reporting cycle since you'll be relying on the schedules of others when producing your Scorecard. The more information you provide here, the easier it will be to begin actually producing Balanced Scorecard reports with real data. Conversely, if you provide vague data sources, or no information at all, you will find it exceedingly difficult to report on the measure later. An admonition: Spend the time you need to thoroughly complete this section. I have seen a number of Scorecards proceed swiftly through the development stage only to stall at the time of reporting because the actual data could not be identified or easily collected.

- *Data Quality.* Use this area of the template to comment on the condition of the data you expect to use when reporting Scorecard results. If the data is produced automatically from a source system, and can be easily accessed, it can be considered "high." If, however, you rely on an analyst's Word document that is in turn based on some other colleague's Access database numbers that emanate from an old legacy system, then you may consider the quality "low." Assessing data quality is important for a couple of reasons: Pragmatically, you need to know which performance measures may present an issue when you begin reporting your results. Knowing in advance what to expect will help you develop strategies to ensure the data you need is produced in a timely and accurate fashion. Second, data-quality issues may also help direct resource questions at your organization. If the information is truly critical to strategic success, but current data quality is low, perhaps the organization should invest in systems to mine the data more effectively.

- *Data Collector.* In the first section of the template you identified the owner of the measure as that individual who is accountable for results. Often, this is not the person you would expect to provide the actual performance data. In the example, L. Hess is accountable for the performance of the measure, but S. Commons serves as the actual data contact.

Performance Information

In the final section of the template you note your current level of performance, suggest targets for the future, and outline specific initiatives you'll use to achieve those targets.

- *Baseline.* Users of the Balanced Scorecard will be very interested in the current level of performance for all measures. For those owning the challenge of developing targets, the baseline is critical in their work.

- *Target.* Some of you may be saying right now, "At this point in the process, we haven't set targets, so what do we do?" Fortunately, some of your measures may already have targets. For example, perhaps you've currently stated an expectation to cut costs by 15 percent next year. Wherever targets exist, use them now. For those measures that don't currently have targets, you can leave this section blank and complete it once the targets have been finalized. For those of you who do have at least some targets, list them based on the frequency of the measure. In this example, I've shown quarterly customer satisfaction targets. Some organizations may find it difficult to establish monthly or quarterly targets and instead opt for an annual target; but track performance toward that end on a monthly or quarterly basis.

- *Target Rationale.* As in the preceding paragraph, this will apply only to those measures for which you currently have a performance target. The rationale provides users with background on how you arrived at the particular target(s). Did it come from an executive planning retreat? Is it an incremental improvement based on historical results? Was it based on a mandate? For people to galvanize around the achievement of a target, they need to know how it was developed, and that while it may represent a stretch, it isn't merely wishful thinking on the part of an overzealous senior management team.

- *Initiatives.* At any given time, most organizations will have dozens of initiatives or projects swirling about. Often, only those closest to the project know anything about it, hence any possible synergies between initiatives are never realized. The Scorecard provides you with a wonderful opportunity to evaluate your initiatives in the context of their strategic significance. If an initiative or project cannot be linked to the successful accomplishment of your strategy, you have to ask yourself why it is being funded and pursued. Use this section of the template to map current or anticipated initiatives to specific performance measures.

TARGETS

What Are Performance Targets? Why Are They Important to the Balanced Scorecard?

Poet, painter, and novelist Kahlil Gibran once noted, *"To understand the heart and mind of a person, look not at what he has already achieved, but at what he aspires to do."* We all have aspirations, which range from the grand—writing the great American novel—to the practical—painting the back fence before the first snowfall. Targets bring our aspirations to life and give us something to shoot for in the quest for improvement. The young writer may set a target of writing 10 pages per day, while the suburban homeowner may vow to paint the fence over two weekends in November. Both actions will lead to improved overall results in their specific situations.

In the context of a Balanced Scorecard, targets represent the desired result of a performance measure. By comparing actual performance results against a predetermined target, you receive information that is imbued with value and meaning. For example, knowing your city can fill a pothole within two days of notice means very little until you know that neighboring jurisdictions can do it in one, and the best organizations can do it in three hours. Armed with this information, you might establish a target of filling potholes within two hours of notification. With the target in place, you have a point of reference toward which to guide your actions, decisions, and resource allocations. As a result, improvement, not the status quo, is reinforced and communicated.

Targets are powerful communication tools, informing the entire organization of the expected level of performance required to achieve success. As a result, they typically drive a focus on continuous improvement, as the organization strives to constantly better its performance. Targets also provide a mechanism for the organization and its customers to gauge management effectiveness and foster accountability. The Environmental Protection Agency (EPA) used performance targets when it launched its "33/50" program in 1988. The goal of the program was to work with industries in an effort to have them voluntarily reduce toxic waste levels a full 50 percent by 1995, with an interim goal of 33 percent by 1992. Before the deadlines were reached, both targets were accomplished.[27]

Types of Performance Targets

If we define a target as "desired result of a performance measure," there is a strong connotation of an orientation toward the future. Targets represent our goals for some period that has yet to elapse. They may be established by month, quarter, half-year, year, or multiyears.

Targets encompassing a longer period of time, generally a number of years, are often termed stretch targets. Their purpose is keeping the organization focused on a long-term goal that is in alignment with its vision and mission. In the EPA example cited, a 50 percent reduction in toxic waste over a seven-year period is clearly a stretch target. The achievement of stretch targets will often require the organization to abandon the status quo and dramatically alter the way it does business in order to meet the dramatic challenge represented by the lofty target.

The caveat with any stretch target is that it contain some semblance of realism. A target that simply reflects the wishful thinking of an overzealous management team is certain to be greeted with tremendous skepticism by employees, and could actually prove debilitating to performance. Before establishing a stretch target you hope will transform your organization:

- Confirm that reaching the target is truly critical to your success.
- Determine whether you possess the skills within your organization to help you reach the target.
- Gauge the organization's willingness to accept a challenge of this magnitude. A workforce lacking the necessary motivation to beat the target will probably result in a Sisyphean endeavor.

Most organizations will develop annual performance targets for their performance measures. In keeping with the theme of cause and effect, which is so critical to the Balanced Scorecard, the achievement of annual performance targets will help lead to the accomplishment of longer-term stretch targets. Whenever possible, it is desirable to decompose annual targets into increments corresponding to your Scorecard reporting frequency. For example, assume you have a customer satisfaction target of 90 percent for the year. If you survey your customers more than once a year, break down the target. Perhaps you'll be shooting for 75 percent in the first quarter, 80 in the second, 85 in the third, and finally 90 at year-end. Rather than waiting until the end of the year to take action on the results, you can now make customer satisfaction a regular and routine part of your operational decision-making process.

Setting Performance Targets

A recent survey of more than 500 studies indicates that performance increases by an average of 16 percent in companies that establish targets.[28] Why have performance targets proven to be so effective? Maybe there is more at work here than just the motivational power of a goal. Actually, social scientists have long argued that we humans will always align with our commitments.[29] As a result, when we make public commitments, such as those in a written performance target, we tend to stick with them. A classic 1955 experiment in which students were asked to estimate the lengths of lines on a screen supports this assertion. Some students were asked to write down their estimates, sign them, and turn them over to the researcher. Others were asked to write them down on an erasable slate, then erase the slate immediately. A third group was instructed to keep their decisions to themselves. The researchers then presented all three groups with evidence that their initial choices may have been wrong. By a wide margin, those most reluctant to shift from their original choices were those in the group who had signed and handed them to the researcher. Those who made a public commitment were the most hesitant to move away from that pledge. This underscores the importance of having written performance targets as part of your Balanced Scorecard. Their achievement may just be human nature!

The advice most often associated with setting targets is to keep them realistic, yet challenging. This is proven and practical advice, especially for closely scrutinized government and nonprofit agencies. Not only will your missteps cause you to lose organizational momentum, but you may be forced to see your results featured on the local news.

Setting targets can represent new territory for some nonprofit and pubic agencies. Often the challenge lies in knowing where to search for meaningful sources of target information. Here are a number of potential areas to consider when setting your targets:

- *Trends and baselines.* The first place to look when setting a performance target is current results on the metric. Examining past data and trends will allow you to choose a target representing a meaningful challenge, while staying within the ballpark of reality.

- *National, state, local, or industry averages.* Many organizations monitor the performance of government and nonprofit agencies, and offer a ready supply of potential target information on wide variety of performance variables. In the public sector, both the Governmental Accounting Standards Board (GASB) and the International City/County Management Association (ICMA) provide relevant performance measurement information.

- *Employees.* Never forget that those closest to the action are frequently in the best position to provide insight on what represents a meaningful target. Involving employees in the process not only makes great sense based on the knowledge they possess, but not approaching them could lead to alienation and lack of buy-in, leading to decreased attention to the target. As Samuel Butler wrote nearly 300 years ago, *"He that complies against his will/Is of his own opinion still."*

- *Other agencies.* While private-sector firms tend to hold their information close to the vest for competitive purposes, public and nonprofit agencies embrace a willingness to share and learn from one another. Talk to your colleagues at other agencies in an effort to glean insights from their experiences.

- *Feedback from customers and other stakeholders.* The goal in all this is improving results for customers, so why not ask them what they expect from your agency?

INITIATIVES

We've covered a lot of ground in the past two chapters. We examined the steps necessary to develop a strategy map of performance objectives, translated those objectives into performance measures, and, most recently, considered the role of performance targets. One step remains in the development of our Balanced Scorecard, one that will translate our targets into reality: initiative setting.

Initiatives are the specific programs, activities, projects, or actions you will engage in to help ensure you meet or exceed your performance targets. An initiative could be anything from building a customer service portal on your Web site to launching a career development program for employees to redesigning your financial management system. While the nature of initiatives will vary tremendously, the common thread that should run through all is a linkage to strategic objectives, measures, and targets.

Most organizations do not suffer from a lack of initiatives. In fact, many government and nonprofit agencies will be bursting at the seams with initiatives, since they frequently begin their performance management efforts with initiative development. The logic works this way: We'll engage in this initiative in order to better meet our needs or our customers' needs, and then we'll develop goals and objectives to track our progress. As I noted earlier in the book, I believe this approach is fundamentally flawed. Mission, values, and vision always come first. Strategy follows, and outlines the broad priorities necessary for success. Next up are performance objectives and measures, which tell us what we must excel at to execute the strategy and how we'll gauge our progress. Targets supply a star to shoot for, and, finally, initiatives are put in place that will help us achieve our targets.

Ensuring That Initiatives Support Your Strategy

A careful analysis of your current crop of initiatives may reveal the seemingly contradictory finding that simultaneously you have too many and too few.[30] You may have any number of initiatives vying for scarce human and financial resources that have literally no effect on the ability to implement your strategy. Concurrently, your Balanced Scorecard may identify entirely new performance objectives and measures that are not represented by a single initiative.

A useful exercise to undertake upon completing your Scorecard is to map current organizational initiatives to your Scorecard objectives. Any initiative that cannot demonstrate a clear linkage to an objective, hence, to your quest of strategy implementation, should be considered a strong candidate for removal. If you're searching for a quick economic payoff to justify your investment in the Balanced Scorecard, this step could be it. Consider the potential drain of organizational resources an ineffective initiative represents. Naturally, financial resources have been committed to it that would be better served elsewhere. Additionally, staff time and attention have been diverted from strategic endeavors in the pursuit of activities that really produce no value. Using the crystal-clear focus provided by the Scorecard, you can put your current initiatives under the microscope and ferret out those that really contribute to value from those that merely suck up all-too-scarce human and financial resources.

The first step in mapping initiatives to objectives involves seeking out each and every initiative currently being sponsored within the organization. Since all initiatives entail the allocation of financial resources, your finance team may be able to provide you with a list of current projects. Next you should create a grid similar to the one shown in Exhibit 9.5. Scorecard objectives are listed on the left side of the document, while initiatives are outlined across the top. Your considerable challenge is to critically examine each initiative in light of all Balanced Scorecard objectives. To conduct such an analysis in a meaningful fashion requires you to perform a good deal of "due diligence" on each of the initiatives. Read background on the project, speak with the sponsor, and review financial information to ensure you have a solid understanding of the project's true essence. For those initiatives that support Scorecard objectives, put a check in the corresponding box of the grid. Any initiatives that do not meet your criteria of being strategic in nature should be carefully reviewed, possibly reduced in scope, or even discontinued.

Exhibit 9.5　Mapping Initiative to Balanced Scorecard Objectives

Perspective	Objectives	Initiatives													
Customer															
Internal Processes															
Employee Learning and Growth															
Financial															

Adapted from material presented in *Balanced Scorecard Step-by-Step: Maximizing Performance and Maintaining Results.*

Eliminating initiatives that don't contribute to your strategy frees up valuable resources within the agency. These resources, both human and financial, can now be directed toward drafting new initiatives that do in fact propel you toward your goals. You'll be amazed at how imaginative your team can be when it comes to creating new initiatives. Take the case of the Boston Lyric Opera (BLO).[31] Employees at this performing arts company rose to the call and suggested a number of inventive approaches to achieving targets. The most successful initiative to emerge was the production of "Carmen on the Common." To meet the Scorecard objective of increasing community support, the BLO staged two free outdoor performances of the classic opera before appreciative audiences of more than 130,000 people. What better way to increase community support than to bring opera to the public? For many who took advantage of this unique opportunity, it was their first exposure to opera, but most assuredly will not be their last. Only a creative approach resulting from the discussion of Scorecard initiatives could lead to such a breakthrough.

SUMMARY

With a strategy map in place, this chapter focused on the remaining components of a Balanced Scorecard system: measures, targets, and initiatives. Performance measures are considered standards used to evaluate and communicate performance against expected results. Many organizations have a long history of performance measurement, but tend to be tracking the wrong things. Gauging actual program results has been absent from most measurement efforts. Three types of performance measures are typically used: inputs, outputs, and outcomes. The Balanced Scorecard should contain all three. Additionally, the Scorecard should include both lag and lead indicators of performance.

Organizations using the Balanced Scorecard do not have to choose one customer group over another for inclusion in the Customer perspective. The many and varied groups representing your customer base may be housed within this perspective. Asking "what do our customers demand or expect from us?" will often yield effective customer measures. Many customer measures will fall under one of four categories: access, timeliness, selection, and efficiency. Customer value propositions have also been used by some organizations to generate customer metrics. Customer intimacy, operational excellence, and product leadership are the value propositions typically encountered.

The Internal Processes perspective challenges the organization to determine the key processes at which they must excel in order to meet or exceed customer needs. Measures for this perspective should "flow," or act as further translations of those appearing in the Customer perspective. Among the key processes frequently analyzed in this perspective are: quality, innovation, partnering, marketing, and fundraising.

Often overlooked during Scorecard development is the Employee Learning and Growth perspective. Despite the fact that over 75 percent of value in today's organizations derives from intangibles, many fail to develop meaningful measures in this perspective. A properly constructed Employee Learning and Growth perspective should contain measures relating to human capital (training, retention, succession), information capital (access to information), and a climate for positive action (communication, satisfaction, alignment).

Every Balanced Scorecard requires a Financial perspective. Public and nonprofit organizations must ensure products and services are delivered with a balance of efficiency and effectiveness. Measures in the Financial perspective help to strike that balance. Elements to consider when creating measures here include: price of the product or service, revenue enhancement, and the state of financial systems.

A number of criteria should be considered when selecting your final group of Balanced Scorecard measures. They include: linkage to strategy, ease of understanding, linkage in the chain of cause and effect, frequency of updating, accessibility, use of averages, date relation, quantitative orientation, and tendency toward dysfunction. The Balanced Scorecard should contain an adequate amount of performance measures to tell your unique story. That said, in practice, a Scorecard with fewer measures will be easier to report and communicate. Before finalizing your measures, employees should be given the opportunity to provide feedback and input on your choices. Open houses, town hall meetings, and direct discussions may all be used when introducing your staff to the measures you've selected. Once you've settled on a group of measures for your Scorecard, cataloging them in a performance measure data dictionary will facilitate the reporting process.

Targets represent the desired result of a performance measure. Balanced Scorecard results have little meaning unless compared to a performance target. Targets may be long-term in nature—stretch targets—or short-term, typically annual in duration. A number of sources exist to help you develop your targets. They include: trends and baselines; national, state, local, or industry averages; employees; other agencies; and feedback from other customers and stakeholders.

Initiatives are the specific programs, projects, or action plans you put in place in an attempt to achieve your performance targets. Ironically, many organizations will have simultaneously too many and too few initiatives in place at any given time. Initiatives used to drive Scorecard targets are strategic in nature. Every organization should analyze their initiatives in light of strategy, and consider discontinuing those that do not assist in its execution.

NOTES

1. From "The President's Management Agenda," at http://www.whitehouse.gov/omb/budget/fy2002/mgmt.pdf, Fiscal Year 2002.
2. Margaret C. Plantz, Martha Taylor Greenway, and Michael Hendricks, "Outcome Measurement: Showing Results in the Nonprofit Sector," *New Directions for Evaluation*, Fall 1997.
3. Deborah L. Kerr, "The Balanced Scorecard in the Public Sector," *Perform Magazine*, Vol. I, No. 8, pp. 4–9.
4. Rudolph W. Giuliani, *Leadership* (New York: Hyperion, 2002), p. 87.
5. As quoted in Peter F. Drucker, *Managing the Non-Profit Organization* (New York: HarperBusiness, 1990), p. 36.
6. Michael Allison and Jude Kaye, *Strategic Planning for Nonprofit Organizations* (New York: John Wiley & Sons, Inc., 1997).
7. Harry P. Hatry, "Where the Rubber Meets the Road: Performance Measurement for State and Local Public Agencies," *New Directions for Evaluation*, Fall 1997.
8. Donald C. Cook, "ACSI Commentary: Federal Government Scores," from www.theacsi.org/government/govt-02c.html. December 16, 2002.
9. Marcus Buckingham and Curt Coffman, *First Break All the Rules* (New York: Simon & Schuster, 1999), p. 128.
10. From interview with Nancy Foltz, September 19, 2002.
11. Jean Philippe Deschamps and P. Ranganath Nayak, *Product Juggernauts: How Companies Mobilize to Generate a Stream of Market Winners* (Boston: Harvard Business School Press, 1995).
12. Christine W. Letts, William P. Ryan, and Allen Grossman, *High-Performance Nonprofit Organizations* (New York: John Wiley & Sons, Inc., 1999), p. 67.
13. Michael E. Porter and Mark R. Kramer, "The Competitive Advantage of Corporate Philanthropy," *Harvard Business Review*, December, 2002, pp. 56–68.
14. Thomas Wolf, *Managing a Nonprofit Organization in the Twenty-First Century* (New York: Fireside, 1999), p. 162.
15. David P. Norton, in Foreword to: Brian E. Becker, Mark A. Huselid, and Dave Ulrich, *The HR Scorecard* (Boston: Harvard Business School Press, 2001).
16. Marcus Buckingham and Curt Coffman, *First Break All the Rules* (New York: Simon & Schuster, 1999), p. 89.
17. Ibid., p. 93.
18. From "The President's Management Agenda," at http://www.whitehouse.gov/omb/budget/fy2002/mgmt.pdf, Fiscal Year 2002.
19. Ibid.
20. Palmer Morrel-Samuels, "Getting the Truth into Workplace Surveys," *Harvard Business Review*, February 2002, pp. 111–118.
21. Ibid.

22. Stephen Taub, "Dazed and Confused," *CFO.com*, September 11, 2002.

23. From "The President's Management Agenda," at http://www.whitehouse.gov/omb/budget/fy2002/mgmt.pdf, Fiscal Year 2002.

24. Institute of Management and Administration, "20 Best Practice Budgeting Insights: How Controllers Promote Faster, Better Decisions," 2001.

25. Paul R. Niven, *Balanced Scorecard Step-by-Step: Maximizing Performance and Maintaining Results* (New York: John Wiley & Sons, Inc., 2002), p. 162.

26. The bulk of this section has been drawn from *Balanced Scorecard Step by Step: Maximizing Performance and Maintaining Results*. Minor modifications have been made.

27. Jonathan Walters, *Measuring Up* (Washington, DC: Governing Books, 1998), p. 74.

28. Edwin A. Locke, "Motivation by Goal Setting," *Harvard Business Review*, November 2001.

29. Robert B. Cialdini, "Harnessing the Science of Persuasion," *Harvard Business Review*, October 2001, pp. 72–79

30. Robert S. Kaplan and David P. Norton, *The Balanced Scorecard* (Boston: Harvard Business School Press, 1996).

31. Robert S. Kaplan, "The Balanced Scorecard and Nonprofit Organizations," *Balanced Scorecard Report*, November–December 2002, pp. 1–4.

PART FOUR

Maximizing the Effectiveness of the Balanced Scorecard

CHAPTER 10

Creating Alignment by Cascading the Balanced Scorecard

Roadmap for Chapter Ten There is a great story about former President Lyndon B. Johnson touring Cape Canaveral during the space race to the moon. During his visit, the president came across a man mopping the floor, and asked him, "What's your position here?" The gentleman looked up from his pail and proudly replied, "I'm sending a man to the moon." Such is the power of alignment, when every person, regardless of role or rank, possesses a clear line of sight between his or her job and the organization's loftiest goals.

You may not be sending a man to the moon, but then again maybe you are. Whatever you're working toward requires the total commitment and alignment of all your people. This chapter will discuss how the Balanced Scorecard can be used to drive organizational alignment from top to bottom, through the process of cascading. We'll explore what the concept is all about, why it's critical to both employees and the organization, and examine techniques you can use to develop aligned Scorecards at your agency.

WHAT IS CASCADING?

A recent study by consulting firm Watson Wyatt revealed that only about half (49 percent) of employees understand the steps their companies are taking to reach new business goals. This represents a 20 percent drop since 2000. Ilene Gochman, Watson Wyatt's national practice leader for organizational effectiveness added, *"There is tremendous positive impact to the bottom line when employees see strong connections between company goals and their jobs. Many employees aren't seeing that connection."*[1] Although nonprofits and public-sector organizations are not bottom-line-driven, you too will benefit greatly when employees see the connection between what they do every day and how those actions affect overall goals.

Cascading the Balanced Scorecard is a method designed to bridge the considerable learning gap that exists in most organizations. Specifically, cascading refers to the process of developing Balanced Scorecards at every level of your organization. The Scorecards constructed at lower levels will align with your highest-level Balanced Scorecard by identifying the objectives and measures lower-level groups will track in order to gauge their contribution to overall success. Some objectives and measures will be used throughout the organization, and appear on every Scorecard; employee satisfaction is a good example. However, in many respects the real value of cascaded Scorecards is evident from the unique objectives and measures lower-level groups engineer to signal their specific contribution to overall strategy implementation. When I introduced this concept to one client recently, a participant half-jokingly commented, "So you're not talking about the stuff I use to clean my dishes?" We're not talking about Cascade™ dishwasher detergent here, but the cascading process will clean away something far more important: the misunderstanding and confusion existing between employee and organizational goals.

Peter Drucker has commented, *"The nonprofit must be information-based. It must be structured around information that flows up from the individuals doing the work to the people at the top—the ones who are, in the end, accountable—and around information flowing down. This flow of information is essential because a nonprofit organization has to be a learning organization."*[2] Every organization today must learn continuously in order to survive the unprecedented changes we witness on almost a daily basis. Cascading facilitates learning by fostering a two-way flow of information up and down the organizational hierarchy (see Exhibit 10.1). As Scorecards are created at lower levels of the organization, employees of every function and rank are given the opportunity to demonstrate how their actions can lead to improved results for everyone. Simultaneously, as results are analyzed across the agency, leaders benefit from the ability to view results that span their organization. Analysis is no longer limited to a few high-level indicators that must serve as abstractions for an entire agency; instead, cascaded Scorecards provide real-time data for decision making, resource allocation, and, most importantly, strategic learning.

In the public sector, cascading should be considered more of a necessity than a luxury or option presented by the Balanced Scorecard. Achieving results in the public domain demands collaboration from a vast web of groups, often spanning levels and service functions. As an example, parents attempting to secure health insurance for their children could simultaneously be interacting with government health insurance specialists, immunization providers, and family counselors. Each of these groups play a vital part in helping the parents achieve their goal of obtaining insurance for their children, therefore, each must document this contribution in the form of performance measures on the Balanced Scorecard. Taken cumulatively, the actions of program providers across the enterprise will move the agency ever closer to achieving its overall mission.[3]

Exhibit 10.1   Knowledge and Information Flow Two Ways When Cascading the Balanced Scorecard

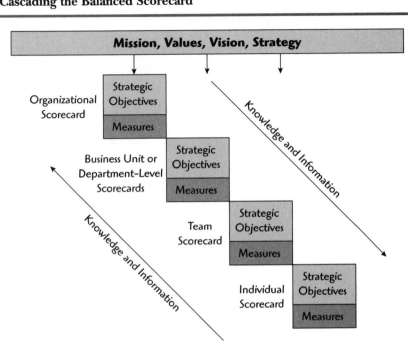

The Search for Meaning

Man's Search for Meaning is among the most powerful and gripping books I have ever read. In it, Austrian psychiatrist Viktor Frankl describes his experiences as he clung to life in a Nazi concentration camp. He had lost everything, and yet it was his discovery that a greater purpose can allow us to rise above even the bleakest of circumstances that led to his psychological emancipation from the Nazis. He used the experience in the development of "logotherapy," which focuses on the meaning of human existence as well as on man's search for such a meaning.[4]

Does man's search for meaning end upon entering the workplace? Does the first ring from the phone on our desk erase any existential cravings? The answer is an unequivocal no. Now, more than ever, people from all walks of life expect more than just a paycheck from their jobs; they demand a higher purpose. Nowhere is this more evident than in the public and nonprofit arenas where employees are typically compelled by the organization's guiding mission and values. Employees are asking, "Why is my organization important to society; how does it contribute something of value?" A lack of alignment between personal objectives and broad organizational goals obscures any hope of discovering true meaning and contribution through our work. Cascading the Balanced Scorecard restores the promise of organizations to help all employees find meaning in their chosen professions. The creation of objectives and measures, which forge a direct link to high-level goals, provides all employees with the opportunity to demonstrate that what they're doing every day is indeed critical to success.

THE CASCADING PROCESS

One very successful corporation that grasps the importance of alignment is Honda Motors. This probably stems from its founder Soichiro Honda, who described the sacred obligations of senior leadership this way:

1. Craft a vision: what we will be.
2. Create goals: what four or five things we must do to get there.
3. Alignment: translate the work of each person into alignment with the goals.

He's really describing the process of cascading performance measures very well. First we craft the vision that will guide the organization. Next we develop key performance measures we can track, and finally we translate the work of each person into alignment with the goals. Honda didn't go on to say how to create alignment, but we now know the best way to do that is through cascading performance measures. Everyone in the organization should develop a few key measures that demonstrate how they can contribute to the organization's overall goals. In this section we'll examine how you can successfully align employee objectives and measures throughout the organization.

Develop Implementation Principles

Just stop for a moment to reflect upon how far you will have traveled to get to this point in your Balanced Scorecard implementation. It began as an idea—perhaps someone read an article, attended a seminar, or learned of the Scorecard from a colleague. You then undertook the challenging tasks of forming your team; gathering materials; reviewing your mission, values, vision, and strategy; and, finally, developing objectives and measures. It would be an understatement to suggest that you learned a thing or two about the Balanced Scorecard and its implementation at your organization along the way. Before you begin your cascading efforts, pause for a moment to reflect on and catalog those key learnings.

The Balanced Scorecard you've created is a true team effort. Your cross-functional team contributed the knowledge that exists in every far corner of your agency to craft a Scorecard that will clearly articulate your strategic story. However, going forward, the cascading process may represent more of a diffused effort. Your team members will now carry forward the responsibility of leading the development of cascaded Scorecards within their work group or business unit. Consistent implementation practices across the organization are an absolute must should you hope to gain the benefits offered by true strategic alignment. To ensure your cascading efforts are consistent and aligned, consider convening your Balanced Scorecard team and all those individuals who will have a hand in leading the development of cascaded Scorecards. A one-day session in which you review the lessons you've learned along the way, and specifically document the principles you expect to employ going forward, will go a long way toward ensuring you create Scorecards that paint a consistent picture.

A client of mine recently devoted an entire day to this process, and developed a number of implementation principles to be used on a go-forward basis. Here's a sampling of those principles:

- The implementation team agreed that cascaded Scorecards should be *content-specific*, representing the unique characteristics of each group. People will only support what they create; therefore, encouraging unique—but aligned—Scorecards is critical to success. Common language will be encouraged where appropriate.

- Terminology must be consistent throughout the organization. We'll all use the four perspectives of the BSC (Customer, Financial, Internal Processes, and Employee Learning and Growth), and the terms objective, measure, target, and initiative. The group agreed that despite the widespread use of these terms, there is a need for further education to ensure we're all speaking the same language.

- At the corporate level, we've made the conscious decision to limit the number of performance measures to only the critical few. The implementation team supports this decision, but does not believe there should be a "cap" placed on the number of measures appearing on a cascaded Balanced Scorecard. Each should have a reasonable number, reflecting the influence of the group. Checks and balances, and reviews will be critical to ensure the Scorecard is utilized as a management tool and not merely a reporting system or "measures inventory."

- Personal performance objectives should be linked to the Balanced Scorecard. All leaders and managers should have the development of a Balanced Scorecard for their area as part of their personal goals, (i.e., advancing the Scorecard among their groups).

- It was recommended that Balanced Scorecard understanding be included as a key leadership competence within the organization. The leadership group is relied upon to embrace and share this tool, and as such must have the requisite knowledge of the tool to make this happen.

- Communication of the Balanced Scorecard and the development process will be critical as we cascade throughout the organization.

- Team leaders (first-level managers) are vital to the acceptance of the Scorecard. The majority of employees receive their information from their managers, and look to them for guidance and support. Among the ideas discussed and tools suggested for this group were: support tools, educational materials, a road show, and a "boot camp." Their commitment and use of the Balanced Scorecard is a critical success factor.

- The group felt we must share learnings as a team, and communicate regularly. Much of the early success of the Balanced Scorecard will be anecdotal in nature, and these stories, learnings, and so on must be circulated and shared. The Web site was proposed as a possible method of distribution. The team also felt that we would need to meet regularly to discuss, monitor, and support a successful implementation.

Notice the broad range of important topics that were discussed, debated, and ultimately agreed upon as core principles in this session. We learned that this organization will focus on aligned, but individualized, Scorecards. They insist on using consistent terminology during the process. While no cap on the number of measures has been suggested, they are providing guidance that a lower number is desirable. In addition to cascading principles, the team deliberated over how to further communicate the Scorecard, the core audience for communication, and how to accomplish their goals for the upcoming year. With these principles clearly articulated and understood by all key players, this organization is in a strong position to achieve great results from its cascading efforts.

Ensure Understanding of Your Highest-Level Scorecard before Cascading

You may have hesitated to write objective statements as described in Chapter Eight, or bristled at the thought of completing the data dictionaries in Chapter Nine, but you're about to receive the payback for those arduous tasks. They are just two of the tools you can use to ensure everyone involved in the Scorecard cascading process has a detailed understanding of your highest-level Balanced Scorecard.

Your high-level Balanced Scorecard represents the starting point for your cascading journey. It contains the objectives and measures that weave through the four perspectives, informing everyone of your strategic story. For those individuals shouldering the responsibility of leading cascading efforts, knowledge of this Scorecard is vital. Imagine someone leading a Scorecard effort in a lower-level department and beginning the session with a comment like this, "Okay, we say here on the high-level Scorecard we're going to delight the customer. I don't really know what that means; what do you think?" Not exactly the stuff oratorical legends are made of. Contrast that with someone who possesses a deep understanding of high-level objectives. He or she is in a position to offer something of this nature: "'Delight the customer' is our first customer objective. This is critical to our strategy of expanding into new services since current clients will often be our best source of referral information. We'll measure it using quarterly surveys consisting of five questions...." Context has been established, which will allow for thought-provoking and beneficial conversations about the objective.

Understanding of your Scorecard is achieved mainly through communication and education. You have a number of tools at your disposal. Consider any of the following: your intranet, presentations from Scorecard team members, Scorecard brochures, newsletters, or town hall meetings.

"Influence" Is the Key to Cascading

The goal of cascading is to provide all groups within your organization the opportunity to demonstrate how their actions contribute to overall success. To do this, each group must ask itself how its members can in fact influence the objectives appearing on higher-level Scorecards. Let's use Exhibit 10.2 to review this concept.

It all begins with your highest-level Scorecard, what some would refer to as the *corporate-level* or *organizationwide Scorecard.* The objectives and measures appearing on this Scorecard represent what you consider to be the critical variables driving your success. Therefore, every Scorecard subsequently created at all levels of the organization should link back to this document.

The first level of cascading occurs as business units (as described in Exhibit 10.2; your terminology may differ) examine the high-level Scorecard and ask themselves, "Which of these objectives can we influence?" The answers to that question will form the basis for their individual Balanced Scorecards. Chances are, they won't be able to exert an impact on each and every objective appearing on the high-level Scorecard. After all, organizations build value by combining the disparate skills of all employees within every function. Therefore, each group should, rightly, focus on the objectives and measures over which they may exert an influence. However, if a group is unable to demonstrate a link to any objectives, you should seriously consider what value they are adding to the whole. The business unit may choose to use the language shown in the high-level Scorecard or create objectives and measures that more accurately reflect the true essence of how it adds value to the organization.

Exhibit 10.2   The Cascading Process

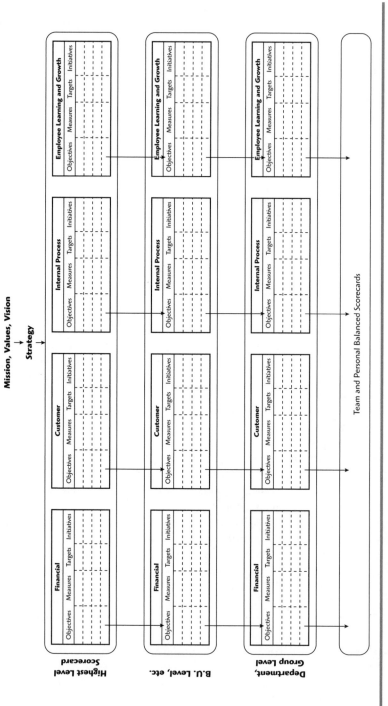

From *Balanced Scorecard Step-by-Step: Maximizing Performance and Maintaining Results*, Paul R. Niven (John Wiley & Sons, Inc., 2002).

Once business units have developed Balanced Scorecards, the groups below them are ready to take part in the process. Individual departments will now review the Scorecard of the business unit to which they report, and determine which of the objectives they can influence. Their Scorecards are formed by making that determination. Once again, they may use similarly termed objectives and measures or develop unique names for their Scorecard elements.

Let's look at an example of cascading using a fictional city government organization. Exhibit 10.3 provides excerpts from Scorecards at three levels of this organization, which will demonstrate the principles of cascading just discussed.

Within the Customer perspective, the city has chosen an objective of providing safe, convenient transportation. To gauge its effectiveness on this objective, it will measure the increase in average ridership of public transportation. A 10 percent increase for the year is the target it is aiming for.

Exhibit 10.3   Cascading the Balanced Scorecard

City Scorecard

Perspective	Objective	Measure	Target
Customer	Provide safe, convenient transportation.	Increase in average ridership of public transportation.	10%

Department of Transportation Scorecard

Perspective	Objective	Measure	Target
Customer	Provide safe, convenient transportation.	Percentage of fleet available	90%

Operations Group Scorecard

Perspective	Objective	Measure	Target
Customer	Provide safe, convenient transportation.	Percentage of vehicle repairs completed within 24 hours	75%

The Department of Transportation is one of several business units within the city. When developing its own Balanced Scorecard, organizers begin by closely inspecting the city's Scorecard to determine which of the objectives appearing on that Scorecard they could influence. As is the case with all city business units, the employees of the Department of Transportation are anxious to show how their important work links to the city's overall goals. When reviewing the city's Customer perspective, they see the objective of providing safe, convenient transportation and feel they have a strong impact on this objective. They too have a goal of providing safe and convenient transportation, so they carry the objective forward to their own Scorecard. However, the measure of increased ridership is not considered appropriate for them. It's a critical indicator, but they would like to develop a measure that indicates how they influence ridership. They conclude that by ensuring availability of the city's entire fleet of public transportation vehicles every day, they can help the city increase ridership. Hence, they measure the percentage of the fleet that is available.

Several groups comprise the Department of Transportation, one of which is the Operations Department. Among its many responsibilities is ensuring that the city's fleet of transportation vehicles is serviced efficiently. When developing the department's Balanced Scorecard, staff begin by reviewing the Scorecard of the business unit to which they report, the Department of Transportation. Upon review, they see the objective of providing safe and convenient transportation. They feel they can impact this objective, and thus choose it for their own Customer perspective. They ask themselves how they might influence the measure of fleet availability, and realize that if they're able to complete vehicle repairs in a timely fashion, the department will have more vehicles at its disposal, and the public will be presented with more riding options. They strive to complete at least 75 percent of vehicle repairs within 24 hours.

Although each of the three Scorecards profiled in this example share a common objective, the measure chosen at each level is representative of what is necessary for the group to contribute to overall success. Those linked performance measures are the key to ensuring alignment throughout the city. Employees in the Operations Department are now able to conclusively demonstrate how their activities link back to a key goal for the city. Likewise, city officials can rest assured that Operations personnel are focused on the necessary elements to drive value for the city's citizens.

Support Group Balanced Scorecards

Support groups such as human resources, finance, and information technology (IT) often feel like the Rodney Dangerfields of the organization: They can't get no respect! Each provides valuable offerings, without which actual service delivery to customers would most likely be severely compromised. However, there exists among public and nonprofits, and in many private-sector firms, a temptation to label these groups as pure overhead, thereby diminishing their valuable role.

The Balanced Scorecard can change all that. Support groups should have the same opportunity as any other department to illustrate their contributions, and the Scorecard provides the forum. Typically, units that have the responsibility for providing services to the entire organization will look to the high-level organizational Scorecard when developing their own objectives and measures. Their quest is to examine the objectives on the "corporate" Scorecard and contemplate how the group plays a role in their success. Human resources departments, for example, will frequently begin their Scorecard development work by transferring all of the Employee Learning and Growth objectives and measures from the high-level Scorecard onto the Customer perspective of their card. The organization is their customer, and as such they have the responsibility to ensure the internal infrastructure of the agency is ready to answer any and all challenges. Similarly, finance departments may assume the objectives and measures appearing in the Financial perspective of a high-level Scorecard.

Unlike their colleagues working with clients and other stakeholders of the organization, support group employees are often shielded from much of the direct service provision that is taking place. Cascading the Scorecard to these units lifts the strategy veil and provides a much-needed line of sight between support work and the mission of the organization.

Checking the Alignment of Cascaded Balanced Scorecards

We all know the many dangers inherent in making assumptions. Cascading the Balanced Scorecard is no different. The act of developing Scorecards up and down the organizational hierarchy can prove to be an exciting and liberating effort, but you must be sure there is true alignment existing from top to bottom. Assuming alignment where none exists could lead to departments inadvertently working against one another, misallocated resources, and a whole lot of confused people.

As each level of cascading is completed, pause to review the Scorecards just created to validate the presence of alignment. Your Scorecard team, with its knowledge and experience, is the best qualified to perform this audit task. Each "chain" of Scorecards should be evaluated to ensure that objectives and measures flow in a demonstrable pattern, leading toward the objectives and measures embodied in the highest-level Scorecard. Upon conclusion of their critique, your team members should meet with Scorecard developers at lower levels and discuss any modifications that would improve the quality of their Scorecards.

Once you've completed your reviews, you should open the feedback process to a wider audience. Give all employees the chance to kick the tires of their colleagues' Scorecards, along the way providing advice and learning a thing or two about what their colleagues actually do! In Chapter Nine, I outlined the "open houses" conducted by the County of San Diego. Employees of the Health and Human Services Agency were invited to a session during which they learned more about the Balanced Scorecard and had the chance to view Scorecards from groups across the agency. Not only did those attending provide great input on the objectives and measures they saw, but they began to see how collaboration between groups could drive overall agency results. I overheard, "Oh, I didn't know you did that...." several times during the events. The inevitable reply was always, "We should meet and talk about this." Rome wasn't built in a day, but when people start talking about strategy, they're thinking about strategy, and when they're thinking about strategy, good things tend to happen.

A Final Thought on Cascading

I have one final piece of advice for you: Of those items within your control, cascading may be the single most important ingredient of a successful Balanced Scorecard implementation. You can't control how much executive sponsorship you receive or predict any crisis that may derail your efforts. You can, however, make the decision to drive the power of the Balanced Scorecard to all levels of your organization.

Developing a high-level Scorecard is a great start, but how many people are really involved in the effort? *Involvement is the key to ownership.* If you want your employees to take true ownership of your success, let them carve out a share for themselves. Allow them to create a language of success with themselves at the center. Everyone wins as interest, alignment, accountability, knowledge, and results are all enhanced in the process. In case only empirical evidence will convince you, how's this: 72 percent of organizations reporting "breakthrough results" from the Balanced Scorecard used the process of cascading to drive goal alignment.

SUMMARY

There has probably been no greater demonstration of the power of alignment in our lifetimes quite like what occurred at Ground Zero in New York City after September 11, 2001. If ever a situation called for a variety of groups to work together toward a common goal, this was it. And work together they did—police officers, firefighters, Health and Human Services personnel, and thousands of volunteers—all aligned toward the common goal of saving as many lives as possible. The results they accomplished in such a short period of time are awe-inspiring, and a testament to what can be achieved when we work together toward a common goal.

Unfortunately, the power of alignment is not altogether evident in most organizations. In one survey of 293 organizations in the United Kingdom, researchers discovered that in poorly performing organizations, two-thirds of employees did not have a good understanding of overall organizational goals.[5] Cascading can bridge this understanding gap by developing Balanced Scorecards at every level of the organization. These cascaded Scorecards align with the organization's highest-level Scorecard by identifying the objectives and measures lower-level groups will track in order to gauge their contribution to overall success. While some objectives and measures may be the same throughout the organization, many will differ (but align), reflecting the opportunities and challenges faced by specific groups. Cascading may be considered a prerequisite of success for public and nonprofits, given the necessity of collaboration from groups spanning levels and functions to drive overall results.

Prior to developing cascaded Scorecards, you should review your implementation efforts to this point and gather all key learnings you've acquired. This knowledge will form the basis for the Scorecards to come. You may determine the terminology you'll use, the number of measures to appear on Scorecards, and so on. Once you're ready to cascade, you must ensure that those individuals responsible for cascading possess a deep knowledge of your highest-level Scorecard, including the operational and strategic significance of performance objectives and measures.

The cascading process is driven by "influence." All groups should look at the Scorecard of the group or unit to which they report, and determine which of the objectives and measures they can influence. Their own Scorecard is formed on the basis of how they impact higher-level objectives.

Support groups such as human resources, finance, and information technology (IT) rarely receive an invitation to the strategy table. However, they should not be overlooked when it comes to cascading the Balanced Scorecard. Support groups have a valuable role to play in the organization and must be given the opportunity to demonstrate their input through the development of aligned Scorecards.

The Balanced Scorecard team should review all cascaded Scorecards to verify that true alignment exists among all groups. This audit will also reveal whether established targets are realistic, and that all organizational objectives are adequately represented on cascaded Scorecards.

NOTES

1. As quoted in Stephen Taub, "Dazed and Confused," *CFO.com*, September 11, 2002.
2. Peter F. Drucker, *Managing the Non-Profit Organization* (New York: HarperBusiness, 1990), p. 182.

3. Paul R. Niven, *Balanced Scorecard Step-by-Step: Maximizing Performance and Maintaining Results* (New York: John Wiley & Sons, Inc., 2002), p. 300.
4. Viktor E. Frankl, *Man's Search for Meaning* (Boston: Beacon Press, 4th edition, 1992).
5. William Fonvielle and Lawrence P. Carr, "Gaining Strategic Alignment: Making Scorecards Work," *Management Accounting,* Fall 2001.

CHAPTER 11

Linking Resource Allocation to the Balanced Scorecard

Roadmap for Chapter Eleven Humorist Will Rogers once remarked, *"The budget is a mythical beanbag. Congress votes mythical beans into it, and then tries to reach in and pull real beans out."* As long as they've existed, budgets have been a source of monetary pain and controversy for public, nonprofit, and private firms alike. Ostensibly designed to pair dollars with results, most budgeting efforts lack a true "strategic stake," and are instead characterized by chicanery and politics of the highest order.

In this chapter we'll examine the role of the Balanced Scorecard in linking resource allocation to strategy. A five-step process will be presented to demonstrate how a series of cascaded Scorecards can drive the budgeting process in any organization. Following the techniques outlined in this chapter will help your agency avoid the dubious distinction of joining the 60 percent of all organizations that do not link budgets to strategy.

HISTORY OF PERFORMANCE AND BUDGETS

Interest in the linkage of performance measures to budgets has been growing in the public sector for many years. The past dozen years, in particular, have introduced a number of elements that improve the environment for a merger of budgets and performance.

In 1990, the Chief Financial Officers Act was passed. While the act's main focus was the improvement of federal financial management, it also referenced the development of performance measures. Following on its heels was the Government Performance and Results Act (GPRA) of 1993. The bill decreed that all federal agencies engage in strategic planning, objective setting, and performance measurement. Going one step further, the GPRA mandated that, beginning in 1999, performance measures be reported in the budgets of federal programs.[1] Budgeting and performance measurement was given yet another attention boost when then-Vice President Al Gore's National Performance Review issued its findings. The

241

report recommended a conversion from budgets based on inputs to a system focused on results. More recently, President George W. Bush has, for the first time in history, sent a budget plan to Congress that will formally assess the performance of government agencies and programs, and to some extent link financing to their results.

All of these initiatives are noble and well intentioned, but results have, thus far, been less than encouraging. In one study by the General Accounting Office (GAO), it was determined that a majority of federal managers are largely ignoring performance information when allocating resources.[2] Part of the problem can be traced to performance measures that are ill conceived and poorly designed. As the backbone of any link to resource allocation, measures must accurately and reliably track outcomes.

As you've read throughout this book, the Balanced Scorecard has been proven to surmount many of the obstacles associated with typical performance measurement systems. Therefore, nonprofits and government agencies wishing to pursue the linkage of budgets to performance measures are well advised to first create a Balanced Scorecard. Assuming you've followed the advice advanced in this book, and have done just that, the remainder of this chapter will itemize the steps necessary to link your resource allocation process back to your Balanced Scorecard.

LINKING BUDGETS AND BALANCED SCORECARDS

The process of aligning budgets and Balanced Scorecard measures is outlined in Exhibit 11.1. As always, the agency's mission, values, vision, and strategy are the starting point in our discussion. These building blocks are translated into a high-level Balanced Scorecard for the organization, which is then used as the key reference point for cascaded Scorecards throughout the organization. As explained in Chapter Nine, all Scorecards include not only objectives, measures, and targets, but equally important, they contain initiatives. These programs, projects, and plans describe how the agency will go about achieving the performance target. As you'll soon learn, it is the initiatives that forge the bond between Scorecards and budgets. Quantifying the initiatives will form the basis for operating and capital budget requests. Let's now turn our attention to the specific steps involved in this process.

Step 1: Develop a Plan

Chapter Four reviewed the topic of communicating your Balanced Scorecard implementation to every person or group with a stake in your organization. Without communication, and a lot of it, even the most well-intentioned change program can die on the vine. The same advice is readily applicable in your quest to transform the budget process. You have to get the word out to everyone involved in the process.

Exhibit 11.1   Linking the Balanced Scorecard to Budgeting

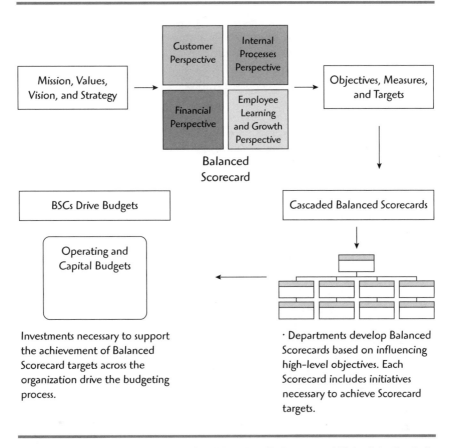

Adapted from *Balanced Scorecard Step-by-Step: Maximizing Performance and Maintaining Results*, by Paul R. Niven (John Wiley & Sons, Inc., 2002).

Communication should center on why the change is being made, how it will benefit the organization, and, recognizing the "WIIFM" (What's In It For Me) principle, how it will make life easier for budget preparers. The plan doesn't end with communication. Templates that facilitate the capture of budget information in as painless a way as possible must be designed and distributed.

Step 2: Develop or Refine Your Highest-Level Balanced Scorecard

This method of Scorecard and budget linkage relies exclusively on the development of cascaded Balanced Scorecards. Therefore, a high-level organizational Scorecard, spelling the key objectives, measures, and targets for the organization must be in place.

Step 3: Develop Cascaded Balanced Scorecards

Cascading, as you learned in Chapter Ten, gives every group within your organization the opportunity to clearly signal how their local actions are contributing to overall results—yet another example of the axiom, "think globally, act locally." Each cascaded Scorecard should include not only objectives, measures, and targets, but initiatives as well. Effective initiatives will help you close any gaps existing between current and desired performance as reflected in your performance targets.

The link to budgeting appears when you calculate the monetary investments necessary to launch the initiative. Every initiative, no matter how big or how small will entail the allocation of resources. Budget requests should be based upon the resources you require to effectively implement your initiatives, which in turn will drive the successful outcomes you're aiming for in your performance targets. All initiatives should clearly document the local and high-level objective(s) they support, resources required to implement (both human and financial), dependencies with other initiatives, and key milestones.

Organizations pursuing this technique will soon have to answer this question: Should typical budget items, which normally do not have supporting initiatives, such as salaries, supplies, and travel, be allocated against the initiatives appearing on the Balanced Scorecard? In other words, how do we support a request for salaries (for example), when there is no supporting initiative? Differences of opinion exist on the subject. Scorecard architects Kaplan and Norton have advocated the use of so-called dynamic budgeting, which represents an amalgam of operational and strategic budgeting.[3] They suggest an operational budget be used to allocate resources necessary for typical, recurring operations. Given the large volume of current service offerings, the majority of an organization's spending would be dictated by the operational budget. The strategic budget is reserved for spending designed to close any significant gaps that exist between current and desired performance on critical performance indicators.

Another school of thought suggests only one budget be used and that it should contain the entire mix of operational and strategic elements necessary to reflect a true picture of the organization. Following this advice forces an agency to consider every possible line item on the budget in light of strategy, which could be a Herculean task indeed. Financial innovations such as Activity-Based Costing, which provide input on cost drivers, are helpful in this regard, but will not eliminate the specter of subjectivity from creeping into the analysis. Proponents of this school also suggest, with some merit, that challenging managers to relate strategy to even the most mundane of activities will bring the concept to the forefront and promote learning through the exchange of ideas around the agency.

The Scorecard and budget linkage process I am describing here will work with either budget school. Your choice will depend on how accurately you can attach costs to strategic initiatives and how motivated your organization is to attempt a change of this magnitude.

Step 4: Compile Spending Requests

Your first task in step four is to provide budget preparers throughout your agency with templates they can use to easily capture resource requirements relating to Scorecard initiatives. Exhibit 11.2 displays a condensed version of such a template. In this example, the Building and Planning department of a city government has proposed three initiatives organizers feel are crucial in helping them achieve an 80 percent customer satisfaction target. Building a customer service portal will allow citizens to find and purchase permits without visiting a city office, which is sure to improve satisfaction. For those who must travel to a local office, the experience will be rendered more pleasant thanks to newly remodeled facilities. Finally, a records management program will provide all departmental staff with the resources they need to respond to customer inquiries in a swift and efficient manner.

Keep in mind this is just one measure. You'll require documents such as this for all measures (no wonder budgets produce so much paper!). Each initiative must be accompanied by supporting documentation as well— costs, timing, dependencies, key milestones, payback periods, and so on.

Exhibit 11.2   A Simplified Budget Submission Form

Business Unit/Department: City Building and Planning Department				
			Resource Requirements	
Measure	Target	Initiatives	Operating	Capital
Customer Satisfaction	80%	Internet Customer Service Portal	$100,000	$50,000
		Remodel of Citizen Service Center	$25,000	$250,000
		Records Management Program	$50,000	$150,000

Adapted from *Balanced Scorecard Step-by-Step: Maximizing Performance and Maintaining Results*, by Paul R. Niven (John Wiley & Sons, Inc., 2002).

In keeping with the title of this step, your next assignment is to compile budget requests from throughout the agency. The rollups should be summarized in relation to their corresponding Balanced Scorecard objective. Exhibit 11.3 provides an example. Here you see the agency has developed a strategy of "making customers the center of everything we do." Three objectives organizers hope will lead to the execution of this strategy have been developed in the Customer perspective: increase customer satisfaction, promote economic opportunity, and provide new services.

The column labeled "Current Scorecard Status" provides readers with a snapshot of performance on the objective in the most recent year. The evaluation uses a traffic-light metaphor: green is synonymous with meeting or achieving the target, red indicates performance requiring improvement, and yellow represents a situation requiring caution and attention. Thus, it's easy to discern that customer satisfaction is performing below expectations, the promotion of economic opportunities is above expectations, and new services require more attention.

The final two columns of the document summarize the total operating and capital dollars requested across the organization on these objectives. You can see that customer objectives represent 35 percent of total operating fund requests and 27 percent of capital. Those responsible for approving budget requests can use this information to determine where the majority of spending requests are being directed, and take action to ensure appropriate balance in the allocation of resources. As is always desirable, this analysis will inevitably produce important questions relating to how funds are expended. In this instance, administrators must determine how much they are willing to spend in order to elevate customer satisfaction to an acceptable level. Similarly, while the promotion of economic opportunities is currently green, how much is necessary to sustain that performance?

Step 5: Finalize the Budget

Once all budget requests have been tabulated, you will almost always discover a gap. Maybe "gap" is too euphemistic a word; "abyss" may be a better description. The gap to which I am humorously referring is the difference between the funds requested by groups throughout the agency and the funds you have available.

To close the gap and finalize the budget, each group leader should deliver a formal presentation to senior leaders, outlining the budget submissions from his or her group, to include: what they encompass, why they are strategically significant, and how they will positively impact Scorecard targets. By clearly demonstrating how initiatives link to Scorecard targets, the information presented will assist leaders in making appropriate resource allocation decisions.

Exhibit 11.3   Budget Requests by Balanced Scorecard Strategy and Objective

Corporate Strategy: Make Customers the Center of Everything We Do

Objective	Current Scorecard Status	Budget Request Operating $000s	Budget Request Capital $000s
Increase customer satisfaction	Red	$XXM	$XXM
Promote economic opportunity	Green	$XXM	$XXM
Provide new services	Yellow	$XXM	$XXM
Percentage of Total Spending		35%	27%

Adapted from *Balanced Scorecard Step-by-Step: Maximizing Performance and Maintaining Results*, by Paul R. Niven (John Wiley & Sons, Inc., 2002).

Now the process becomes iterative in nature, with executives reviewing and questioning the proposals, attempting to determine which are worthy of inclusion in the budget. To ease the decision-making process somewhat, you may wish to develop an internal ranking system for the initiatives you propose. A simplified rating system may be devised to represent the potential impact of removing a specific initiative from the Balanced Scorecard. For example, the number 1 might indicate an initiative that could be eliminated and have minimal impact on the ability of the group to achieve its target. A 2 might translate to an initiative that could be cut, but with a definite effect on the group's chances of meeting targeted expectations. Finally, initiatives awarded a 3 could represent projects that are deemed as crucial to the successful achievement of Scorecard targets. The ratings will be necessarily subjective, but they will serve as a powerful impetus for conversations centered on establishing spending priorities.

BENEFITS TO EXPECT FROM THE PROCESS

Have you ever found yourself in a situation where you felt like a fish out of water? It happens to all of us from time to time. An old friend in the consulting business told me this story that demonstrates the surprising outcomes that can result when we find ourselves in a seemingly uncomfortable situation. Fresh out of graduate school, he was immediately dispatched by his new employer, a large and prestigious consulting firm, to an important client on the East Coast. The consulting firm's leaders felt my friend's liberal arts background would serve him well in any and all situations. However, they gave little consideration to the fact that he had taken only one finance course during his entire academic career, and they were thrusting him into a lion's den of financial professionals, who were demanding instant answers to their budgeting problem. Decked out in his freshly pressed suit, he arrived at the client's office radiating confidence and ready to solve any problem they threw at him. When the meeting began, he quickly realized that it was nothing like the philosophy seminars he had attended in school. The topic was budgeting, and hard as he pressed his mental accelerator, he had nothing in the tank. Finally, exasperated, and feeling his short-lived consulting career was over anyway, he asked this seemingly simple question: "Why do you budget?" The room fell silent. He was preparing for the inevitable tirade focusing on his utter incompetence when suddenly, from the head of the table, a voice was heard. It was that of the company president, who said, "He's right; why do we budget?" The next thing he knew, the entire group was engaged in a spirited discussion on the underlying rationale for their budget; and before long, they had developed several recommendations based on an examination of their true purpose. My friend was branded "a brilliant consultant" and never looked back.

The point of the story is this: Sometimes simplicity is the best approach. We have a tendency in modern organizations to make things appear more complicated than they really are. Budgeting is a case in point. Some readers may regard the process I have laid out as unduly simplistic and, as such, not worthy of implementation. But what, I ask, is the fundamental purpose of a budget? To allocate scarce resources among a variety of possible alternatives. What better way to do that than to use the Balanced Scorecard that represents a direct and faithful translation of our strategy. Only those initiatives that provide a meaningful contribution to the fulfillment of strategic objectives should be undertaken. Simple yes, but effective as well. Listed next are some of the benefits associated with this process.

- *Develops budgets based on facts, not emotion.* The typical budgeting process is fraught with extensive game-playing, as each department postures and engages in whatever histrionics are necessary to secure adequate funding. Persuasive arguments tend to hold as much weight as strategic needs during these entertaining, yet ineffective, proceedings. The Balanced Scorecard levels the playing field for all participants, forcing all groups to demonstrate a clear link between budget requests and strategic impact. The Ministry of Defence (MoD) in the United Kingdom discovered the difference a Balanced Scorecard can make at budget time. *"The MoD now uses its Scorecard during funding negotiations with the Treasury. By removing the emotion from funding discussions and enabling the MoD to dispassionately demonstrate the impact of various funding scenarios, the Scorecard helps focus the conversation on the facts and key priorities."* [4]

- *Builds collaboration.* Admiral Raymond A. Archer, former vice director of the Defense Logistics Agency, described the use of the Balanced Scorecard in the budgeting process this way. *"We decided that the only way to make the Balanced Scorecard work was to put our money where our Scorecard was. So we made a rule: investment initiatives had to be in the Balanced Scorecard. If they weren't, they wouldn't be funded. What used to be a painful investment strategy process became quite simple. In fact, the Scorecard eliminates turf battles."*[5] Eliminating turf battles is a tremendous enhancement to the budgeting process, but the Scorecard can take it one step beyond. With strategy at the center of the discussions, an open dialog is encouraged, in which groups actively look for opportunities to collaborate and share resources. Perhaps an initiative won't be funded on its own, but when combined with another group's plan, there may be synergies that make both more appealing. This facet of the Scorecard and budget link is very appropriate for nonprofits and governments where so many of the outcomes require cross-collaboration.

- *Reinforces the strategy.* In order to effectively create a budget request with a clear link to a strategy, there is an implicit assumption that individuals preparing budgets understand the strategy. A poor grasp of the strategy will be revealed in initiative and budget requests that have little impact on driving overall outcomes. Linking dollars to the Scorecard is a great opportunity to enhance learning, since knowledge of the strategy will become a prerequisite to generating budget dollars.

SUMMARY

Efforts to link budgets and performance measures have existed for some time, but have been significantly hampered by poor measure design. The Balanced Scorecard has demonstrated the capability to overcome many of the shortcomings associated with typical performance measurement efforts, and therefore, offers a powerful platform for the linkage of budgets, performance measures, and strategy.

Using the Balanced Scorecard to drive the resource allocation process is accomplished through a five-step process:

1. *Develop a plan.* Communicate the new budget process to all stakeholders. Provide information on why the change is necessary and how it improves the prospects of organizational success and eases the burden of those responsible for preparing budgets.

2. *Develop or refine the highest-level Scorecard.* The method presented relies heavily on cascaded Balanced Scorecards. Therefore, a high-level Scorecard from which to launch the cascading efforts must be in place.

3. *Develop cascaded Scorecards.* Scorecards from throughout the agency should be developed and should include not only objectives, measures, and targets, but initiatives as well. The initiatives describe the processes or projects that will be undertaken to achieve Scorecard targets. The investments necessary to support the initiatives forge the bond between budgets and the Balanced Scorecard. All initiatives entail the allocation of resources. They should be quantified and form the basis of the budget request.

4. *Compile results.* Budget submissions gathered from all groups are compiled on templates. The "rollup" of spending requests is often displayed in relation to strategies and Scorecard objectives.

5. *Finalize the budget.* Normally, a gap will exist between budget appeals and what is feasible for the agency. Unit leaders will deliver presentations outlining the budget submission, highlighting the strategic significance of initiative requests, and focusing on the link to Scorecard targets. Following the presentations, the process becomes iterative in nature, with senior leaders discussing and debating the relative merits of all requests. A simple Scorecard ranking system often facilitates these discussions.

Organizations pursuing the link between budgets and Balanced Scorecards have discovered a number of benefits associated with the process, including: the elimination of emotion, placement of facts as the driver of budget discussions, ability to build collaboration, and reinforcement of the organization's strategy.

NOTES

1. Philip G. Joyce, "Using Performance Measures for Budgeting: A New Beat, or Is It the Same Old Tune?" *New Directions for Evaluation,* Fall 1997.
2. From the President's Management Agenda at http://www.whitehouse.gov/omb/budget/fy2002/mgt.pdf, Fiscal Year 2002.
3. Robert S. Kaplan and David P. Norton, *The Strategy-Focused Organization* (Boston: MA, Harvard Business School Press, 2001).
4. As quoted in Lauren Keller Johnson, "Making Strategy a Continual Process at the U.K. Ministry of Defence," *Balanced Scorecard Report,* November–December, 2002, pp. 5–8.
5. Raymond A. Archer, "Enabling a Whole New (and Customer-Focused) Structure at the DLA," *Balanced Scorecard Report,* November–December, 2002, pp. 8–9.

CHAPTER 12

Reporting Results

Roadmap for Chapter Twelve Reflecting on the future of management reporting, General Electric Chief Executive Jack Welch once commented, *"Most of the information a manager will need to run a business will reside on a computer screen in a digital cockpit. It will contain every piece of real-time data, with automatic alerts spotlighting the trends requiring immediate attention."* Well, the future is here. Today's Balanced Scorecard reporting tools can perform all of Welch's prognostications and 101 other tasks. In this chapter we'll explore the role of technology in reporting your Balanced Scorecard results and go through the steps you should follow when choosing a software solution.

But technology is not for everyone, so in this chapter you'll also learn that many Scorecard pioneers used simple paper-based results to drive breakthrough results for their organizations. Key considerations when developing an in-house system will also be provided.

Results can only generate improvement and learning if analyzed and shared. The Balanced Scorecard provides governments and nonprofits with the mechanism to redefine and invigorate an often-tired and ineffective management meeting process. We'll look at the specifics of this new and exciting process.

FROM THEORY TO PRACTICE

A public-sector client recently introduced me to an acronym I had never heard before: SPOTS. Any guesses? It stands for "strategic plan on the shelf." The term is indicative of those organizations that go to great and painstaking lengths to develop a strategy, only to have it sit on a shelf or be used to prop up projectors during presentations. Both fairly ignominious results for the much-vaunted strategic plan! The last thing you want is a "BSCOTS." Okay, it's not as catchy as SPOTS, but you get the picture.

Developing performance objectives on a strategy map and translating them into measures, targets, and, later, supporting initiatives, is a challenging task. However, people also find it exhilarating and thought-provoking. With a frenetic pace characterizing most organizations, there is precious little time reserved for actually contemplating high-level strategy and how it will be executed. Creating a Balanced Scorecard provides that opportunity, that mental fresh air, revealing a new perspective on your organization. Beneficial and thought-provoking, yes, but it's still largely an academic exercise. It's not until you begin reporting your Balanced Scorecard results that the tool is transformed from a cognitive simulation to a real business solution.

Every organization will launch the Balanced Scorecard for individual reasons; however, improving results and enhancing accountability are frequently cited. These Scorecard traits are not introduced until you begin reporting your results. Only then will you see the true power of the Balanced Scorecard, the power to drive alignment from top to bottom, to improve communication, and to learn about your business through strategic conversations arising from an analysis of reported results.

BALANCED SCORECARD SOFTWARE

Ever curious as to the latest developments in the Scorecard field, I recently typed "Balanced Scorecard" and "software" into a search engine to see how many hits I would receive. Forty-four thousand is the jaw-dropping answer. By the time you read these pages, the number will inevitably be higher. Mercifully, the search result doesn't indicate the presence of 44,000 Scorecard software vendors or programs; but it does present strong evidence of the rapidly growing interest in the topic.

When I started working with the Balanced Scorecard several years ago, reports generated using an Excel spreadsheet with some clip art were considered avant-garde and often yielded expressions of awe from Scorecard reviewers. Whenever I mention that, I feel as though I'm recounting one of those stories you might hear from your grandfather: "When I was your age, we walked 12 miles to school...in the snow...uphill...both ways." We weren't suffering in our technology-deprived state, but in retrospect we could have achieved much more from the Scorecard had we been able to avail ourselves of the many benefits offered by even the most modest of Scorecard software systems on the market today.

As the Balanced Scorecard evolved in the mid-1990s from a pure measurement system to a strategic management system, the paper-based reports used by early adopters were hard-pressed to keep up with progress in the field. Organizations were cascading the Scorecard from top to bottom, linking it to budgeting and, in many cases, compensation as well. The reporting, analysis, and communication requirements represented by these advances required new tools. Software providers were swift in their response, and soon developed a number of sophisticated programs capable of everything from simple reporting to strategy mapping and scenario planning.

Selection of the right software for your organization is a crucial decision. Not only are you shopping for a system to report your Scorecard results and provide a platform for future evolution of the tool, but you must be sure that whatever you buy will suit the needs of your workforce and be accepted as a useful tool. Software selection is typically a process of five sequential steps[2]:

1. *Form a software team.* Just as you used a cross-functional team to develop your Scorecard, so too will you rely on a number of people to make the crucial software decision. Include your executive sponsor, Balanced Scorecard champion, a representative of your information technology (IT) group, and an individual representative of the typical Scorecard user. The team should begin their work by reviewing the current landscape of Scorecard software and by speaking to end users regarding their requirements for this tool. Remember that different users will demand specific functionality. Executives may, for example, simply be interested in one-page summary reports, whereas analysts may focus on data input, retrieval, and complex reporting. The team should also develop a software project plan, outlining key dates and milestones on the path to the software decision.

2. *Develop a short list of candidates.* You'll find dozens of potential vendors ready and willing to supply you with Scorecard software. Use the criteria presented after these steps to help you determine three or four finalists.

3. *Submit a request for proposal (RFP).* Compile your needs and specifications into a document for distribution to your finalists. Each organization you contact should provide you with a written summary detailing how its product stacks up to your requirements.

4. *Arrange demonstrations.* Invite software candidates to conduct a demonstration of their product at your facility. To ensure the demonstration is relevant to your needs, send in advance a copy of your strategy map and measures to the vendor and have them base the demonstration on your data. This is important since many vendors will default to manufacturing or service examples that bear little resemblance to the world of public agencies and nonprofits.

5. *Write a summary report and make your selection.* Determine which functionality and specifications are most vital to you, and rank each product against them. Select the software program that most closely matches your requirements.

Criteria for Selecting Software

Design Issues: Configuration of the Software

In this section we'll examine a number of the Scorecard software setup and design elements.

- *Setup wizards.* Your software solution should provide easy-to-use-and-understand "wizards" to guide new users through the initial setup process.

- *Time to implement.* Software programs for the Balanced Scorecard can run the gamut from simple reporting tools to sophisticated enterprisewide management solutions. That means major differences exist in the time and resources necessary to implement the system. You must determine what your thresholds are in terms of timing and resource requirements necessary to have the system up and running. Carefully consider the resource requirements you have, and are willing to dedicate to, the Scorecard software.

- *Various Scorecard designs.* This book focuses exclusively on the methodology of the Balanced Scorecard; however, you may at some point wish to track other popular measurement alternatives, such as the Baldrige award criteria, TQM metrics, or any number of different methodologies. The software should be flexible enough to permit various performance management techniques.

- *User interface/display.* Most Balanced Scorecard software will feature a predominant display metaphor. It may use gauges similar to those you'd see in the dashboard of a plane or automobile, boxes that are reminiscent of organizational charts, or color-coded dials. Some of these simply look better (i.e., more realistic and legitimate) than others. That may sound insignificant but, remember, you're counting on your workforce to use this software faithfully, and if they find the "instrumentation" unrealistic or, worse, unattractive, that could significantly impact their initial reaction and ongoing commitment.

- *Number of measures.* In all likelihood, you will use the Scorecard software for tracking performance measures from around your entire organization. Ensure your software is equipped with the flexibility to handle a significant volume of measures.

- *Strategies, objectives, measures, targets, and initiatives.* As the backbone of the Scorecard system, you should be able to easily enter all of these elements in the software. The software should also allow you to specify cause-and-effect relationships among the objectives and measures.

- *Strategy maps.* Capturing the strategy map with compelling and easy-to-understand graphics is critical should you hope to benefit from the information sharing and collective learning to be derived from the Balanced Scorecard.

- *Multiple locations.* The software should accommodate the addition of performance measures from a variety of physical and nonphysical locations.

- *Descriptions and definitions.* Simply entering names and numbers into the software is not sufficient for communication and eventual analysis. Every field in which you enter information must be capable of accepting textual descriptions. Upon launching the software, the first thing most users will do when looking at a specific performance indicator is examine its description and definition.

- *Assignment of owners.* The Scorecard can be used to enhance accountability only if your software permits each performance indicator to be assigned a specific owner. Since you may also have another individual acting as the owner's assistant, and yet another as data enterer, it is beneficial if the software provides the capability to identify these functions, as well.

- *Various unit types.* Your performance indicators are likely to come in all shapes, sizes, and descriptors, from raw numbers to percentages to dollars. The tool you choose must permit all measure types.

- *Appropriate timing.* Your performance measures are sure to have variable time increments. Spending may be tracked monthly, while customer satisfaction is monitored quarterly. The software should accommodate varied reporting frequencies.

- *Relative weights.* All measures on the Balanced Scorecard are important links in the description of your strategy. However, most organizations will place greater emphasis on certain indicators. For public and nonprofit organizations, customer indicators are of vital importance and may warrant a higher weight. A good Scorecard tool should permit you to weight the measures according to their relative importance.

- *Aggregate disparate elements.* That description sounds a little complicated, but it simply means your program should deliver the capability to combine performance measures with different unit types. This can best be accomplished with the use of weighting (see the preceding element). Measures are accorded a weight that drives the aggregation of results regardless of the specific unit type of each indicator.

- *Multiple comparatives.* Most organizations will track performance relative to a predefined target, for example the financial budget. However, it may be useful to examine performance in light of last year's performance, relative to your peers, or a best-in-class benchmarking number. Look for the software to allow a number of comparatives.

- *Graphic status indicators.* At a glance, users should be able to ascertain the performance of measures based on an easy-to-understand status indicator. Many programs will take advantage of familiar color metaphors, using for example, red (stop), yellow (caution), and green (go). Fortunately, they usually offer greater color ranges. This is particularly important to public agencies and nonprofits that may feel hesitant to attach red lights to performance.

- *Dual polarity.* For the software to produce a color indicating measure performance, it must recognize whether high values for actual results represent good or bad performance. Up to a certain point results might be considered good, but beyond a certain threshold they may be a cause for concern. For example, it may be perfectly appropriate for a call center representative to answer 12 to 15 calls an hour, whereas responding to 30 might indicate the representative is rushing through the calls and sacrificing quality for the sake of expediency. The software solution should be able to flag such issues of "dual polarity."

- *Cascading Scorecards.* Users should be able to review Balanced Scorecards from across the organization in one program. Ensure your software allows you to display aligned Scorecards emanating from throughout the organization.

- *Personal preferences.* "My" has become a popular prefix in the Internet world, with "My Yahoo" and "My Home Page" as two prevalent examples. The information age has heralded a time of mass customization. And so it should be with your Balanced Scorecard software. If desired, users should be able to easily customize the system to open with a page displaying indicators of importance to them. Having relevant information immediately available will greatly facilitate the program's use.

- *Intuitive menus.* Menus should be logical, easy to understand, and relatively simple to navigate.

- *Helpful help screens.* Some help screens seem to hinder user's efforts as often as they help them. Check the help screens to ensure they offer relevant, easy-to-follow information.

- *Levels of detail.* Your software should allow users to quickly and easily switch from a summary view of performance to a detailed view comprising a single indicator. Navigating from data tables to summary reports back to individual measures should all be easily accommodated. The user community will demand this functionality as they begin actively using the tool to analyze performance results.

Reporting and Analysis

Any software solution you consider must contain robust and flexible reporting and analysis tools. In this section we'll explore a number of reporting and analysis factors you should consider during your selection process.

- *Drill-down capabilities.* A crucial item. The tool must allow users to drill down on measures to increasingly lower levels of detail. Drill-down might also be considered in the context of strategy maps, which should be easily navigable at the click of a mouse.

- *Statistical analysis.* Your software should include the facility of performing statistical analysis, for example trends, on the performance measures making up your Balanced Scorecard. Additionally, the statistics should be multidimensional in nature, combining disparate performance elements to display a total picture of actual results. Simply viewing bar charts is not analysis. Users require the capability to "slice and dice" the data to fit their analysis and decision-making needs.

- *Alerts.* You will want to be notified automatically when a critical measure is not performing within acceptable ranges. Alerts must be built into the system to provide this notification.

- *Commentaries.* This is particularly crucial for government and nonprofit users, most of whose work is contextual and requires explanation. Whether a measure is performing at, above, or below targeted expectations, users (especially managers) need to quickly determine the root cause of the performance and be aware of the associated steps necessary for sustaining or improving results. Commentary fields are essential to any Scorecard software program, and most, if not all, will include them.

- *Flexible report options.* "What kind of reports does it have?" is invariably one of the first questions you'll hear when discussing Scorecard software with your user community. We're a report-based and -dependent culture, so this shouldn't come as a surprise. What may in fact be surprising is the wide range of report capabilities featured in today's Scorecard software entries. Test this requirement closely, because, simply put, some are much better than others. An especially important area to examine is print options. We purchase software to reduce our dependency on paper, but as we all know it doesn't necessarily work that way. Ensure the reports will print effectively, displaying the information clearly and concisely.

- *Automatic consolidation.* You may wish to see your data presented as a sum, average, or year-to-date amount. The system should be flexible enough to provide this choice.

- *Flag missing data.* At the outset of their implementation, most organizations will be missing at least a portion of the data for their Balanced Scorecard measures. This often results from the fact that the Scorecard has illuminated entirely new measures never before contemplated. The software program should alert users to those measures that are missing data, whether for a single period or because the measure has never been populated.

- *Forecasting and what-if analysis.* Robust programs will be capable of using current results to forecast future performance. It's also very useful to have the capability to "plug in" different values in various measures and examine the effect on related indicators. This what-if analysis provides another opportunity to critically examine the assumptions made when constructing the strategy map.

- *Linked documents.* At a mouse click users should be able to put measure results into a larger context by accessing important documents and links. Media reports, executive videos, discussion forums, and a variety of other potential links can serve to strengthen the bond between actual results and the larger context of organizational objectives.

- *Automatic e-mail.* To harness the power of the Balanced Scorecard as a communication tool, users must be able to launch an e-mail application and send messages regarding specific performance results. Discussion forums, or "threads," may develop as interested users add their perspective on results and provide insights for improvements.

Technical Considerations

In this section, we'll examine the technical dimensions of both hardware and software to ensure the tool you select is right for your technical environment.

- *Compatibility.* Any software you consider must be able to function in your current technical environment. Most employ client/server technology and will run on Windows 95, 98, XP, 2000, NT, and UNIX.
- *Integration with existing systems.* Data for your Balanced Scorecard will probably reside in a number of different places. Your software should be able to extract data from these systems automatically, thereby eliminating any rekeying of data. Those users who appear reluctant to use the Scorecard software will often point to redundant data entry as a key detraction of the system. Therefore, a big win is scored should you have the capability to automatically extricate information with no effort on the part of users.
- *Acceptance of various data forms.* In addition to internal sources of data, you may collect performance information from third-party providers. The software should therefore be able to accept data from spreadsheets and ASCII files.
- *Data export.* Sometimes, getting information out is as important as getting it in. The data contained in the Balanced Scorecard may serve as the source for other management reports to boards, regulators, or the general public. A robust data export tool is an important component of any Scorecard software.
- *Web publishing.* Users should have the option of accessing and saving Scorecard information using a standard browser. Publishing to both an internal intranet and the Internet is preferable.
- *Trigger for external applications.* Users will require the capability of launching desktop programs from within the Balanced Scorecard software.
- *Cut and paste to applications.* Related to the preceding, users may wish to include a graph or chart in another application. Many programs will provide functionality that enables users to simply copy and paste with ease.

- *Application service provider (ASP) option.* An ASP is a company that offers organizations access over the Internet to applications and related services that would otherwise have to be located in their own computers. As information technology outsourcing grows in prominence, so does the role of application service providers. A number of Scorecard software vendors now offer this service, which gives anyone direct access to the Balanced Scorecard for a monthly (normally) fee based on the number of users.

- *Scalability.* This term describes the capability of an application to function well and take advantage of changes in size or volume in order to meet a user need. Rescaling can encompass a change in the product itself (storage, RAM, etc.) or the movement to a new operating system. Your software should be scalable to meet the future demands you may place on it as your user community and sophistication grow.

Maintenance and Security

Ensuring appropriate access rights and ongoing maintenance are also important criteria in your software decision. Here are a few elements to consider.

- *System administrator access.* Your software should allow for individuals to be designated as system administrators. Depending on security (see the third and fourth entries in this list), a number of these users may have access to the entire system.

- *Ease of modification.* Altering your views of performance should be facilitated easily, with little advanced technical knowledge required.

- *Control of access to the system.* My proclivities are toward open-book management with complete sharing of information across the organization. Agencies practicing this participative form of management give it glowing reviews for the innovation and creativity it sparks among employees. The Scorecard facilitates open sharing of information both through the development of a high-level organizational Scorecard and the series of cascading Scorecards that allow all employees to describe their contribution to overall results. However, not all organizations share this view and many will wish to limit access to the system. Therefore, a software program should allow you to limit access to measures by user, and develop user groups to simplify the measure publishing process.

- *Control of changes, data, and commentary entry.* Related to the preceding, not all users will necessarily be required to make changes, enter data, or provide result commentaries. Only system administrators should have the power to change measures, and only assigned users will have access to entering data and commentaries.

Evaluating the Vendor

Chances are, you'll be presented with a wide array of software choices from both industry veterans and upstarts you've never heard of. Either way, performing a little due diligence on the vendor is always a good idea.

- *Pricing.* As with any investment of this magnitude, pricing is a critical component of the overall decision. To make an informed decision, remember to include all dimensions of the total cost to purchase and maintain the software. This includes the per-user license fees, any maintenance fees, costs related to new releases, training costs, as well as salaries and benefits of system administrators.

- *Vendor viability.* Is this provider in for the long term, or will any vicissitudes of the economy spell its demise? Since the vendor is in the business of providing Scorecard software, you would expect it to steer its own course using the Balanced Scorecard. Ask representatives to review their Scorecard results with you. For reasons of confidentiality, they may have to disguise some of the actual numbers, but you should still glean lots of valuable information on the organization's future prospects.

- *References and experience.* By examining the profiles of past clients, you can determine the breadth and depth of experience the vendor has accumulated. While no two implementations are identical, it will be reassuring to know the software company has completed an installation in a public-sector or nonprofit environment. References are especially important. When discussing the vendor with other organizations that have been through the process, quiz them on the vendor's technical skills, consulting and training competence, and ability to complete the work on time and on budget.

- *Long-term service.* You'll inevitably encounter many bumps in the road as you implement your new reporting software. Bugs hidden deep in the program will be detected, patches will be required, and thus a lifeline to the vendor is crucial. How much support are reps willing to offer, and at what cost? Do you have a dedicated representative for your organization, or are you at the mercy of the vendor's call center? These are just a couple of questions to ask. And never forget that software companies owe a lot to us, the users. New functions and features are very often the product of intense lobbying on behalf of function-starved users who sometimes end up knowing more about the product than the vendor. So don't be shy about making requests!

Exhibit 12.1 displays an easy-to-use template that will assist you in ranking various software choices. This example includes only the configuration and design elements, but you can expand it to include all aspects of the decision. In this example, the configuration and design items have been weighted at 50 percent of the total decision. Specific elements comprising the category are listed in the first column, and the competing vendors are shown in the third, fourth, and fifth columns. Each vendor is accorded a score out of a possible 10 points demonstrating how well it satisfies each element of the decision. For example, vendors 1 and 3 both have easy-to-use setup wizards and are awarded 10 points. On many elements of the analysis, subjectivity is sure to creep into the decision. All vendors may offer the option of graphically displaying your strategy map, for example. Your point decision will then be based on ease of importing the map, graphical appearance, and so on. Once all evaluations have been made, total the points for each vendor. In this example, vendor 3 has scored perfect 10s on all points and therefore receives the full 50 points available.

Exhibit 12.1   Ranking the Software Alternatives

CRITERIA	WEIGHT	VENDOR 1	VENDOR 2	VENDOR 3
Configuration and Design	50%			
Setup wizards		10	9	10
Time to implement		9	10	10
User interface/display		8	8	10
Various Scorecard designs		8	9	10
Number of measures		9	9	10
Strategies, objectives, measures, targets, initiatives, and cause and effect		8	7	10
Strategy maps		8	7	10
Multiple locations		8	5	10
Cascading Scorecards		7	8	10
Descriptions and definitions		5	9	10
Assignment of owners		10	10	10
Various unit types		6	10	10
Varied reporting frequencies		6	10	10
Relative weights		10	8	10
Aggregate disparate elements		9	7	10
Multiple comparatives		10	10	10
Graphic status indicators		6	9	10
Dual polarity		5	10	10
Personal preferences		5	10	10
Helpful help screens		9	8	10
Levels of detail		7	8	10
Total		163	181	210
Total Points		38.80	43.10	50.00

PROS AND CONS OF USING AN AUTOMATED SCORECARD SOLUTION

Pros

Recent surveys suggest upwards of 70 percent of Scorecard-adopting organizations are considering technology tools.[3] Those that have made this decision report a number of benefits to using Scorecard software tools. Perhaps the most important benefit conferred by software is enhanced acceptance of the Balanced Scorecard. The Michigan Department of Transportation is just beginning its Scorecard journey, but has already seen the power of software in driving acceptance. According to Scorecard team member Nancy Foltz, *"At this point, we would say the use of technology has accelerated the acceptance of the Scorecard. One of the immediate and obvious concerns is the volume of data that is produced and the time and resources it would take to manage the data without such technology. We believe the Scorecard would not be accepted and used without the availability of software."*[4] Undoubtedly, the potential of data piled as high as Mt. Everest is intimidating to those developing Balanced Scorecards. The promise of software to tame the data beast is a strong selling point for every vendor, and can have a strong positive impact on the Scorecard's acceptance.

I've discussed the importance of cause and effect at several points throughout the book. Scorecard applications that display these interrelationships in an easy-to-understand and aesthetically appealing way also promote the Scorecard's acceptance. With acceptance, actual use often follows. Once users feel comfortable with the software, and can competently navigate, decision-support and management decisions can be greatly enhanced as a result of the advanced analytics offered in today's Scorecard packages. Cause-and-effect relationships can be probed, what-if analyses conducted, and questions raised—all of which lead to increased learning. Exhibit 12.2 shows a screenshot from one Scorecard software provider, QPR.

Software also supports true organizationwide deployment of the Balanced Scorecard. Even relatively small organizations can rapidly spawn dozens or hundreds of performance measures as they widely cascade the Balanced Scorecard. Facilitating the process and ensuring alignment of all Scorecards is far more manageable using an electronic solution. Consider the challenge faced by the United Nations Development Programme (UNDP). The UNDP is the United Nations' global development network, advocating for change, and connecting countries to knowledge, experience, and resources to help people build a better life. With offices in more than 140 countries around the world, each using the Balanced Scorecard, it would have been virtually impossible to aggregate data on a real-time basis without the use of enabling technology. Whether you operate from a single location or from around the globe, technology will facilitate the sharing of information generated by your Balanced Scorecard system.

Exhibit 12.2   Screenshot from a Balanced Scorecard Software Program

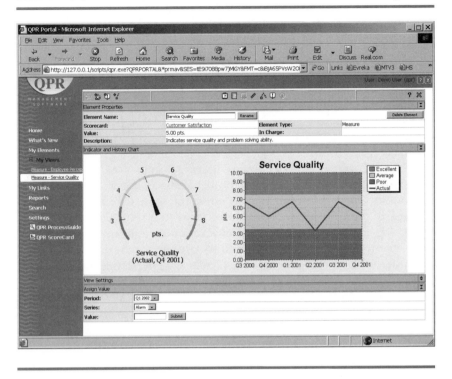

Communication, information sharing, and knowledge can all be enhanced using an automated system. Documents linked to the Scorecard package may lead interested users to mission statements, strategies, media stories, and any number of places that could stimulate ideas on improving performance. Commentaries provided as explanations for measure performance can often lead to the spontaneous formation of discussion groups throughout the organization. Technology also allows users to join a wider fraternity of colleagues embracing Scorecard software. Most vendors will sponsor "user conferences" at least annually, at which they tout their latest features, offer training classes, and feature presentations from lead users. These events offer a great opportunity to influence product upgrades, learn about the latest features, and network with other Scorecard-adopting agencies.

Cons

First off, it's not cheap. Do you need to read anymore? In actual fact, that's a bit of a generalization. Scorecard packages run the gamut in pricing from a few hundred dollars to several hundred thousand (depending on the number of users you'll supply with the new system). In addition to the cost of the software itself, you should consider training fees, annual maintenance agreements, and possible consulting assistance. However, the cost can often be justified based on the elimination of manual tasks. That was the case for the Texas State Auditor's Office, which discovered that, *"technology enhances data retrieval and tracking, which in turn leads to better accuracy, reliability, and timeliness. We estimate that our office saved about $3,000 per month when we stopped generating, copying, and distributing all the paper reports we used to make management decisions in the past."*[5] Performing a cost-benefit analysis that factors in current costs of performance measurement activities will help you determine whether software makes sense for you.

A potential danger in using technology is the temptation for organizations to introduce the automated system at the same time as the Balanced Scorecard, and in effect introduce it as the Balanced Scorecard. Technology is an enabler of the Balanced Scorecard. It will often help you derive the maximum benefits from the Scorecard, but it does not act as a substitute for the challenging work of selecting objectives and measures that depict your strategy. Some packages will come stocked with libraries of performance measures for virtually any organization of any size. View these with caution. While you will undoubtedly share measures with other organizations, you should make sure that a number of your measures are unique and reflect the specific actions you're taking to implement your strategy. Imitation may be the purest form of flattery, but it won't help you execute your strategy and improve your operations.

The section on software pros led off with the notion that acceptance of the Scorecard could be enhanced with the use of technology. Let's balance the ledger by looking at the flip side of that coin. Acceptance can sometimes be hampered by the introduction of technology. Many public and nonprofits are relatively technology-starved, and as a result employees may be justifiably intimidated by the latest gizmo being hawked by stampeding software vendors. The elegant simplicity of the Scorecard model and concept may be compromised by the complexity and enormity of a new software system that must be mastered in order to use the Scorecard.

This con can be mitigated, if not entirely eliminated, through communication and education efforts. A case in point is the Public Safety Group of the County of San Diego, California. The transition to an automated software solution at this public agency was eased through a series of performance measurement workshops for all employees who would be receiving the new package. Rather than focusing exclusively on the software, the workshops discussed the need for change within the group, demonstrated how performance measurement could help, and provided Balanced Scorecard basics in an easy-to-understand and nonthreatening way. The workshops

concluded with a hands-on Scorecard training session during which participants were led through several facilitated exercises designed to introduce
them to the basics of the new tool. Following the event, in an effort to avoid
the "out of sight, out of mind" phenomenon, Public Safety Group Scorecard
Champion Nicole Alejandre sent each workshop participant an e-mail package including a welcome letter, software brochure, glossary of terms, and tips
sheet.

DEVELOPING YOUR OWN BALANCED SCORECARD
REPORTING SYSTEM

Investing in a technological solution to report your Scorecard results is neither a guarantee nor a prerequisite of success. Long before software companies sensed the burgeoning Scorecard opportunity, many early adopters
were blazing their own trail with paper-based reports created on desktop
computers. The success of the Balanced Scorecard today is due in large
part to the efforts and tenacity of these pioneers who quickly grasped, and
gained, the Scorecard benefits of alignment, accountability, and strategy
execution with nary a thought to "graphic user interfaces" or "data import
functions." You may be surprised to learn that the City of Charlotte, North
Carolina, widely considered the single best example of Balanced Scorecard
use in a government setting, has never used a software program to report
its results since it began using the Scorecard in the mid-1990s. In Chapter
Thirteen, you will learn how Charlotte reported results and why implementors resisted the alluring glare of technology.

Necessity is the mother of invention, and when it comes to building in-
house Scorecard applications, creativity can surge. I've witnessed everything
from humble paper reports with a few graphs and charts to large whiteboards
custom-designed to hold Scorecard data to relatively sophisticated intranet
applications. One term that tends to pop up quite frequently in nonprofit
and government circles is "dashboard." Although they vary widely in design
and content, these reporting tools all focus on one key attribute: displaying
performance in a clear and unambiguous way. The Minnesota Department
of Transportation (Mn/DOT) has used the dashboard technique to broad-
cast its performance on a number of performance variables. Its snow-and-ice
dashboard is featured in Exhibit 12.3.

Mn/DOT's Dennis Feit explains the benefit of dashboards: *"The dashboards provide clear and universal presentations. So, as the commissioner walks
throughout our offices, he doesn't have to see 100 different formats of performance
reports. There are no charts, graphs, and spreadsheets stapled all over the place, each
requiring a different interpretation. With the dashboard setup, everybody presents
their information the same way: red, amber, green, or blue."*[6]

Exhibit 12.3   Minnesota Department of Transportation Performance Dashboard

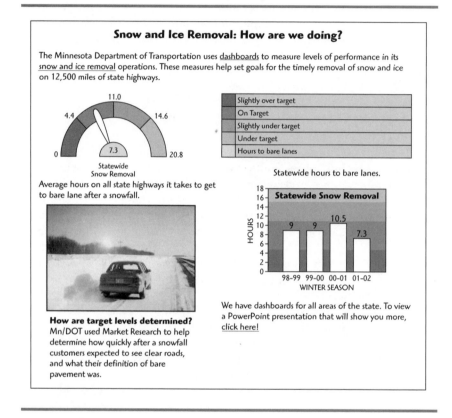

Your choice of reporting formats will depend on a number of variables, including: the resources you're willing to expend, available expertise to craft the reports, and, of course, the preferences of your senior managers. Here are a couple of key guidelines to keep in mind before developing any in-house reporting tool:

- *Before producing the first manual Balanced Scorecard report, create a mock-up with dummy results.* Circulate it to the executive group for their approval. This is important since senior leaders may have different style preferences and wishes. By creating a mock-up, the team has the opportunity to incorporate executive feedback to the process and design a reporting tool that satisfies all. And, as I've discussed at other points in the book, involvement tends to breed acceptance.

- *Be cognizant of the data collection issues that may accompany your in-house solution.* Virtually all software solutions will provide "bridges" from the system to various data sources spread throughout your organization. Should you build your own system, however, manual data entry is a distinct possibility. Possibly the least favorable association for the Balanced Scorecard is with the word "redundancy." If those charged with the task of loading Scorecard data feel it is a task being duplicated in other areas, resistance, if not downright anarchy, will surely follow. Manual data entry also introduces the attendant risks of errors from the miskeying of performance data. Unreliable data is a major Scorecard momentum killer.

USING THE BALANCED SCORECARD TO DRIVE THE AGENDA OF MANAGEMENT MEETINGS

This chapter has been devoted to the topic of reporting Balanced Scorecard results. Now the question is, what do you do with those results? Virtually all organizations hold some form of management review meetings, during which recent performance is critiqued and plans are established for the future. Bill Catucci, former chief executive at AT&T Canada described the pre-Balanced Scorecard dynamics typically encountered at these gatherings this way: *"People told you what they did last month and what they were going to do next month. It was show-and-tell with no focus. Operational reviews and discussions of tactical issues dominated the typical meeting. Little time was left for strategic issues."*[7] Little time indeed; as you may recall from Chapter One the typical management team spends less than one hour per month discussing strategy.

In the defense of those organizations practicing this "show-and-tell management," they may have been limited in their discussion options due to the narrow focus of performance data at their disposal. Perhaps financial data was all their meager performance measurement systems could muster. The Balanced Scorecard provides the opportunity to dramatically alter the agenda and, more importantly, the results, of management meetings. Scorecard reports cover the broad spectrum of metrics necessary to drive improved results, and as such provide a platform for analyzing, debating, and learning about your strategy.

The "new" management meeting puts the Scorecard at the center of discussion. Take, for instance, the case of the Boston Lyric Opera. Janice Mancini Del Sesto, the general director, began each weekly staff meeting by writing the company's three strategic themes on the whiteboard. Her aim was to ensure that all conversation generated during the meetings was related to the three themes and that staff were constantly focused on what was necessary to achieve their goals.

Rather than rote oratories delivered to an often disinterested audience, discussions of this nature frequently spawn new ideas, and maybe even some creative tension. That was the case in New York City. While mayor, Rudy Giuliani held twice-weekly meetings during which precinct police commanders from each of the city's boroughs analyzed their unit's performance. The mayor later recalled, *"The dynamic [of the meeting] created a marketplace for ideas, in which the best strategies got adopted through true competition. Say the commander of the 44th precinct in the Bronx had reduced shootings by placing more undercover officers on quality-of-life duty. It was only a matter of time before other commanders, eager to outperform their buddy in the 44th, would implement his strategy, often adding improvements."*[8] Analyzing performance in an environment characterized by a desire for learning and improvement is the surest path to breakthrough results.

Listed next are the steps you can take when using the Balanced Scorecard to drive the agenda of your management review meeting:

1. *Invite based on knowledge.* The old guard of management meetings is typified by a list of attendees representing only the senior management ranks. In stark contrast, meetings with the Balanced Scorecard at the helm base attendance on knowledge, not chain of command.

2. *Review performance on all Scorecard measures.* One school of thought suggests skipping any measures that are operating at or above target, and instead focusing immediately on those measures under target. The sense of urgency committed to the improvement of ailing measures is admirable, but equally important is the ability to sustain success. What can you learn from those measures at which you excel? Are there initiatives or resources that could be applied with equal effectiveness to other measures? Perhaps your target does not represent a meaningful challenge. Success always demands as much scrutiny as failure.

3. *Ask more questions.* Learning demands a dedication to constantly striving for additional information. Simply examining measure results and asking "Why are we off target?" is not sufficient. If results on a measure are lower than your expectations, why not ask:

   • Is the target appropriate?

   • What supporting initiatives are devoted to this measure?

   • How are we progressing on those initiatives?

   • Do these results imply a flaw in our strategy?

   • How have other measures in the chain of cause and effect reacted to this performance?

4. *Track issues.* Uncovering answers to the questions raised in step 3 will inevitably lead to a number of issues. Develop a tracking device to ensure that commitments made in the meeting are kept and that progress is taking place.

If you're not asking the questions just raised, and many more, you can be certain your employees won't be asking them either. If you do take the time and effort to learn from your Scorecard, it can prove to be just the start of a powerful new voice of strategy to be heard throughout your agency.

SUMMARY

It's not until you begin reporting Balanced Scorecard results that the tool transcends the academic world and is viewed as a valuable management resource. As the Scorecard has grown in use and prominence, so too has the number of software providers attempting to assist organizations in their quest to maximize the Scorecard's effectiveness. A number of sophisticated tools offering robust reporting and analysis options are available to today's Scorecard adopters. There are five steps in the selection of Balanced Scorecard software:

1. Form a software team.
2. Develop a short list of candidates.
3. Submit a request for proposal.
4. Arrange product demonstrations.
5. Create a summary report and make your selection.

There are a number of criteria to help you make the software choice. Design issues focus on the configuration of the software, and include: setup wizards, user interface, number of measures accommodated, unit types, weighting, and personal preferences. Reporting and analysis features are also critical. You should examine your potential tool's capability to provide: drill-down capabilities, statistical analysis, and flexible report options. Technical considerations of the tool include compatibility with your current IT infrastructure and scalability. Maintenance and security features will also require scrutiny. Look for ease of modification and controlled access to the system. Conclude your analysis by evaluating the vendor. Discuss past engagements with clients, carefully review pricing, and always ask for references.

Technology adoption features both pros and cons. Decision support, resource allocation, alignment, and accountability may all be enhanced with the use of software. Additionally, organizationwide cascading and deployment of the Scorecard is simplified with the aid of enabling technology. Communication, information sharing, and knowledge are also potentially increased through the application of software. Cost is typically a significant inhibitor for organizations wishing to pursue a technology solution. When software, training, maintenance and license fees are accumulated, the total can prove cost-prohibitive for many nonprofits and governments. Another risk of software implementation is the elevation of the tool to the same level as the Scorecard concept. Software is an enabler, but must never be considered tantamount to the Scorecard itself.

Many successful Scorecard-developing agencies have chosen to use paper-based reporting systems. A pioneer in public-sector Scorecard use, the City of Charlotte, North Carolina, still relies on the power of paper reports to tell its Balanced Scorecard story. When developing in-house solutions to your Scorecard reporting needs, be sure to create a prototype report for review and discussion, and be aware of the data collection issues that can accompany the Scorecard reporting process.

It's one thing to gather results, but another thing entirely to take action based on those results. Using the Balanced Scorecard as the centerpiece of your management reporting system allows you to do just that—take action on, and learn from, performance results.

NOTES

1. Jack Welch with John A. Byrne, *Jack: Straight from the Gut* (New York: Warner Business Books, 2001)
2. Christopher Palazzolo and Kent Smack, "The Four Steps to BSC Software Selection," *Balanced Scorecard Report,* November–December, 2002, pp. 15–16.
3. From "The Global BSC Community: The 2002 Report on Technology Implementation Experiences," presented by Laura M. Downing at the 2002 Balanced Scorecard Summit, San Francisco, California, October 8, 2002.
4. From interview with Nancy Foltz, September 19, 2002.
5. Deborah L. Kerr, "The Balanced Scorecard in the Public Sector," *Perform Magazine,* Vol. I, No. 8, pp. 4–9.
6. From interview with Dennis Feit, October 4, 2002.
7. Robert S. Kaplan and David P. Norton, "Leading Change with the Balanced Scorecard," *Financial Executive,* September 2001.
8. Rudolph W. Giuliani, *Leadership* (New York: Hyperion, 2002), p. 90.

CHAPTER 13

The City of Charlotte: A Balanced Scorecard Success Story

Roadmap for Chapter Thirteen The City of Charlotte, North Carolina, is widely considered the best example of Balanced Scorecard success in a public or nonprofit setting. An "early adopter," the city implemented its first Balanced Scorecard in 1996. Adhering to a firm belief that "measurement matters," leaders have continuously fine-tuned their efforts, maximizing the benefits of the Scorecard as a measurement system, strategic management system, and communication tool. Their success has not gone unnoticed; in fact, it has resulted in a long list of accolades, including: entry into the Balanced Scorecard Collaborative's Hall of Fame (2002), and University Best Practice from the International City/County Manager's Association (2001). Charlotte's City Manager, and Scorecard guiding force, Pam Syfert, was named a top 10 public official in 1999 by *Governing Magazine*.

This chapter contains a wide-ranging interview, in which you'll hear the Charlotte Balanced Scorecard story recounted by three people instrumental in its successful implementation: Lisa Schumacher, Tiffany Capers, and Matt Bronson. Lisa has been with Charlotte's Budget and Evaluation Office for 17 years, and has worked with the Balanced Scorecard since its inception in 1996. She has spoken on the Charlotte experience at seminars and conferences throughout North America, and has co-authored articles on the use of the Balanced Scorecard. Tiffany and Matt are also key players contributing to the success of Charlotte's ongoing Balanced Scorecard implementation. They have shared the Charlotte story with conference audiences in the United States, Canada, Ireland, and Singapore.

The interview has been structured so that topics flow in a pattern resembling the subject matter of this book. Readers interested in specific subjects may refer to the italicized text, which outlines the key topic represented in each question. However, I would highly recommend enjoying the entire learning experience.

Paul Niven (PN): Who *introduced the Balanced Scorecard* to the City of Charlotte, and when?

Lisa Schumacher (LS): Pam Syfert was deputy city manager in 1994, and at that time she read the first *Harvard Business Review* article on the Balanced Scorecard.

PN: Did she just happen to come across the article or was there interest in the topic of performance measurement and, specifically, the Balanced Scorecard at that time?

LS: We were interested in a new Performance Management system. We had been doing management by objectives (MBO) since the early 1970s and had been looking at what other cities were doing. We were kind of "shopping around"' for a better and more meaningful way to approach performance management. The article Pam read in 1994 was the first we heard of the Balanced Scorecard.

PN: Were you concerned that this was a tool conceived for, and used primarily by, the private sector, and therefore it wouldn't be *appropriate for a pubic-sector organization?*

LS: The initial reaction was intrigue. The idea of being able to measure and report on our strategy was something that we had never really attempted with our Performance Management system. I think we knew that it would be a leap, in the sense that it was designed for the private sector, and most of the literature and the training available was designed for the private sector. So that was a bit of an adjustment in the beginning, to take a private-sector idea, private-sector language, and figure out how to make that work and be meaningful for a city organization.

PN: Were you able to get *executive sponsorship* for implementing the Balanced Scorecard? And, how did you win the *support of your mayor and city council?*

LS: When we implemented the Scorecard in 1996, Pam Syfert, who had originally introduced the concept to us, had become the city manager. So she was our most visible champion. We also had a mayor and city council members who had been urging us to emulate the best practices in the private sector whenever possible. When they learned the Scorecard would help us become more strategic and give them better information for making decisions, they were onboard.

PN: What were your *objectives* in launching the Balanced Scorecard?

LS: In the past, any links between our Performance Management system and strategic plan were coincidental. So we wanted to tie our Performance Management system and city strategy together. We wanted the ability to measure our strategic plan.

PN: How did you *adapt the Kaplan and Norton model of the Balanced Scorecard* to fit the City of Charlotte?

LS: If you look at our Scorecard, you'll see the first thing we did was to move the Customer perspective to the top. We initially attempted to develop the Scorecard with the Financial perspective on top but found that we were spinning our wheels because financial results don't represent our "bottom line." Financial measures are important, but the customers' view of our performance is much bigger in government.

Tiffany Capers (TC): Putting the Financial perspective at the top of the Scorecard would also have sent the wrong message. Being a public-sector organization, we are funded by citizens, by taxpayers, so we didn't want to send a message that we were in this "for the money," that is, for a profit. We really wanted to convey that we are providing services as an organization to meet the needs of our citizens, meet the needs of our customers. By reorganizing the perspectives, it conveyed a more accurate and more appropriate message to our customers and our organization on how we view our customers and deliver services to them.

A more recent adaptation for our 2004/2005 Scorecard is renaming the perspectives. We recommended changing the names of the perspectives so that they were more consistent with the language we use internally. For example, the city manager doesn't talk about "Internal Processes"; instead, she talks about "Running the Business." Similarly, rather than simply using the word "Customer," we say "Serve the Customer." The perspectives are now more representative and more consistent with our organizational culture and management expectations [see Exhibit 13.1].

Exhibit 13.1   The City of Charlotte's Strategy Map of Objectives

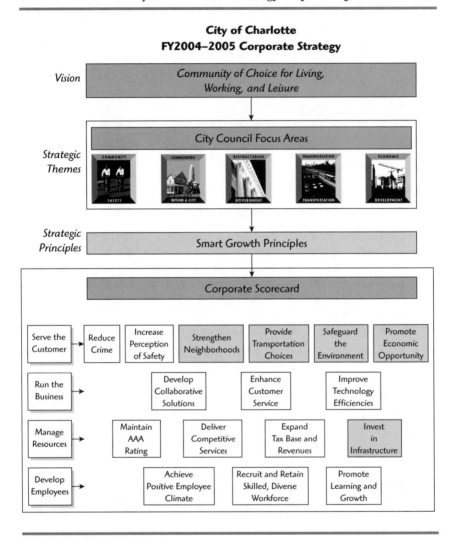

PN: Did you use the typical Kaplan and Norton *terminology* of *objectives, measures, targets,* and *initiatives?*

TC: For the most part we were very consistent with using the terminology that's presented in the original Balanced Scorecard book. We use *objectives, measures, targets,* and *initiatives.* However, we expanded the types of measures. Specifically, we use four types of measures: activity measures, input measures, output measures, and outcome measures.

Outcome measures, the results measures, were a struggle for us initially—understanding them conceptually, and then actually trying to define and describe what an outcome would be for a city organization in a fiscal year, or even within two fiscal years. There was a learning curve, and to some extent, we still have opportunities in those areas. We've done a lot over the past year or so to make sure our vocabulary, our definitions, our lexicon is consistent.

PN: Can you describe some of the *methods you've used to educate employees* about key Balanced Scorecard concepts and terms?

TC: We've done several things. Discussing the Scorecard in our newsletter is one method we've used. We've also developed a glossary of all the terms we use in describing performance measurement. We conduct Balanced Scorecard training sessions through our organization training department. Finally, we developed a *Balanced Scorecard Handbook*, which includes a lot of useful Scorecard information.

PN: Where did you *build your first Balanced Scorecard?* Was it a high-level Scorecard for the city or did you choose a department to "pilot" the Balanced Scorecard?

TC: It was a combination. At the outset we did build a Corporate Scorecard. After we had the initial 21 objectives described for the Corporate Scorecard, there were two other processes that went on simultaneously: Focus-area cabinets developed Scorecards, and four key business units (KBUs) also built Scorecards.

PN: Can you describe what is meant by a *focus-area cabinet?*

TC: In 1991, our current City Manager, Pam Syfert, had a conversation with the city council during one of their retreats and essentially shared with them that the city organization can't be all things to all people. She strongly suggested a need to define and describe the areas that we could most impact as a city organization. That conversation ultimately resulted in what we know as our five focus areas: community safety, city within a city (now communities within a city), transportation, economic development, and restructuring government.

Each of the focus areas has a cross-functional staff team that meets on a regular basis to discuss the corporate strategy relative to the respective focus areas, and how the city as an organization can impact, influence, and achieve the overall vision for the focus areas by identifying strategic initiatives and measures. During our initial rollout of the Balanced Scorecard, those teams were responsible for developing focus-area cabinet Scorecards.

PN: Which *process*, or *processes*, did you use to *actually develop your Scorecards?*

TC: We contracted with a consulting firm that, over a period of weeks, gave us a crash course on the Balanced Scorecard as a concept, as a tool, and how we could use it in the city organization. We then adopted a train-the-trainer model and facilitated the development of KBU Scorecards. Initially, two staff members, Lisa Schumacher and Nancy Elliot, were primarily responsible for facilitating the implementation of the Balanced Scorecard for the organization. Nancy Elliott spent over a year working with each key business unit. Now the Balanced Scorecard is administered by a team of five members from the Budget and Evaluation Office.

PN: Public and nonprofit organizations often have a difficult time determining what to measure in their Customer perspective. *Who or what did you measure in your Customer perspective and how did you make that determination?*

TC: I don't think we had as much difficulty because we had our focus areas in place, which represent strategic focus. I think for a lot of nonprofits and governments, implementing a Balanced Scorecard requires some conversation at a high level in the organization to decide the organization's strategy—what is it that the organization wants to accomplish? What is the organization's focus, mission, and vision? To what end or for what outcomes should we be dedicating our resources? We had wrestled with these questions and more before deciding to implement a Balanced Scorecard.

PN: By looking at your Scorecard, it's apparent you don't *advocate focusing on one customer group*. You look at the broad spectrum of customers.

TC: That's correct. We look at the broad spectrum of customers. We view our customers as the donor, the taxpayer, as well as the service recipient. So, in defining and describing our Customer perspective, we really try to think about what it is we want to accomplish. Quite honestly, we try to answer the fundamental questions the Balanced Scorecard poses, which are: "At what must we excel to satisfy our customers?" "At what must we succeed to satisfy our customers?" The objectives appearing in our Customer perspective represent what the citizens and city council have indicated as being critical to providing customer and taxpayer value—value in terms of what they pay and the services they receive.

PN: *How many measures* do you have on your Balanced Scorecards?

TC: Before the Balanced Scorecard, we had about 900 measures across 13 key business units. After we implemented the Scorecard, that number dropped down to about 260. Right now we have approximately 375 measures across all 14 of our key business units. We felt a little apprehensive when we saw the number of measures gradually increasing; however, our concerns subsided because we were getting a better balance of measures. Government is process-oriented. Often it takes more than a fiscal year to achieve or to accomplish the ultimate goal. We had to become more comfortable with the fact that we're not going to have only outcome measures on our Scorecard or in key business unit business plans. There will undoubtedly be some process measures as well [see Exhibit 13.2].

Exhibit 13.2   Sample of Charlotte's Corporate-Level Scorecard Measures

Perspective	Objective	Sample Measure	Target
Serve the Customer	Strengthen Neighborhoods	Number of stable neighborhoods as measured by the Quality of Life index	102 Stable Neighborhoods
Run the Business	Develop Collaborative Solutions	Percent of strategic transportation and land use projects utilizing integrated land use and transportation planning	100%
Manage Resources	Expand Tax Base and Revenues	Percent change in tax valuation in targeted neighborhoods	10% increase in tax valuation
Develop Employees	Recruit and Retain Skilled, Diverse Workforce	Percent increase in city average turnover rate	<5% increase in turnover

PN: Did you *cascade the Balanced Scorecard* across the city, and if so how did you accomplish that task?

Matt Bronson (MB): Yes, we designed the Scorecard to really cascade the corporate strategy and vision down to the departments. We focused on translating the five focus areas into tangible objectives that could then be adopted by departments in guiding their initiatives. We began with the four pilot KBUs Tiffany mentioned, and then we rolled it out to other departments over an 18-month period.

There were varying degrees of success in developing KBU scorecards. All of the departments developed Scorecards, but with mixed results. Some departments really grabbed on to the concept of taking those objectives and developing meaningful and specific measures. Other departments found it more difficult. Over the past year and a half, we've really reinvigorated the KBU Scorecard development process. We have been leading a number of retreats and discussions and facilitating brainstorming sessions—really challenging the departments to look at the Scorecard, identify which of the corporate objectives they relate to, and develop some key measures and targets based on those objectives [see Exhibit 13.3].

Exhibit 13.3   Charlotte's Strategy Pyramid

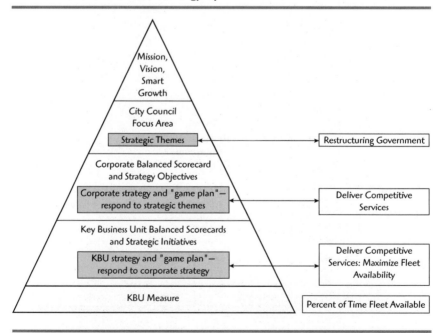

PN: Have you *linked the Balanced Scorecard to budgeting* and, if so, do you think that link has proven effective?

MB: Very timely question because that's an area we're spending a lot of time on right now. In the past, we've always had some linkage between budgeting and performance management, particularly with the focus areas. For many years we've been able to say, for example, "Because of council's priority in community safety, we've identified $X million in community safety initiatives in the recommended budget." What we haven't always done is really to show how service-level changes and resource requests tie back into specific Scorecard objectives. For example, "How does X request tie back into 'strengthen neighborhoods'?" "How does this request tie back into 'deliver competitive services'?" That's the missing piece that we were always faced with.

Another complicating factor is the fact that our budget requests were developed in the fall and winter, while departmental Scorecards and business plans were developed in the spring. So, in essence, we had the budget driving the business planning. We're changing that now by developing a "strategic operating plan" that integrates business planning and budgeting. The strategic operating plan starts off with developing KBU scorecards and business plans, with departments then identifying the resources necessary to carry out these strategic priorities.

PN: Who *owns or manages* the Balanced Scorecard process at the city?

MB: The Scorecard is primarily managed and coordinated by the Budget and Evaluation office. This office has been the traditional home of Performance Management at the city. Three of us, in addition to two other analysts, are the primary Scorecard coordinators for the organization. We're charged with helping implement corporate strategy throughout the organization, monitoring performance, advising the leadership team on scorecard-related issues, and consulting with departments across the organization.

PN: How do you *report your Balanced Scorecard results*? Are you using an off-the-shelf software package? Is it something you built in-house? What do you use?

TC: We've taken a look at a couple of off-the-shelf systems, and our dilemma has been that those systems tend to be extremely quantitative in their orientation and in the reports they generate. As I was alluding to earlier, because of the processes involved with government work, there wasn't really a good fit with what we were seeing from off-the-shelf providers and what we felt we needed to provide as management information. We've also explored trying to develop something internally that allowed for more qualitative and more anecdotal data collection and data retrieval, but we've not landed on a perfect solution for how to automate that, yet. At the present time, our reporting system is paper-based. We produce midyear and year-end reports.

LS: We really wanted to get it right on paper. A big part of our challenge has been defining and describing those measures that provide management information. That's really where we're trying to move our organization: to being a strategy-focused organization that uses data to make decisions to move forward.

We've used Word and Excel because we have to report a good bit of narrative. If we do have a number to report, we usually need to give context. You just can't just look at spreadsheets of columns and numbers and make judgments about whether that was particularly outstanding or not. That's one of the things people are often surprised about us, that we've not wanted technology or a system to drive the Scorecard. We've wanted to have it right on paper; automation will come whenever automation comes.

PN: What has been the *effect of new administrations coming in,* a new mayor if that has occurred, or new city council members? How has that affected the Balanced Scorecard, if at all?

LS: We have been fortunate to have a good deal of consistency in our elected leadership. There have been some new faces on our city council in the last six to eight years, but there has also been a lot of consistency as far as people serving for six and more years on city council, as well as the mayor who is now in his fourth two-year term. So that has certainly helped us.

I also think if you look at our strategic themes, in some ways they are timeless. I don't know that we'll ever raise the flag and say that we have conquered community safety or that we have arrived at economic development. Maybe that is a test of good strategy.

As council members change, the only thing that really changes is agreement on the initiatives. It's not that they disagree with the ultimate outcome of economic development, but there can be some disagreement about what the appropriate role of government is. So we see some adjustment in the initiatives we may be undertaking.

PN: What do you feel have been the biggest *benefits to using the Balanced Scorecard* for the City of Charlotte?

MB: This can be a very challenging question because it's often difficult to identify tangible, specific benefits from the Balanced Scorecard in terms of cleaner streets, a safer neighborhood, or other tangible services citizens expect of government. The benefits we point to are more internal in nature—really developing a strategy-focused organization.

The first benefit we tout is emphasizing strategy throughout the organization. Taking the five themes of the city council and really articulating what those mean. Community safety to us means reduced crime, increased perception of safety. The Scorecard has also been an important tool to help us integrate strategy with budgeting. It's really helped us view the budget as those resources necessary to achieve the community goals articulated through the Scorecard.

The Scorecard also represents a one-page game plan that shows what we're about as an organization. We can take that one-page sheet and say this is who we are as the city of Charlotte. This is our direction for the next two years. Additionally, the Scorecard helps us develop consensus through the process of coming up with these objectives, developing the measures and initiatives.

It helps improve management decisions by developing more relevant performance measures based on strategy, based on our council focus areas and our key themes. Last, it reports outcomes to elected officials and the community. We can show exactly what we're doing to achieve those key Balanced Scorecard objectives: reducing crime, creating economic opportunity, and so on.

LS: Another benefit to using the Scorecard is an understanding of the city's strategy. In our 2002 employee survey, 57 percent reported that they understood what the city's overall goals are. And I believe almost 70 percent reported that they understood the goals of the specific business unit that they work in. We think that's a good baseline; it actually increased from the 2000 survey, but our goal is to see that number go up over time. The Scorecard also gives nonprofit and government organizations a platform to discuss employee growth and development. Sometimes a tenuous subject to broach in nonprofit and government organizations, the Scorecard clearly positions the employee as being integral to the successful achievement of organizational strategy. By doing so, it allows organizations to ask: "What do employees need to be successful and, in turn, to help the organization succeed?" The Balanced Scorecard truly "balances" success on the four critical pieces—the customer, the business, the resources, and the employees.

PN: What *roadblocks did you face in your implementation,* and how did you overcome them?

MB: We faced some initial challenges from KBUs in trying to develop the Balanced Scorecard. One KBU had a director who really viewed this as a "flavor of the month," a management tool that had come up in a magazine, and he wasn't quite sold on it. I will say, however, that this particular director has since become a strong champion and ally of the Scorecard, which is a testament to the time and effort we have invested into making the Scorecard meaningful for the organization. It was also perceived by some as too top-down, as coming from the top of the organization, being pushed down to those in departments, particularly at a time when the organization was moving toward more of a decentralized format. We have worked with departments to see how they can be creative in selecting key strategic initiatives and measures based on a set of core organizational objectives.

Tiffany mentioned the private-sector orientation earlier. It can be challenging with terminology: lead and lag measures are one example. Trying to familiarize these terms in a public-sector organization has been a challenge for us.

"Strategic selection" is another challenge. A Scorecard can't include everything we do as a city. Some departments had difficulty finding themselves in the Scorecard, and felt they were strategically ignored. Pam's [City Manager Pam Syfert] challenge to the departments was: Find where you support the organization internally in a way that helps us all deliver those services to our customers. The Scorecard can't include every particular service that we provide to the community, but we can still build the organization internally. It can be very difficult to strike the right balance of measures to really show meaningful performance; particularly with so many of our measures being multiyear measures, we also need to keep working on developing shorter-term measures to give us information to make decisions.

PN: What *advice would you have for other organizations,* particularly nonprofit and government, that are just starting out on their Balanced Scorecard journey?

LS: I'd say it looks easier than it is. It is hard work. You should begin with a commitment to devote time to it. Our implementation period was longer than was desirable, but that was a result of juggling competing priorities. If you have staff available who can jump on it and spend six months, that's terrific. Our reality was that we didn't have that level of resources to devote to it, so we had to do a slower implementation than we would have liked. But even if you can launch a quick implementation, it still takes time and commitment. There will be some bumps and frustrations. Also, don't hold out for the perfect Scorecard the first time around; get the first one on paper, then in the next year build and improve from there.

MB: It's also critical to have a high-level champion, an executive champion visible throughout the organization. The Balanced Scorecard has to have this kind of champion to be a success. Team members can do the legwork and coordinate, but unless you have the high-level champion visible and supporting it, the Scorecard will not go far.

A second thing is that you can't overcommunicate the Scorecard to employees. We've built partnerships with Corporate Communications, our Training Team, and the City Manager's Office to really communicate the importance of the Scorecard and strategic planning, and how it's part of everyone's job. That is one of our biggest ongoing challenges—communicating the Balanced Scorecard and communicating strategy.

TC: The Balanced Scorecard is ultimately a tool for change—it's a change agent. With change you have potential benefits and risks. Organizations should not underestimate the extent to which the Balanced Scorecard can and will and should change the way they think about strategy, the way they view strategy, and, hopefully, the way they evaluate the successful achievement of strategy.

SUMMARY

The City of Charlotte has been measuring its performance for over 25 years. In 1996, it became one of the first organizations to apply the Balanced Scorecard concept to a public-sector or nonprofit organization. Thanks to a lot of hard work and dedication to the concept, the Balanced Scorecard has paid tremendous dividends to the city's performance management efforts.

In this interview with three of Charlotte's key Balanced Scorecard ambassadors, you were treated to an illuminating view of how, specifically, the city has been able to accomplish such significant results. Outlined here are some of the key points raised during this very insightful dialog.

- The Balanced Scorecard was introduced to the City of Charlotte by then-Deputy City Manager Pam Syfert in 1994. Leaders had been engaging in Management by Objectives (MBO) since the 1970s, but were interested in a new system that would help them measure and report on their strategy.

- The Scorecard was championed by Syfert, who became city manager in 1996. The city's mayor and council, who were very interested in any tool that would promote improved decision making, were also supportive from the start.

- Adaptations were made to the private-sector model of the Balanced Scorecard. The first change was to move the Customer perspective to the top of the model. While financial measures are important, they are not the "bottom line" for a public-sector organization. Recently, the city has decided it will change the names of the perspectives to more accurately reflect discussions that take place internally.

- Consistent with the model advocated by Kaplan and Norton, the City of Charlotte's Scorecard implementors have used the terms objective, measure, target, and initiative in articulating their strategy. They do, however, expand on the term measure. Four types of measures are used: activity, input, output, and outcome.

- Employee training has been stressed throughout the Scorecard implementation. Among the training vehicles utilized are: newsletters, glossaries of terms, Scorecard training sessions, and handbooks.

- A high-level "Corporate Scorecard" was constructed for the city first. Implementors then developed Scorecards for their focus-area cabinets and four key business unit (KBU) Scorecards.

- Prior to launching the Balanced Scorecard, the city monitored more than 900 performance measures. Since the development and use of the Scorecard, that number has dropped to a more manageable 375 measures spread across 14 KBUs.

- The Scorecard has been cascaded to all KBUs throughout the city.

- Linking the Balanced Scorecard to budgeting is accomplished through the development of cascaded Scorecards. Each KBU identifies the resources required to achieve Balanced Scorecard objectives.

- Many benefits have accrued to the City of Charlotte as a result of implementing the Balanced Scorecard. Among the benefits cited are:
  - Awareness and understanding of strategy
  - Linkage of budgets and strategy

- Enhanced consensus and teamwork throughout the organization
- Improved management decision making
- Ability to report outcomes to the community

- The city did encounter some roadblocks during its implementation. To counter the notion that the Scorecard represented a management "flavor of the month," technique was a key issue. Others protested the use of the Scorecard, believing it represented a top-down approach of management.

- The city has this advice for others implementing a Balanced Scorecard:
  - A high-level champion is crucial.
  - It's difficult work!
  - It requires time and commitment.
  - Don't attempt to build the perfect Balanced Scorecard with your first attempt.
  - Communicate, communicate, communicate!

CHAPTER 14

Sustaining Balanced Scorecard Success

Roadmap for Chapter Fourteen A Balanced Scorecard is more akin to a marathon than a sprint. To ensure your Scorecard has the staying power of a champion, this chapter will provide you with two key ingredients of success: updating your Balanced Scorecard's key elements to reflect current realities, and the roles necessary to sustain success.

UPDATING THE BALANCED SCORECARD

"Does our Balanced Scorecard stay the same?" is a question I often hear from those who have recently developed Scorecards. Some fear that, once established, the strategy map, objectives, and measures are cast in stone, never to be altered. Fortunately, that is definitely not the case. The Scorecard was designed to help you navigate the changing tides your organization must ride, and as such must be occasionally updated to ensure it remains relevant and effective.

Chapter Seven examined the role of the Balanced Scorecard in the context of your wider Performance Management system. Many of the elements of that framework, including budgets and operating plans, will be updated annually to reflect changing conditions. Likewise, it is a very good idea to critically examine the Scorecard at least annually and determine if its core elements are still appropriate in telling an accurate strategic story. A "best practices" benchmarking study suggests a majority of Scorecard practitioners do just that. In the study, 62 percent of participants updated their

Balanced Scorecards annually, 15 percent updated every 6 months, while 23 percent updated every 3 months.[1] Let's look at the core elements comprising a Balanced Scorecard and consider how they may change over time.

- *Mission, values, and vision.* The mission defines your core purpose and, as a result, will seldom change. In a similar fashion, values reflect the timeless and deeply held beliefs of your organization and guide day-to-day actions. Unless you determine your value system to be undermining your efforts, it is unlikely you would advocate a wholesale change. The vision represents a word picture of what the organization intends to become, maybe 5, 10, or 15 years into the future. Unlike the mission, which is foundational and permanent, the vision can be accomplished and may change. Should you feel you've reached the aspirations articulated in your vision, it will be time to retool it for the next generation of your existence. Balanced Scorecard objectives and measures should be translated to ensure alignment with any changes in direction.

- *Strategy.* Strategy represents the broad, overall priorities adopted by the organization in recognition of its operating environment and in pursuit of its mission. Obviously, your operating environment will change; it's probably changing as you read this. Any number of areas could affect your strategy going forward: changes in federal, state, or local laws; changes in the target population you serve; new members on your board; newly elected officials; or changes in funding levels. Each of these will entail a strategic response, and since the Scorecard is designed to translate your strategy into action, it would require modifications as well.

- *Strategy map and objectives.* Should you experience a change in mission, values, vision, or strategy, your map and objectives will inevitably require updating. Aside from those "structural" elements, you may deem other alterations desirable. For example, many agencies will change the wording of objectives to more accurately represent their core purpose or to clarify potentially confusing terminology.

- *Measures.* In addition to the preceding structural items, measures are subject to many changes over time. You may alter the method of calculation to better capture the true essence of the event under investigation; or the description may be enhanced to improve employee understanding of operational and strategic significance. Frequency of reporting could also be changed. For example, you may have attempted to track customer satisfaction monthly, but the logistics of gathering the data simply proved too challenging. In that case, you wouldn't abandon this important metric, but would simply change the reporting period to something more amenable to measurement, perhaps quarterly. Another important measure change is the raw number appearing on the Scorecard. The majority of agencies, as they become more accomplished in the use of Performance Measurement, will decrease the number of indicators they track over time.

- *Targets.* Targets will normally change on an annual basis as you review your Balanced Scorecard. Midyear "course corrections" are also a possibility should you believe you've set the bar too high or too low.

- *Initiatives.* Like targets, initiatives will be updated annually, and should be reflected in your budgeting process as discussed in Chapter Eleven.

Updating the Scorecard is a normal process that should be embedded in your annual operating procedures or plans. Whenever, possible it's always a good idea to invite feedback from employees and other stakeholders on any proposed changes. As discussed throughout the book, involvement and communication are key elements of Scorecard success.

KEY BALANCED SCORECARD ROLES

Being labeled a "project" is a significant risk for your Balanced Scorecard efforts. The word "project" connotes something of a short-term duration, an item that can be completed and checked off a list. Unfortunately, some organizations do treat their Scorecards as mere action items on a master to-do list. Sustaining the Scorecard, and deriving long-term value from this tool, requires that it become a fixture in your management processes. The obvious method for accomplishing this task is the simple and repetitive use of the Balanced Scorecard in decision-making, resource allocation, and every other facet of your operations. Additionally, however, transitioning the Scorecard from a short-term fix to a long-term solution requires resources, namely many of the roles identified in Chapter Three. Let's consider them now in the context of your ongoing Scorecard development.

The key role required to ensure unabated Scorecard momentum is that of the Balanced Scorecard champion or team leader. This individual guided the initial process of Scorecard development and should be responsible for shepherding the tool to the next phase of its evolution. Scorecard policies and procedures, recommended changes, data issues, and a dozen other considerations require a point of contact. The Scorecard champion is that contact. Building on his or her organizational knowledge and influence, as well as Scorecard wisdom, this person crafts the future development of the Scorecard. The cheerleading and ambassador aspects of the role remain relevant as long as you have a Scorecard. The champion must take advantage of every opportunity that presents itself to herald the Scorecard as a key tool in the organization's quest to improve results, execute strategy, and work toward the mission.

The influence yielded by the Scorecard champion will be sharply diminished, if not entirely eradicated, without the presence of an executive sponsor. A senior leader dedicated to the Scorecard is critical at every juncture of the tool's ongoing development. I have seen more than one fine Scorecard implementation crumble upon the departure of a sponsoring executive. More than anyone else, the executive sponsor has the responsibility of keeping the Scorecard relevant as conditions change. New opportunities, new challenges, and a changing environment should all be examined through the lens of the Scorecard. The sponsor has the power to ensure this can, and does, occur. True sponsorship is often evidenced by the willingness of executives to share information on the Balanced Scorecard with colleagues at other agencies. Networking, collaboration, and learning opportunities will frequently result.

Original members of your Balanced Scorecard team remain important contributors to Scorecard success, although their role will most certainly change. Rather than occupying center stage in the Scorecard drama, their important work shifts behind the scenes: rallying support within their own groups, liaising with colleagues, and acting as sounding boards for future Scorecard work, such as links to budgeting. Your team should convene periodically in order to share learnings from within their respective groups, provide feedback on Scorecard progress, and offer input on key Scorecard processes and procedures being undertaken.

Depending on the sophistication of your reporting tool, you may require the services of a system administrator. An in-house paper-based reporting solution will most likely fall under the Scorecard champion's sphere of responsibility. However, a packaged software system may require an individual with more specific expertise in the information technology field. The system administrator holds the ultimate responsibility of scheduling results reporting, ensuring Scorecard data is gathered on a timely basis and entered accurately into the tool. He or she also makes changes to Scorecard elements (objectives, measures, and targets), provides technical support to users, upgrades to new versions of software, and supplies training. The management review process discussed in Chapter Twelve will also benefit from the competent guidance of the system administrator. Should you choose a technology system to display results during the meeting, having a technical resource on standby is a must.

THE BALANCED SCORECARD IS ABOUT CHANGE

You're introducing far more than a new measurement system when you launch the Balanced Scorecard. A host of changes will accompany this powerful framework for gauging performance. You can anticipate a new language emerging, one focusing on strategy and results. Accountability will be enhanced as a result of the Scorecard's emphasis on gauging the effectiveness of your operations. Resource allocation is linked to results and strategy, not to last year's numbers. Alignment will be positively influenced as employees from across the agency are given the opportunity, through cascading Scorecards, to demonstrate how their roles contribute to long-term, sustainable success for the agency. The Balanced Scorecard combines all of these powerful elements to create the alchemy of positive results you need to thrive in today's challenging times.

Undoubtedly, some among your ranks will resist the changes discussed in this book. We all know resistance to change is natural. I believe the techniques presented throughout this book will equip you with the tools you need to disarm cynicism and resistance wherever it resides in your organization. The Balanced Scorecard holds tremendous promise when wielded with passion and commitment. For those dedicated to the constant pursuit of improvement and an unwavering desire to advance toward your mission, you will find a powerful ally in the Balanced Scorecard. As difficult as the road of change may appear, always recall the words of inventor and change advocate, Charles F. Kettering, who reminds us, *"The world hates change, yet it is the only thing that has brought progress."*

SUMMARY

The Balanced Scorecard is a dynamic tool, capable of, and indeed requiring, change as an organization encounters new business conditions. The Scorecard should be reviewed at least annually in conjunction with a normal planning cycle. The Scorecard's core elements—objectives, measures, targets, and initiatives—will most likely undergo changes each year. Objectives may be reworded to better reflect their core purpose or to clarify any potentially confusing terminology. Measures are subject to a number of changes, including: the method of calculation, description, and reporting frequency. Additionally, the number of measures may be reduced as organizations become more comfortable operating within the confines of the Balanced Scorecard system. Targets may be updated annually, or midyear in the case of those that are either too demanding or, conversely, offer little incentive for improvement. Initiatives are reviewed annually in conjunction with the budgeting process.

Several roles are required on an ongoing basis in order to achieve the maximum benefits offered by the Balanced Scorecard. The Balanced Scorecard champion guides the future development of the Scorecard system, while simultaneously acting as the organization's ambassador for the tool. An executive sponsor is critical in all phases of Scorecard development. As the tool matures, the sponsor provides strategy updates, and continues to positively influence other senior leaders regarding the role of the Scorecard.

Team members continue to play a part in the Scorecard's success, but will do so mainly in a behind-the-scenes fashion. Rallying support in their home departments and providing feedback on proposed Scorecard practices are two of their key tasks. Finally, a new role, that of system administrator, may be required within organizations pursuing sophisticated reporting solutions.

NOTE

1. Best Practices Benchmarking Report, "Developing the Balanced Scorecard" (Chapel Hill, NC: Best Practices, LLC, 1999).

Glossary of Key Balanced Scorecard and Performance Management Terms

In Chapter Seven we examined the critical nature of terminology in any change effort. Noted Organizational Development expert Peter Senge reminded us that leaders rely almost entirely on communication to drive results in their organizations. As such, they must impose a discipline on the domain in which they spend most of their time: the domain of words.

When developing a Balanced Scorecard system, you'll quickly discover that even within your own organization different individuals and groups will have different meanings for commonly used terms. This glossary will help you find some common ground by offering descriptions and definitions that have been used successfully in many Balanced Scorecard implementations. However, as noted in Chapter Seven, while I recommend these definitions, what matters most in the end is not the definitions you use, but the *consistency* of their use. Everyone must be speaking the same language if you expect the Balanced Scorecard, or any change initiative, to be understood, accepted, and to produce results.

Activity measures These measures typically track the actions or behaviors an organization performs using its inputs of staff time and financial resources. Performance measures are covered in Chapter Nine.

Balanced Scorecard An integrated framework for describing and translating strategy through the use of linked performance measures in four balanced perspectives: Customer, Internal Processes, Employee Learning and Growth, and Financial. The Balanced Scorecard acts as a measurement system, strategic management system, and communication tool.

Benchmarking The comparison of similar processes across organizations and industries to identify best practices, set improvement targets, and measure progress. Benchmarking results may serve as potential targets for Balanced Scorecard measures.

Cascading The process of developing aligned Scorecards throughout an organization. Each level of the organization will develop Scorecards based on the objectives and measures it can influence from the Scorecard of the group to which they report. For example, a city's transportation department will develop objectives and measures based on how they influence overall city Balanced Scorecard objectives and measures. Cascading allows every employee to demonstrate a contribution to overall organizational objectives. See Chapter Ten for a discussion of cascading.

Cause and effect The concept of cause and effect separates the Balanced Scorecard from other performance management systems. The measures appearing on the Scorecard should link together in a series of cause-and-effect relationships to tell the organization's strategic story. Chapters Eight and Nine provide further information on cause and effect. *See also* Strategy map.

Customer perspective One of the four standard perspectives used with the Balanced Scorecard. The role of the Customer perspective is often elevated to the top of the Balanced Scorecard model in public-sector and nonprofit organizations. See Chapters Eight and Nine for more on the Customer perspective of the Balanced Scorecard.

Efficiency measures These measures evaluate the cost of each unit of service delivered. They typically begin with "cost per..." See Chapter Nine for more on performance measures.

Employee Learning and Growth perspective One of the four standard perspectives used with the Balanced Scorecard. Measures in this perspective are often considered "enablers" of measures appearing in the other three perspectives. Employee skills, availability of information, and organizational climate are often measured in this perspective. See Chapters Eight and Nine for more on the Employee Learning and Growth perspective.

Financial perspective One of the four standard perspectives used with the Balanced Scorecard. In public-sector and nonprofit applications of the Balanced Scorecard, measures in the Financial perspective are often viewed as constraints within which the organization must operate. The Financial perspective is discussed in Chapters Eight and Nine.

Government Performance and Results Act (GPRA) Signed into law in 1993, the GPRA requires federally funded agencies to develop and implement an accountability system based on performance measurement, including setting goals and objectives and measuring progress toward achieving them. The law emphasizes what is being accomplished, as opposed to what is being spent.

Human capital May be considered a metaphor for the transition in organizational value creation from physical assets to the capabilities of employees—knowledge, skills, and relationships, for example. Human capital is closely related to terms such as *intellectual capital* and *intangible assets*. Recent estimates suggest that as much as 75 percent of an organization's value is attributable to human capital.

Initiatives The specific programs, activities, projects, or actions an organization will undertake in an effort to meet performance targets. See Chapter Nine for a discussion of initiatives.

Input measures These measures track resources used to drive organizational results. Typical inputs include staff time and financial resources. Chapter Nine discusses performance measures.

Internal Processes perspective One of the four standard perspectives used with the Balanced Scorecard. Measures in this perspective are used to monitor the effectiveness of key processes the organization must excel at in order to continue adding value for customers, given the finite resources available. See Chapters Eight and Nine for more on the Internal Processes perspective.

Lagging indicator Performance measures that represent the consequences of actions previously taken are referred to as lag indicators. They frequently focus on results at the end of a time period and characterize historical performance. Employee satisfaction may be considered a lag indicator. A good Balanced Scorecard must contain a mix of lag and lead indicators. See Chapter Nine for additional information on types of performance measures.

Leading indicator These measures are considered the "drivers" of lagging indicators. There is an assumed relationship between the two that suggests that improved performance in a leading indicator will drive better performance in the lagging indicator. For example, lowering absenteeism (a leading indicator) is hypothesized to drive improvements in employee satisfaction (a lagging indicator). See Chapter Nine for additional information on types of performance measures.

Measure A standard used to evaluate and communicate performance against expected results. Measures are normally quantitative in nature, capturing numbers, dollars, percentages, and so on. Reporting and monitoring measures help an organization gauge progress toward effective implementation of strategy. Measures are discussed in depth in Chapter Nine.

Mission statement A mission statement defines the core purpose of the organization—why it exists. The mission examines the *raison d'etre* for the organization, and reflects employee motivations for engaging in the organization's work. Effective missions are inspiring, long-term in nature, and easily understood and communicated. Mission statements are discussed in Chapter Five.

Objective A concise statement describing the specific things organization must do well in order to execute its strategy. Objectives often begin with action verbs such as "increase," "reduce," "improve," "achieve," and the like. Chapter Eight has more on objectives.

Outcome measures These measures track the benefit received by stakeholders as a result of the organization's operations. They may also be known as *impact measures*. Outcome measures track the extent to which an organization has achieved its overall goals. Possible examples include: "Reduce incidence of HIV" and "Increase perception of public safety." Measures are discussed in detail in Chapter Nine.

Output measures These measures track the number of people served, services provided, or units produced by a program or service. Number of inoculations provided and number of potholes filled are examples. Measures are discussed in detail in Chapter Nine.

Perspective In Balanced Scorecard vernacular, perspective refers to a category of performance measures. Most organizations choose the standard four perspectives (Financial, Customer, Internal Processes, and Employee Learning and Growth); however, the Balanced Scorecard represents a dynamic framework, and additional perspectives may be added as necessary to adequately translate and describe an organization's strategy.

Stakeholder Any person or group that has a "stake" in the success of the organization. Stakeholders for public and nonprofit organizations may include: employees, customers and clients, funders, elected officials, citizens, special-interest groups, suppliers, media, financial community, and partners. All stakeholders must be considered when developing mission, values, vision, strategy, and Balanced Scorecard objectives and measures.

Strategic management system Describes the use of the Balanced Scorecard in aligning an organization's short-term actions with strategy. Often accomplished by cascading the Balanced Scorecard to all levels of the organization, aligning budgets and business plans to strategy, and using the Scorecard as a feedback and learning mechanism.

Strategic resource allocation The process of aligning budgets with strategy by using the Balanced Scorecard to make resource allocation decisions. Using this method, budgets are based on the initiatives necessary to achieve Balanced Scorecard targets. Chapter Eleven is devoted to the topic of linking the Balanced Scorecard to budgeting.

Strategy Represents the broad priorities adopted by an organization in recognition of its operating environment and in pursuit of its mission. Situated at the center of the Balanced Scorecard system, all performance measures should align with the organization's strategy. Strategy remains one of the most widely discussed and debated topics in the world of modern organizations. See Chapter Six for further details.

Strategy map Balanced Scorecard architects Kaplan and Norton coined this term to describe the interrelationships among measures that weave together to describe an organization's strategy. Chapter Eight discusses the development of strategy maps. *See also* Cause and effect.

Target Represents the desired result of a performance measure. Targets make meaningful the results derived from measurement and provide organizations with feedback regarding performance. Targets are discussed in Chapter Nine.

Value proposition A value proposition describes how an organization will differentiate itself to customers and the particular set of values it will deliver. To develop a customer value proposition, many organizations will choose one of three "disciplines," articulated by Treacy and Wiersema in *The Discipline of Market Leaders*: operational excellence, product leadership, or customer intimacy. Using value propositions to develop customer measures is discussed in Chapter Nine.

Values Values represent the deeply held beliefs within the organization and are demonstrated through the day-to-day behaviors of all employees. An organization's values make an open proclamation about how it expects everyone to behave. Values should endure over the long term and provide a constant source of strength for an organization. See Chapter Five for more on values.

Vision A powerful vision provides everyone in the organization with a shared mental framework that helps give form to the often abstract future that lies ahead. Effective visions provide a word picture of what the organization intends ultimately to become—which may be 5, 10, or 15 years in the future. This statement should not be abstract; it should contain as concrete a picture of the desired state as possible, and provide the basis for formulating strategies and objectives. Vision statements are discussed further in Chapter Five.

Index